A Series from
Southern
Illinois
University
Press

ROBERT A.
SCHANKE
Series Editor

Other Books in the Theater in the Americas Series

The Theatre of Sabina Berman: The Agony of Ecstasy *and Other Plays*
Translated by Adam Versényi
With an Essay by Jacqueline E. Bixler

Composing Ourselves: The Little Theatre Movement and the American Audience
Dorothy Chansky

Broadway's Bravest Woman: Selected Writings of Sophie Treadwell
Jerry Dickey and Miriam López-Rodríguez

Women in Turmoil: Six Plays by Mercedes de Acosta
Edited and with an Introduction by Robert A. Schanke

Staging America: Cornerstone and Community-Based Theater
Sonja Kuftinec

Stage, Page, Scandals, and Vandals: William E. Burton and Nineteenth-Century American Theatre
David L. Rinear

"That Furious Lesbian": The Story of Mercedes de Acosta
Robert A. Schanke

Caffe Cino: The Birthplace of Off-Off-Broadway
Wendell C. Stone

Teaching Performance Studies
Edited by Nathan Stucky and Cynthia Wimmer
With a Foreword by Richard Schechner

Our Land Is Made of Courage and Glory: Nationalist Performance of Nicaragua and Guatemala
E. J. Westlake

Unfinished Show Business

Unfinished Show Business

Broadway Musicals as Works-in-Process

Bruce Kirle

Southern Illinois University Press ◆ *Carbondale*

Printed in the United States of America
08 07 06 05 4 3 2 1

Library of Congress Cataloging-in-Publication Data
Kirle, Bruce.
Unfinished show business : Broadway musicals as works-in-process / Bruce Kirle.
p. cm. — (Theater in the Americas)
Includes bibliographical references (p.) and index.
1. Musicals—History and criticism. 2. Musicals—Production and direction. I. Title. II. Series.
ML2054.K57 2005
782.1'4'097471—dc22 2005003767
ISBN 0-8093-2666-3 (cloth : alk. paper)
ISBN 0-8093-2667-1 (pbk. : alk. paper)

Printed on recycled paper. ♻

The paper used in this publication meets the minimum requirements of American National Standard for Information Sciences—Permanence of Paper for Printed Library Materials, ANSI Z39.48-1992. ♾

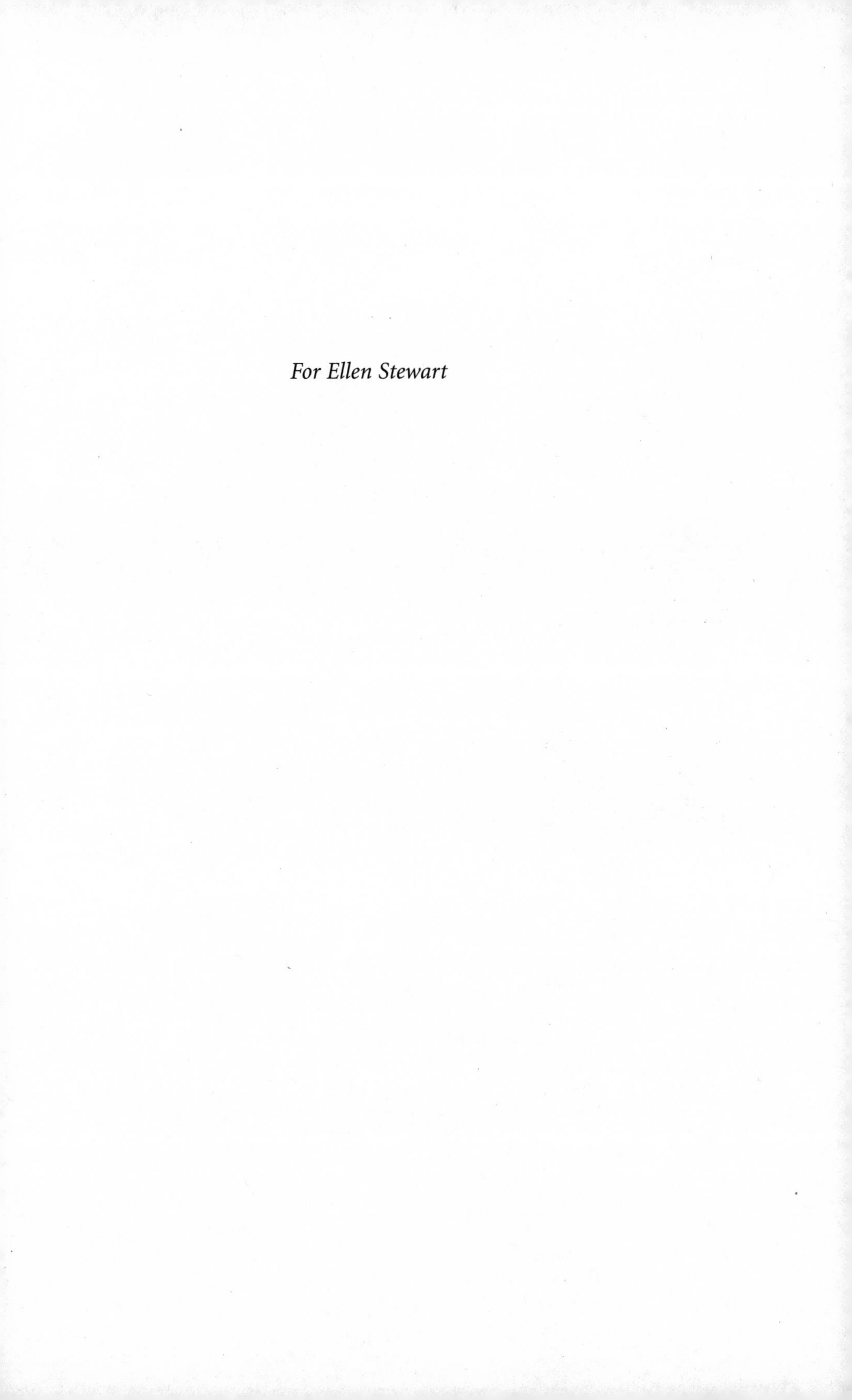

For Ellen Stewart

The drama's laws the drama's patrons give,
And we that live to please must please to live.
—*Dr. Samuel Johnson*

◆ ◆ ◆ ◆ ◆ ◆ ◆

Contents

◆ ◆ ◆ ◆ ◆ ◆ ◆

Illustrations

◆ ◆ ◆

ILLUSTRATIONS

◆ ◆ ◆ ◆ ◆ ◆ ◆

Preface

Unfinished Show Business is the result of my distrust of linear, text-based historiographical approaches to the Broadway musical. It is also the product of my own experience as a practitioner and my work as the director of the musical theatre programs at Roosevelt University in Chicago.[1] My early career was spent at La MaMa Experimental Theatre Club in New York City, where I collaborated with Tom Eyen on several shows during the late 1960s and into the 1970s, including the opening show for La MaMa's current theatre on East Fourth Street in 1969. My perspective on musical theatre, and theatre in general, was formed there. I was part of a larger, nonmusical community that included writers such as Eyen, Julie Bovasso, Rochelle Owens, Sam Shepard, Maria Irene Fornes, Paul Foster, and Megan Terry, and directors such as Ron Link and Tom O'Horgan. The work process in which I participated and to which I was exposed was not unlike that of the Open Theatre, where director, playwright, and actor were unafraid to decompartmentalize and play with each other's roles in contributing to the rehearsal process. Certainly this kind of fluidity was typical of the way I worked with Eyen and the way I have preferred to work ever since. Even as a composer, I learned to distrust the absolute autonomy of text and score.

Let me give some examples of my distrust of the text by itself. In 1982 I musical-directed a revival of a Cole Porter show in New York entitled *Something for the Boys.* One of the numbers, "By the Mississississinewah" was not working during rehearsals, even though in the original 1943 production it was the showstopper of the evening. The song is tangential to the World War II plot. Two Indian squaws appear for no logical reason to complain about sharing the same Indian chief, their mutual husband. Our actresses, both seasoned professionals, did not think the lyrics were funny and were incredulous that this song had ever stopped the show. Since I had previously worked with Paula Laurence, who had created the number with Ethel Merman, I invited her to attend a rehearsal. After she watched our version, she explained that the humor was not in Porter's double entendres or clever rhymes but in the deadpan, silly repetition of the phrase, "By the Mississississinewah." I slowed the tempo down to draw out the title phrase, and we suddenly got laughs. Laurence also showed me some comic business she and Merman had performed with their pigtails. The answer to my problem was in performance, not in the sheet music.

A second example involves Ann Corio's *This Was Burlesque,* a re-creation of the form that played on Broadway, across the country, and on an HBO television special. The comics were all veterans of the burlesque of the 1920s and 1930s. Often we would be called to go out on the road with only a few days' notice. Corio would gather whichever comics were still alive, available, and capable of working; consequently, the cast varied from engagement to engagement. Invariably there was an attempt at a run-through before opening. Even though all the comics had done the same sketches for fifty years, each was used to a variation based on his or her own ad-libs and comic tricking. After ten minutes the rehearsal would stop as the comics argued with each other about which one-liners and stage business were correct. There was no written text for *This Was Burlesque,* only the performers' own oral histories. Often comics would lift a line from one sketch and arbitrarily insert it in another for a laugh. Since they all had been doing this for fifty years, any question of authenticity had long become moot. Blackout lines often depended on comic tricking or shtick and were subject to debate. For example, in "School Daze," the elderly comics impersonated unruly grade school students disciplined by their teacher (Corio), who asked them a series of questions and whacked them over the head with a rolled-up newspaper if they responded incorrectly. One comic insisted that the blackout occur as he ogled the teacher's breasts and delivered a wisecrack. Another argued that the blackout should come after he kissed the teacher goodbye. She was then supposed to ask him where he had learned to kiss like that, whereupon he would open his mouth and unroll a foot-long tongue. When I first joined the show, I had three days to learn it, obviously without benefit of a script or a dress rehearsal. On that first opening night, I remember sheepishly knocking on Corio's door at half hour to ask her for the blackout lines so that I could cue the orchestra. She looked at me, laughed, and told me not to worry. Nothing can go wrong in a burlesque show, she promised. Nothing really did, despite the absence of a stable script or score.

As a final example, I musical-directed three companies of *Hair* when the show was relatively new. Eventually I was hired to conduct the Guber-Gross tour, which was a circuit of twenty-five-hundred-seat theatres-in-the-round on the East Coast. To save on production costs, the producers allowed for one day of rehearsal—three hours in the morning for a band read-through and a three-hour dress the afternoon of the day we opened. To facilitate this policy, the Guber-Gross management, apparently subscribing to the notion that all productions are interchangeable, customarily hired only those who had already done the show previously on Broadway or on tour. What the producers failed to realize was that no two companies of *Hair* were the same. Rather than identical, touring national companies, *Hair* was unique in that it installed autonomous companies in major cities across America, including Boston, Los Angeles, San Francisco, Chicago, and Philadelphia. The running order varied from city to city, and dialogue, often ad-libbed, was altered to suit individual performers in each production. If one saw *Hair* in Boston, Philadelphia, and Chicago, one saw three significantly different shows. As a result, the afternoon dress rehearsal was chaotic. No one wanted to alter his or her version of the "authentic" show. On opening night, I cued the band for "Hare Krishna," while Shelley Plimpton came onstage to sing "Frank Mills." Again, there was no stable script or fixed text.

If these examples seem biased or weighted, they were more typical than one might imagine of my twenty-five-plus years in the business, especially in terms of musical comedy. When I musical-directed *Sugar* with Bobby Morse, at least fifteen minutes of the show were ad-libbed each night and appear in no scripted version that I have ever seen. I found myself looking forward each night to the names that Morse would arbitrarily attach to the chorus girls. Sometimes they sounded like a smorgasbord of Tennessee Williams's heroines: Miss DuBois, Miss Wingfield, Miss Del Lago, and Miss Winemiller. Similarly, when I musical-directed *Funny Girl* with Mimi Hines, who replaced Barbra Streisand on Broadway, the performer defined the show. The score was played in alternate keys nightly, depending on Hines's voice. Her years as a nightclub entertainer and her improvisatory skills were apparent in her timing and comic business, which she changed shrewdly according to audience response. As a practitioner I was obviously inculcated with the importance of performance and reception.

Conversely, musical theatre histories tend to be based primarily on a reading of the printed texts (book and lyrics) and to reiterate the same litany in different ways. When did operetta and musical comedy fuse? Were Rodgers and Hammerstein responsible for the revolution in integration of book, dance, and score, or did it happen earlier with Kern, Bolton, and Wodehouse? Historians write passionately, even hyperbolically, about their enthusiasms and convictions, but unfortunately they tend to focus on the same question of integration. The abundant value judgments about the respective worth of musical comedy, operetta, and the integrated musical at times make the historians' conclusions suspect and feed skepticism about the objectivity of the scholarship. A few musicologists—surprisingly few of them until recently—add one further text to the stew: the printed piano-vocal score. Even so, the questions they ask remain fundamentally the same. At a time when theatre studies recognize the importance of performance analysis and reception, it seems to me that new questions need to be asked if one is to examine seriously the development of the form and to question how musicals have evolved or where they are going.[2]

Musicals are read by their audiences in theatres, not through scripts in a library. I do not wish to overstate my case; it is hard to imagine a musicologist well versed in Wagner who does not appreciate the complexity of performance. Nor do I in any way advocate that we abandon the study of the text. But the text by itself is incomplete.

Moreover, the reading of musicals involves the wedding of text not only with performance and reception but also with historical context. It is impossible to evaluate musicals of the past without examining the cultural moment that produced them. We can look at *Oklahoma!* (1943), *Show Boat* (1927), or *Lady in the Dark* (1941) with an early-twenty-first-century critical eye; we cannot receive them as they were originally mounted. Not only do we live in a different time and culture, but also it is difficult, if not impossible, to reconstruct the conditions of performance. It is certainly impossible to reconstruct the audience. Blackface, for example, was very much a part of the original production of *Show Boat* and was obviously received very differently in 1927 than it would be today. Similarly attitudes toward psychoanalysis and the role of women in the workplace have changed drastically since *Lady in the Dark* was originally mounted. Rather than assume a formalistic approach to musical theatre and agonize about which texts were responsible for *Oklahoma!*'s integration of book, music, and dance, I prefer to acknowledge that *Oklahoma!*, mounted during World War II, was a product of its cultural moment in much the same way that *Hair* (1968) was the product of a different moment twenty-five years later, and the revival of *Chicago* (1996) was able to exploit the headlines from the O. J. Simpson trial. Historical context not only influenced the texts of these musicals but also helped shape the way these productions were performed and received by their audiences. New productions of these musicals will inevitably adapt to new cultural moments and to new audiences. As such, the musical is innately open, subject to a plurality of readings.

This book, then, focuses on musicals as peculiarly unfinished show business. The complex process by which musicals are produced and mounted invites great discrepancy between the page and the stage. Battles for authority among author, director, and star are common enough in nonmusical theatre; the vast collaborative machinery of the Broadway musical causes even greater variation in the way texts are actually translated into performance. The material conditions that influence musicals as works-in-process fascinate me far more than speculations about authorial intent, which inevitably will undergo permutations with time as new productions take on lives of their own.

I will try to privilege gaps and absences in the text throughout this book, but I acknowledge from the start that some of this evidence is limited. Autobiographies tend to be self-serving, and show business biographies often are hagiographies. Much of the material that has been written about star performers and Broadway productions is anecdotal, which makes for entertaining reading but which is often pretty thin as history. Many of the key figures of the Broadway musical may be deceased; however, their wives, husbands, mistresses, lovers, and offspring are very much alive. As a result biographies and histories have carefully evaded elements of the personal lives of these authors and performers for a variety of reasons, not the least of which are potential lawsuits. Unfortunately, much of the knowledge in the field of musical theatre has been passed down through word of mouth but cannot be authenticated, although it is potentially revealing. For example, Jerome Robbins was such a powerful figure in the field that no one dared tackle his biography until after his death. Although Greg Lawrence, Robbins's biographer, has filled in many of the gaps, much of what made Robbins so enigmatic and fascinating is buried with him.[3] If I am arguing that the form of musicals is innately open and ambivalent, unfortunately, so is much available source material that cannot be authenticated.

I also freely acknowledge that there will be gaps and absences in this study. *Unfinished Show Business* is not intended to be all-encompassing. My purpose is to raise as many questions as I answer about the complex interrelationship of text with performance, reception, and historical context. The book is not a survey of all significant Broadway musicals, nor is it meant to address all those who contributed significantly to the form. I particularly regret that there is not space for separate chapters devoted specifically to the African American's contribution to musical theatre and to female stars, who often subversively (and humorously) challenged essentialist notions of gender. These subjects are fodder for a second and third book. Some readers inevitably will be irritated that I have chosen to discuss some musicals and ignored their favorites. This book is a counterhistory that celebrates the openness of the form and questions what becomes privileged and what does not. My hope is that it will encourage others to think about musicals in different ways and make the form relevant not only to musical theatre buffs but also to a larger community interested in the sociology of culture and the reflexive relationship that Broadway musicals have with shifting notions of American identity.

Chapter 1 lays out the theoretical underpinnings of the book. I argue that musicals, both integrated and nonintegrated, are a particularly open theatrical genre in which text interacts with performance, reception, and historical context. In celebrating this incompleteness, I question previous histories that have privileged integrated musicals as closed, autonomous texts and that, on the other hand, have dismissed nonintegrated musicals as jerry-built vehicles that existed to showcase star turns. Part of this privileging involves the veneration of so-called authorial intent and the quest for authenticity, which musicologists refer to as the nineteenth-century concept of *Werktreue.* Until the past forty or fifty years, historians of opera similarly privileged Wagner's *Gesamtkunstwerk* and denigrated Baroque opera as unfinished, since it depended on the improvisations and embellishments of great virtuosi, most notably castrati, as cocreators. Just as "new" musicologists now find excitement in a form that was never meant to be complete in the first place, I argue that the virtue of the nonintegrated musical lies in its looseness of structure. It is this very flimsiness that enabled great comics and entertainers to perform as cocreators. Integrated texts, on the other hand, are often far less authentic and complete than historians would have us believe. Authorial intent is lost over time as texts are filtered through new audiences during different cultural moments. As a result, the supposedly closed texts of integrated musicals are often surprisingly open in performance.

In celebrating the openness of the nonintegrated, star-based vehicle, chapter 2 focuses on the great comics whose performance of Jewishness during the white melting pot (roughly between the second decade of the twentieth century and the mid-1960s) helped audiences to realize that the Jewish experience provided insights into the struggle for assimilation not only of Jews but also of other marginalized ethnoracial groups. That time span roughly coincides with the tension between the white melting pot and Horace Kallen's cultural pluralism, which championed the hyphenated American. Jews were one of the marginalized, off-white groups that carefully negotiated the thin line between ethnicity and race. Part of the challenge for Jewish performers was to play both sides of the bargain: to maintain their ethnoracial identity and still become sufficiently "whitened" to gain limited assimilation. Jewish performers, in effect, were guides who devised fluid, assimilationist strategies to subvert stable notions of Anglo-American identity. Using theatricality, playfulness, and improvisation, these comic cocreators appropriated numerous racial, ethnic, and gendered disguises not only within the musical as a whole but often within a given scene or song. The chapter includes discussions of performers such as Eddie Cantor, Al Jolson, Bert Lahr, Ed Wynn, the Marx Brothers, and Fanny Brice.

In building my case for the openness of the form, chapter 3 identifies integrated musicals as works-in-process that constantly reinvent themselves as products of their cultural moments. The chapter traces the musical's striving toward integration from *Show Boat* until today. Rather than a linear outgrowth from the Hammerstein model, however, the integrated musical has consistently borrowed from prevailing theatrical conventions, the sociocultural zeitgeist, and an eclectic variety of sources. In exploring the material conditions in which these texts were created and mounted, I also address the complex collaborative process of mounting a musical, from casting choices to directorial auteurship, both of which often subvert the written word.

Chapter 4 addresses four musicals whose popularity, at least in part, sprang from their ability to provide utopian solutions to social problems experienced by audiences during specific cultural moments. By promoting an assimilationist strategy within a grassroots, populist setting, *Oklahoma!* helped heal New Deal–Conservative tensions as well as America's own anti-Semitism during World War II. *Fiddler on the Roof* (1964) reflects the generational conflict between middle-class values and an emerging youthful counterculture in the 1960s. *A Chorus Line* (1975) negotiates the tension between individual autonomy and capitulation to an increasingly corporate America within the context of the 1970s "me" generation. Finally, *Les Misérables* (1987) endorses the power of the individual to create change during a period of cynicism and apathy about the possibility of larger social reform. (*Les Mis* raises the intriguing complication of a work that was written and first performed abroad but with one eye trained on its eventual performance in New York and in cities across America.)

Chapter 5 begins with a discussion of enigmatic, unfinished characters, which I then apply to three musicals produced within a year after the Stonewall riots: *Company* (1970), *Coco* (1969), and *Applause* (1970). Each of these musicals involves or suggests sexually ambiguous characters, but the texts are left open, subject to a plurality of readings that will inevitably change with time and in performance. I have made the issue of homosexuality salient here because the three musicals are so obviously products of an important cultural marker, the Stonewall riots. Although the texts of each survive, they are incomplete by themselves. Their authenticity is inextricably linked with performance, which is a function of their historical moment of production. It is this interplay that provides audiences with answers for reading and decoding the provocative issues these musicals raise in terms of gendered identity.

Musicals, both integrated and nonintegrated, thrive on ambiguity and openness. By overprivileging the text in such a collaborative form, historians tend to ignore what makes musical theatre so vital to American popular culture; its complex relationship to its historical moment of creation and performance.

◆ ◆ ◆ ◆ ◆ ◆ ◆

Acknowledgments

I owe a great debt of thanks to the archivists who have helped me research this book and secure permissions. In particular, I thank Maryann Chach of the Shubert Archives; Marty Jacobs and Marguerite Lanvin of the Museum of the City of New York; Jeremy Megraw of the Lincoln Center Library of the Performing Arts; Robin Walton, Karen Smith, and Carol Cornicelli of the Rodgers and Hammerstein Organization; Roberta Staats of the Cole Porter estate; and Dave Olson of Warner Music. Thanks also to the Johns Hopkins University Press, the publishers of *Theatre Journal.*

This book grew from my dissertation at the City University of New York. Three distinguished scholars guided me throughout the project: Jill Dolan, who supervised the dissertation, Judith Milhous, and Marvin Carlson. Through patience and gentle prodding, Jill encouraged me to find my own scholarly voice, for which I will always be grateful. It was Judy who taught me that practitioners have an obligation to document what they have assimilated in production, a lesson I faithfully pass on to my own graduate students. Marvin's own work on semiotics and reception has inspired much in this book and done much to shape the way I read musicals and theatre in general. I cannot thank them enough for teaching me to see theatre in new ways and for helping a practitioner develop a new vocabulary and perspective. Their professional generosity has been ongoing, and their influence on my work has been enormous.

Ralph Locke at Eastman painstakingly went through an early version of this book manuscript. His ability to make me see both sides of any issue has been invaluable. I particularly thank Stacy Wolf for her comments on the *Oklahoma!* material in chapter 4. Her scholarship on musical theatre performance, especially her book *A Problem Like Maria,* has significantly affected my own work. Thanks also to Alisa Solomon and to the Center for Lesbian and Gay Studies for awarding me the first annual Monette-Horwitz dissertation prize, which provided an incentive to transform my writing into a viable book. David Román and Harry Elam did much to help shape the section on *Oklahoma!* that appeared in *Theatre Journal.* Steven Carr's work on anti-Semitism and the film industry inspired many of the observations about *Oklahoma!,* and he has encouraged my ongoing research in performing Jewishness, not only in America but in France. Rob Hume's generosity demystified a rather complex indexing program, and I thank him for that kindness, among others. Special thanks go to Alisa Roost, who has consistently been a valued sounding board and friend.

At Roosevelt University, Belinda Bremner plowed through an earlier version of this manuscript on short notice, offering much appreciated editorial suggestions. Thanks also to Brigitte Erbe, without whom this book would not have been written. She managed to find summer grant money throughout my career at Roosevelt and was instrumental in securing additional funds to secure permissions. Similar thanks go to my chair, Joel Fink, who supported my research leave to complete this project. Above all I owe an ongoing thank you to my students at Roosevelt, who invariably force me to reevaluate my positions and ideas about musical theatre. I am fortunate, for they teach me; their enthusiasm for the form does much to keep mine kindled.

Since this is a performance-based history, I believe it is necessary to thank the many practitioners who, over the years, have helped teach me about the practice of musical theatre and theatre in general: Ellen Stewart, Tom Eyen, Joe Papp, Fred Ebb, Ron Field, Denny Shearer, Chita Rivera, Robert Morse, Mimi Hines, Dorothy Collins, Ruby Keeler, Ann Corio, Michael Iannucci, Carleton Carpenter, Helen Gallagher, Sue Ane Langdon, Michael Callan, Gordon MacRae, Maria Karnilova, Tammy Grimes, Julie Wilson, Paula Laurence, Van Johnson, Rosemary Prinz, Peter and Aniko Palmer, Jack Cassidy, and Bill Hayes, among many others. Judy Insell shared many insights about the production history of Alan Jay Lerner's musicals. Marvin Hamlisch and Mitzi Hamilton provided information about *A Chorus Line,* and Tony Stevens shared some of his experiences working with Gower Champion and Bob

Fosse. Stephen Schwartz generously discussed the production history of his musicals with my students at Roosevelt, not once but twice. These artists may not agree with what I have written, but certainly their knowledge and expertise has been a catalyst for my own research.

I particularly thank Guy Little for thirty years of unconditional friendship and professional mentoring. Thanks also to Jerry Bell, with whom I have been playing Botticelli for a similar amount of time and who has devoted more than twenty-five years to the restoration and revival of lost musicals. Bill Gile has been a valued collaborator, longtime friend, and source of information. Thanks to Joy Hawkins, a wonderful director and actress, for providing an artistic home for me in Key West; Albert Bermel for being a long-time teacher, friend, and collaborator; Jane Phillips for her incredible support; and the late Frank Taylor for encouraging me to find a way to make musical theatre accessible to a wider, cross-disciplinary audience. Sir John Tydeman has been a terrific sounding board about British musicals and performers, and I cherish our visits in London. Patrick Honoré has kept me abreast about musical theatre and dance in Paris and has been a gracious host. Thanks also to Jay Jeffries and David Cleaver for their insights and conversations and to all my friends at Marie's Crisis, whose limitless passion for the Broadway musical helps keep New York so special. I also acknowledge my nephew, Zachary DeLuca, whose love of magic reminds me of my love for musical theatre.

I am especially grateful to Robert Schanke, my series editor at Southern Illinois University Press, for his perceptive and canny editorial suggestions. His comments have contributed significantly to reshaping, refocusing, and reorganizing the book. Working with him has been a joy, and I am fortunate to have had such a fine series editor. Many thanks also go to Karl Kageff, the acting editor-in-chief at SIU Press, for caring about the project, treating it with importance, and facilitating each step of the publishing process.

I thank Maggie Wirth for providing me with a base in New York to complete research and to secure permissions, for her own astute feedback as a longtime practitioner, for Christmas and Thanksgiving dinners, for learning how to make pot-roasted tongue, and for being the best of friends. Finally, thanks to Ixann, who found a fantasy cottage for me to finish rewrites while in Paris and who has encouraged my work with an astonishing intelligence as well as with the best *rognons* and *poivrons* in the world.

Unfinished Show Business

1

◆ ◆ ◆ ◆ ◆ ◆ ◆

Celebrating Incompleteness

A theatre experience which lives in the present must be close to the pulse of the time, just as a great fashion designer is never blindly looking for originality but is mysteriously blending his creativity with the ever-changing surface of life.—Peter Brook, *The Open Door*

Musicals wed text, performance, and reception to create meaning within specified historical contexts. Works-in-process, they are open and fluid, subject to a great deal of variation, even subversion, in the way they are performed. As such, in their original productions or over time, they often assume lives of their own that can be quite independent from the original intentions of their authors. It is their innate incompleteness—the gaps and absences caused by performance and reception—that this book celebrates. Truly they are unfinished show business.

Formalistic histories have tended to regard nonintegrated, pre–Rodgers and Hammerstein musicals as unfinished or open texts and assumed their artistic inferiority, while privileging the artistic aspirations of the post–Rodgers and Hammerstein texts as closed, autonomous, and artistically superior. Part of my goal is to challenge assumptions about what has been privileged and what has not. When considered in performance, integrated musicals are often much less complete and autonomous than we would have them be. Similarly, nonintegrated musicals, in which the star performer was often cocreator, were never meant to be fixed or closed in the first place. To study and compare musicals, we need to look at them alongside one another, which, at best, becomes difficult once one makes formalistic, hierarchical assumptions about value.

Speaking of labels, categories, and aesthetic value judgments in a larger, historiographical sense, Lawrence Levine challenges the "world of adjectival boxes . . . of continual defensiveness and endless emendations, this world in which things could not be truly compared because they were so rarely laid out horizontally, next to one another, but were always positioned above or below each other on an infinite vertical scale."[1] Rather than a formalistic look at the development of the genre, my interest is in the material conditions that produce musicals, not only in terms of the process whereby a text is transformed through a complex, collaborative production machine into performance but also in sociocultural terms.

As a strand of popular culture, musicals have been characterized by their playful acknowledgment of the messiness of American identity since the days of Ned Harrigan and Tony Hart in the late 1870s. Even the most serious musicals often offer happy or at least uplifting endings. These happy endings inevitably suggest that there are no insuperable class barriers in America and that all ethnicities, races, and genders can triumph and transcend perceived notions of identity through will and desire. These happy endings are deceptive, however, just as happy endings are deceptive in Euripides' plays and Shakespeare's comedies. If the deus ex machina at the end of a play by Euripides only highlights the disturbing and seemingly insolvable problems raised during the course of the drama, musicals similarly are far more interesting for the provocative issues they raise in terms of American attitudes toward race, ethnicity, class, and gender than for the happy endings they tack on at the final curtain. Since these attitudes shift with time, musicals intrinsically become works-in-process or unfinished business.

The idea that theatrical texts are innately open and incomplete is certainly not a new concept. Roland Barthes develops the notion of the death of the author and of authorial intent in *Image, Music, and Text* (1977). According to Barthes, the text is a paradox and involves a plurality of readings rather than the autonomous, authentic reading modernist critics ascribed to authorial intent before postmodernism: "Hence, no vital 'respect' is due to the Text: it can be broken (which is just what the Middle Ages did with two nevertheless authoritative texts—Holy Scripture and Aristotle); it can be read without the guarantee of its father, the restitution of the intertext paradoxically abolishing any legacy. It is not that the Author may not 'come back' in the Text, in his text, but he then does so as a 'guest.'"[2] In terms of postserial music, Barthes applies the same principle. The interpreter no longer tries to follow any authentic text but, as in opera seria, becomes a coauthor of the score: "We know that today post-serial music has radically altered the role of the 'interpreter,' who is called on to be in some sort the co-author of the score, completing it rather than giving it 'expression.' The Text is very much a score of this new kind: it asks of the reader a practical collaboration."[3]

Directors such as Tyrone Guthrie and Peter Brook follow the same line of reasoning. In championing a relativistic, historical approach to production, Guthrie argues against an ideal performance of Shakespeare. Marvin Carlson summarizes his position: "Any work of art will always be a partial perspective of that observer at that historical moment, and every performance can only be that performing group's comment on the play, their interpretation of an open-ended score, to which the audience will add yet another level of interpretation."[4] Brook echoes Guthrie's open-ended approach to the text: "Many years ago, it used to be claimed that one must 'perform the play as Shakespeare wrote it.' Today, the absurdity of this is more or less recognized: nobody knows what scenic form he had in mind. All that one knows is that he wrote a chain of words that have in them the possibility of giving birth to forms that are constantly renewed."[5] Since the text is a function of a given cultural moment, both in terms of performance and reception, it is logical that the text, by itself, is open-ended and incomplete.

In a similar vein, William E. Gruber maintains that performance must call the text into question.[6] Gruber cites Nahum Tate's version of *King Lear* (1681), in which Cordelia was played by the promiscuous Mrs. Barry, who was greeted with laughter when she referred to her "virgin innocence." Gruber also notes that the character of Lysistrata, in its original ancient Greek incarnation, was played by a man. How, he wonders, does this affect a play about a patriarchal society and its attitudes toward women, particularly revolutionary women? Just as a musical score is a blueprint for performance, a text is open, subject to performance and to the stage conventions of its time. Similarly, J. L. Styan insists that because of the uniqueness of each performer who interacts with a role, "we should no longer look for definitive characterization, but rather for the spectrum of a character."[7] Commenting on Styan, Gruber asserts, like Barthes and Guthrie, that the theatrical text is incomplete, characterized as it is by absences and gaps:

> The hermeneutics of drama must not automatically presuppose a stable text, nor can the text stand as an ideal which any performance in any age must realize. As no narrative is ever independent of the occasion of its telling, so no play is ever independent of its performance. This dependence does not radically diminish the text's importance in criticism of drama. The text is still primary, but it is no longer separate from the needs of its viewers or from other contemporary forms of expression.[8]

Gruber's attack on a stable text and Barthes' insistence on the death of the author mirror the attack of postmodern musicologists on the authenticity of text. By *authenticity* I refer here to musicology's concern with recreating the intentions of the composer in terms of performance.

Richard Taruskin adapts Barthes' theory of the death of the author to music, advocating an aesthetic that attributes real authenticity not to authorial intent but to the creation of something new from an incomplete text from the past. He is opposed to the belief that reimagining something old is better than creating something new. Rather than naively trying to replicate the impossible, authenticity, for Taruskin, would be better defined by the representation of the times and tastes of contemporary performers and audiences. In attacking textual completeness and authorial intent, Taruskin goes beyond early music. Modernist musicologists, he argues, are devoted to the nineteenth-century concept of *Werktreue,* which posits that since Bach, it is possible to ascertain, through original manuscripts and musicological scholarship, a recreation of the composer's intentions during the original performance. According to Taruskin, if musicians believe this postulate, how do they justify the greatness of Fürtwangler, who freely interpreted seemingly inviolable Beethoven texts, adding unnotated nuances and varying tempi?[9] Fürtwangler's embellishments were a product of his own imagination and artistic sensibility, not of historical or textual authenticity.

Composition concerns are different from performance concerns. Once a composer completes his composition, he relates to it as a performer, if he is one, or as a listener. Taruskin quotes Irving Berlin, who said of Fred Astaire, "I like him because he doesn't change my songs, or if he does, he changes them for the better."[10] Modernists, on the other hand, cling to the notion that Romantic music is verifiable and can be performed authentically:

> I have seen a review of a recording of Liszt's keyboard arrangements of Beethoven symphonies in which the pianist is reproached for vio-

> lating the letter of the score; and even one in which an authentically Ivesian performer of the Concord Sonata (that is, one who attempted to capture something of the perpetually evolving and contingent character the composer prized as the very essence of that work) was dourly enjoined "to learn humility in the face of the text."[11]

This kind of criticism is common in theatre as well. Purists criticized Peter Brook for stripping down *Hamlet* (2001) to two hours to find the essence of the text. Similarly, in the 1920s, George Bernard Shaw attacked John Barrymore's acclaimed portrait of Hamlet (1922–24). The Barrymore production took many liberties with the text. After watching a performance in London, Shaw sent Barrymore a telegram admonishing him for presuming to rewrite Shakespeare.[12] Despite Shaw's privileging Shakespeare's text as inviolable, Barrymore's Hamlet was regarded as one of the great performances of his generation.

Musicologists attack Taruskin's postmodern antagonism toward the notion of *Werktreue* and authenticity, just as musical theatre historians cling to the authority of a fixed text. Musicologist Roland Jackson laments the postmodern tendency to denigrate the timeless and the universal:

> [Taruskin's views are] typical of the swing towards subjectivism in current critical thought, of a movement away from the single work, from the search for objective reality, to pluralism and individuality of interpretation, away from the notion of the "timeless" work (or "timeless" performance) to a consideration of the personal responses of those who at various times have experienced (or will experience) the work. Implicit in the new scepticism and subjectivity are its anti-textuality (did the work exist in a single form? Did the composer have only one performance in mind?), its refunctioning (the work is simply adapted to new situations), its conceptualism (works are as we perceive them), and its historicism (history and its manifestations "exist" only in accordance with our view of them).[13]

Taruskin's response is that Jackson sounds like a musicological T. S. Eliot in his modernism:

> Prof. Jackson's "timeless" is a familiar euphemism for "inviolate" or "sacred," perhaps taboo. Performance practice, on this account, is a sacrament that aims at something akin to transubstantiation. The reality it seeks is not objective but transcendent. The singleness to-

> ward which it aspires is to be found not in the untidy world we all inhabit (still less the one Bach or Mozart inhabited) but in the realm of romance. I cannot see what it has to do with scholarship.[14]

For Taruskin, tradition is an invention that is designed to suit contemporary purposes. Rather than debunking historical performances as inauthentic, he argues that reconstructing performance or reviving the past enables one to be original in today's musical world. This belief echoes Nietzsche, who wrote, "We try to give ourselves a new past from which we should have liked to descend instead of the past from which we actually descended."[15] In other words, historians write the past in terms of the present to read the present in terms of the past.

The questions Taruskin raises about authenticity and the privileging of the musical text can easily be applied to musical theatre. Jérome Savary, the most successful director of musical theatre in Paris for the past thirty years and the current head of the Opéra-Comique, agrees. Noted for his sometimes radical reenvisioning of French operettas and musicals, Savary advocates seeking new, relevant productions to "restore the theatre to its true dignity."[16] Savary's ideas are not uncommon in Europe. Peter Brook's reinvention of *Carmen* recognized that Bizet's text was filled with the conventions of nineteenth-century opera rather than the musical theatre of today. In staging a contemporary *Carmen,* Brook dispensed with many of the conventions that he believed were outmoded and interfered with the purity of the plot. According to Brook, he realized that much in *Carmen* seemed boring to him, including the reliance on colorful scenery, spectacle, and processions. He also questioned the necessity of a chorus of eighty invading the stage for no particular reason except to dress it and to provide a choral framework that he felt unnecessary to the story.[17] Brook's revisionist approach no doubt superseded even postmodern musicology in that he altered the score to strip away the fat and focus on the opera as a piece of compelling musical theatre:

> Sacrilegiously, we confessed to ourselves that the music was not consistently of the same quality. What was quite exceptional was the music which expressed the relationships between the protagonists, and we were struck by the fact that it was into these musical lines that Bizet had poured his deepest feelings and his finest sense of emotional truth. Thus we made the decision to see if we could extract from the four hours of the full score what we deliberately called

> the *Tragedy of Carmen,* referring to the concentrated interrelation of a small number of protagonists in Greek tragedy.[18]

Brook's extreme tampering with the Bizet score raised many a musicological eyebrow. At the same time, Brook and Savary, who has done much the same kind of tampering with operetta in France, are not alone in advocating a historically relativistic, open-ended approach to the texts of musical theatre and opera. American directors, on the other hand, both in opera and in musical theatre, tend to be more cautious and positivistic in their privileging of the text and reluctance to veer from traditional approaches.

The notion that historians of the American musical should privilege text over performance is puzzling. Authenticity, in terms of authorial intent, is, if anything, more tenuous in the collaborative medium of musicals than in other forms of theatre. The very process of mounting a Broadway musical precludes the ultimate authority of the text. To an extent, this preclusion is also true of nonmusical theatre, which foregrounds a long history of collaborative production work in which authorial intent is ignored or glossed over. Chekhov fought bitterly with Stanislavsky over interpretations of his plays; *The Seagull* (1896), however, was a dismal failure until Stanislavsky restaged it for the Moscow Art Theatre. Tennessee Williams and Elia Kazan were famously at loggerheads over *Cat on a Hot Tin Roof* (1955). Kazan urged Williams to rewrite the final act to guarantee the play's commercial success. William Inge and Joshua Logan had similar battles over *Picnic* (1953). Inge finally acceded to Logan's demands to change the ending of the play, then spent the rest of his career fussing about the rape of his text. Both Williams and Inge happily spent the royalties earned by their artistic compromise during production and were bitterly disappointed when Kazan and Logan were loathe to work with them again.

One must be similarly skeptical of authorial intent in terms of the texts of musicals. The original production of *Pippin* (1972) was certainly not faithful to the writer and composer's original text or intentions. In fact, director-choreographer Bob Fosse banned Stephen Schwartz (composer) and Roger O'Hirson (librettist) from rehearsals. Like Williams and Inge, the authors complained bitterly over Fosse's appropriation of their work for his own purposes, but, arguably, *Pippin*'s commercial success was due to Fosse's production rather than the text. Certainly Jerome Robbins and George Abbott invariably shaped and often helped rewrite and refashion the musicals they directed. Out-of-town tryouts were opportunities for collaboration among authors, director, choreographer, designers, and stars.

Gower Champion turned *Hello, Dolly* (1964) into a hit before it came to New York by altering the script to accommodate the big production numbers at which Carol Channing excelled. Whatever the final commercial outcome, the privileging of an authentic, inviolable text is antithetic to the collaborative way in which musicals are created. Often the scripts originally submitted by authors of integrated musicals were virtually unrecognizable by the end of the rehearsal and tryout process. One is reminded of Jewish writer Bert Shevelove's famous quip that he only wished Hitler could have authored a Broadway musical and suffered the tortures of an out-of-town tryout.

Much of the privileging of musical theatre texts stems from the policy of the Rodgers and Hammerstein office, whose published scripts included stage directions taken from performances of the original Broadway productions that became a mark of textual authenticity. When the shows were remounted for the road or internationally, Rodgers and Hammerstein often hired stage managers to duplicate the exact Broadway production rather than adapt their text to a different company, locale, or even country, a practice that still exists today in remounting both national and international productions of Broadway successes. The Rodgers and Hammerstein office was notoriously vigilant in assigning the rights to their canon, both to professionals and to amateurs, and often sent representatives to monitor mountings throughout the country and abroad to guarantee the authenticity of the performance. If the representatives questioned faithfulness to the authors' original intent, production rights were withdrawn. Perhaps the most notorious example of this was the 1983 Anne Bogart production of *South Pacific* at New York University, an experimental piece set in a mental hospital that featured multiple actors playing Nellie Forbush. The Rodgers and Hammerstein office withdrew the rights after sending representatives to see one performance. The reason for this vigilant monitoring of productions is not difficult to fathom. The Rodgers and Hammerstein organization asserted the autonomy of the composer, lyricist, and librettist (and, depending on how Rodgers and Hammerstein were getting along with Agnes de Mille at any given moment, at times the choreographer). Integration, for which Rodgers and Hammerstein carried the banner, supposedly depended on the autonomy of the closed text and the faithful reproduction of the "definitive" Broadway production.

Prior to the development of the Rodgers and Hammerstein integrated musical play, producers sent shows out on the road, sometimes with the original Broadway cast, sometimes with replacement stars who demanded the shows be tailored to their specific needs and talents. With the privileging of the integrated musical over the nonintegrated musical, the authority seemingly reverted from performer to text. In asserting the autonomy of the text and, by implication, the idea that the original production was the ideal, Rodgers and Hammerstein insisted on duplicate productions. One salient example is the London remounting of *South Pacific*, in which Mary Martin recreated her role as Nellie Forbush and about which Richard Rodgers and Joshua Logan have conflicting stories. Rodgers had sent stage manager Jerome Whyte to reproduce the New York production and brought Logan in at the last minute to touch it up. Logan, expecting to see a nearly finished product, was appalled at the state of the performance: "Every move on the stage was within a millimeter of the move that was made by the New York company, and every reading was a tape recording played at the right speed. It was perfect—and at the same time perfectly awful."[19] Even worse, Logan found Martin lacking the spontaneity of her original performance. What remained was mechanical and strident. Rodgers, on the other hand, "was appalled at the staging he saw in the London rehearsals, as was Martin," since Logan attempted to inject life into the London production by slowing it down for English audiences, and by making amendments to the staging as well as to the text.[20] Indeed, when Logan directed the film version, he incorporated significant changes in the text to adapt the show to a cinematic form, much to the frustration and displeasure of Rodgers and Hammerstein. The point is not whether Logan's changes were improvements or detriments but that the authors believed there was a definitive version of their work that had to be reproduced, not reenvisioned.

Ted Chapin, currently in charge of the Rodgers and Hammerstein organization, apparently has realized that much of this canon, if it is to survive, needs reenvisioning. Its future popularity lies in its relevance to contemporary audiences. As a result, a revisionist, multiracial production of *Carousel* was mounted at London's National Theatre and at New York's Lincoln Center; an interracial, textually altered *Cinderella* starring Brandy was presented on television and later transferred to the stage in a national touring production; and a drastically rewritten *South Pacific* (2001), starring a middle-aged Glenn Close in the unlikely role of Nellie Forbush, was broadcast on network television. In 2002, David Henry Hwang, author of *M. Butterfly* (1988), rewrote the libretto for *Flower Drum Song* (1958) to make it reflect contemporary Asian American sensibilities.

Cameron MacIntosh, the producer of a string of phenomenally successful British "poperettas" since the 1980s, vigilantly guards his properties in much the same fashion that Rodgers and Hammerstein guarded theirs for so many years.[21] MacIntosh brags that his productions are interchangeable. According to MacIntosh, it doesn't matter if one sees *Les Misérables* in London, on Broadway, or in Peoria. The productions are identical, which is counterintuitive to Peter Brook's argument that "the same play put on today in Paris, in Bucharest, or in Baghdad will obviously be very different in form. The locale, the social and political climate, the prevailing thought and culture, must all have their influence on what makes a bridge between subject and the audience, what affects people."[22] *Les Misérables* is an international hit, playing to a variety of cultures and social and political climates, not the least of which reside in the United States itself. Interchangeable, duplicate productions seem more like mass-produced technology than theatre to me. MacIntosh's boast that his productions are all the same also denigrates the importance of the performer, since the privileging of an absolute text promotes interchangeable performance. This kind of theatrical mass production reminds me of Norma Desmond's famous line in *Sunset Boulevard,* in which she extols the art of silent film by declaring that the actors had faces then. Valuing interchangeable actors, unless one wants to advocate an übermarionette school of musical theatre, does not make for exciting performance. Time, however, will no doubt temper MacIntosh's vigilance, as it has tempered the policy of the Rodgers and Hammerstein office about authenticity in production and the privileging of closed texts (including stage directions). Many of the MacIntosh musicals involve complex technology, such as the falling chandelier in *Phantom of the Opera* (1988) and the onstage helicopter of *Miss Saigon* (1991). How will these shows be reenvisioned for regional theatres or venues with less spectacular budgets in the future? Musicals that run fifteen years on Broadway become tourist events rather than reflections of a dynamically changing culture. This duration in itself helps sap the vitality from the form. As of now MacIntosh's musicals are regarded as universal, but universality is mythical and consequently has a pitifully short life. Text and performance are products of given cultural moments; when those moments change, what seems closed magically opens.

The privileging of the closed text is inextricably linked with the idea of definitive performance. If popular culture is a product of its given cultural moment, how can one subscribe to the idea of a definitive performance, since that very notion is dependent on historical relativism? The French director Michel Saint-Denis, a nephew of the text-centered Copeau and lifelong admirer of Stanislavsky's productions of Chekhov, nevertheless argues against ideal, definitive productions, since text and performance are subject to historical subjectivity. Saint-Denis argues that each country has a constantly changing historical personality. Since a theatre practitioner inevitably filters a text through his own country and his own time, works from other countries and other periods must be recreated in contemporary terms. The challenge, for Saint-Denis, is to meld contemporary performance style with the flavor of the original to create something new and relevant. One must take the historical style of a piece into consideration, but reconstruction is impossible with modern acting styles and modern audiences.[23] For instance, Thomas Betterton's approach to playing Restoration comedy would differ markedly from that of any actor in 2005. The twentieth century itself has seen radical changes in acting training, with the advent of film, television, and the privileging of a more naturalistic style of acting. The celebrated performances of John Barrymore, along with those of Katherine Cornell and Lunt and Fontanne, theatrical icons of the early to mid twentieth century, might well seem stilted and stagy to contemporary audiences.

The same is true of musical theatre. Both Arthur Laurents and Stephen Sondheim question whether Ethel Merman's presentational performance of Mama Rose in *Gypsy* (1959) would be palatable to contemporary audiences. Merman related a telling story when she was featured on Ralph Edwards's *This Is Your Life* in the mid-1970s. One of the guests paying tribute to Merman's career was Benay Venuta, her longtime friend and standby. Venuta recounted having to go on for Merman as Mama Rose in *Gypsy* and telephoning her for advice on how to play the song "Small World." With a mixture of incredulity and affection, Merman recalled instructing Venuta to simply sit on the trunk, sing the song, and, at the end, get up, walk downstage, and take a bow. Merman was a marvelous performer trained in a different era. Words such as characterization, intention, motivation, and tactics were foreign to her actorly vocabulary. As a result, years after working with her, Sondheim unkindly likened Merman to "a talking dog."[24] Similarly, Laurents maintains acting was not her long suit: "Acting hadn't made Ethel Merman Ethel Merman. . . . To help the acting, I wrote stage directions for her speeches: 'slower,' 'softer,' 'louder,' 'faster,' 'starting flat, then building.' An actress would have broken pencils furiously crossing them out; Ethel quoted them if any of her line readings were questioned."[25]

I loved her; however, one can only speculate how today's younger audiences would respond to her performances. The saddest aspect of live performance is that it is so ephemeral. Once the performance is over, the memory lives only with those fortunate enough to have been audience members. On the other hand, perhaps this is fortuitous. New generations, used to different acting styles and theatrical conventions, would undoubtedly respond less enthusiastically. I have shown my musical theatre students a videotape of the 1958 television production of *Kiss Me, Kate,* which featured Alfred Drake and Patricia Morison, the stars of the original 1948 production. The students much preferred the performances of Marin Mazzie and Bryan Stokes Mitchell, the stars of the 1999 revival, who, in my opinion, work a lot harder with significantly less result and belabor their laughs. I was raised, however, on different musical theatre conventions and an older style of musical theatre performance. My students were raised on MTV and a different performance aesthetic. Which is preferable? It depends on the conventions one is used to.

The idea of the "definitive," closed performance also is a result of the marketing of original Broadway cast recordings beginning in the 1940s. When these "authentic" cast albums first emerged, "definitive" performances were recorded for posterity and subsequent studio recordings were denigrated as inauthentic. With the passage of time and the popularity of revivals on Broadway, however, other "definitive" performances of these same musicals have been recorded. Again, the post–Rodgers and Hammerstein musical is only sixty years old. "Definitive" is a function of age in a form as relatively new as the integrated musical. Which is the definitive recording of *Follies*? One can choose from the original Broadway cast, the London production, the concert version at Lincoln Center, the 2000 Paper Mill Playhouse revival, and the 2001 Broadway revival. The text and score of each of these productions were altered. Those who saw the original production of *Follies,* for example, claim it was definitive. Those who did not see it probably may never see a definitive performance because nothing can live up to its legend. It is the *Rebecca* of musicals. This comparison would be true of Richard Burbage or Thomas Betterton if anyone who had seen these legendary actors still lived. I suspect definitive performances survive far better in the imagination than they would in revival.

To underscore my point that there can be no definitive production of a musical apart from a given cultural moment and that, consequently, the texts of musicals are in themselves necessarily incomplete, many musicals written before the women's movement need to be altered in revival today, either through script or through performance, if they are to be successful (or even simply if they are not to be laughed or booed off the stage). Rather than closed, the texts become unfinished, because the characters must be played to conform to changing societal conventions and audience tastes.

The comic soubrette, for example, a longstanding line of business in musical theatre, is difficult to recreate thirty years after the women's movement. Many were originally written as bimbos, which would alienate contemporary audiences whose attitudes toward women have changed drastically since these roles were first written.

For instance, *Kiss Me, Kate* (1948) features the Lois Lane–Bianca character. Lois is an ambitious performer, in love with her hoofer boyfriend, Bill Calhoun, but not averse to accepting gifts from other men in exchange for sexual favors, which she bestows on the producer of the show in which she and her boyfriend are currently appearing. As originally written and as played by Lisa Kirk, Lois was dizzy and dumb, which somehow excused her behavior and caused audiences in 1948 to laugh at her antics, particularly the showstopping "Always True to You in My Fashion," in which she celebrates her mental fidelity to her boyfriend while enumerating a long list of sexual-financial conquests. The part is challenging to play today. What are contemporary audiences to make of an ambitious woman who sells her sexual favors? Is she so dizzy she truly is not aware of what she's doing? Do we close our eyes when she obviously cheats on her boyfriend? Characters in musicals, generally, must be likable. How does a performer approach Lois so that she is not a dirty joke in a post–women's liberation environment? One choice is to emphasize her genuine love for the irresponsible Bill Calhoun, who is obviously incapable of taking care of her (not to mention himself) or providing her with future security. This approach might justify Lois's doing whatever she can to build a nest egg so she and Bill can share a future together. In the 1999 revival Amy Spanger did little to soften the character's promiscuous edges. Rather than establishing love for her boyfriend, her relationship with Bill was obviously "hot" and based purely on sex. Lois, in effect, became a glorified hooker, who enjoyed sleeping with her boyfriend for sexual pleasure and sleeping with her producer to advance her career. This Lois was far from lovable. Usually, the gangsters and Lois walk off with the show. In this case, everyone but Spanger was nominated for a Tony award.

Wonderful Town (1953) poses similar problems. The musical focuses on Ruth and Eileen, two sisters trying to make their fame and fortune in New York during the 1930s. Ruth is an aspiring writer whose intelligence frightens away potential suitors. Eileen, an aspiring actress, is a blond-haired, blue-eyed mantrap. She manages to charm free dinners and groceries from male admirers by flirting with them but is morally indignant if one comes on to her sexually. This behavior was acceptable and cute in 1953, when Edie

Adams played Eileen in the original production. Eileen's willingness to use men and her dependent nature threaten to be painfully coy and cloying today. In the 2003 Broadway revival, Jennifer Westfeldt approached the role with sincerity and quirkiness, rather than with the wide-eyed, self-consciously cute narcissism that was hailed in 1953 on Broadway and in 1957 in the televised version with Jacquelyn McKeever. A recording in 1999 featured Audra MacDonald, an African American, in the role intended for a blond, blue-eyed man killer. This casting obviously produced a very different Eileen: honest, forthright, and assertive, yet sweet and a bit naive. The performance provided an acceptable enough contrast with Kim Criswell's self-deprecating, wizened Ruth. MacDonald's casting is but one of a variety of acting or directing choices available to make Eileen viable. What was regarded as a closed text in 1953 was necessarily incomplete and opened in a different historical time frame and cultural context.

Similarly, how do we take Ado Annie today? *Oklahoma!* is a product of a considerably more innocent sexual era. Do we pretend that Annie is just innocently kissing lots of boys or is she sexually promiscuous? If she is sexually promiscuous, how does that open the character of Will Parker? How does a contemporary actress approach Hedy LaRue in *How to Succeed in Business Without Really Trying* (1961)? In essence, Hedy is a dirty joke—the whore without a heart of gold. How does one make her likable? Rosemary, in the same show, is a stereotype of the prefeminist woman, who longs to live in New Rochelle and play mah-jongg with her girlfriends while she happily keeps her husband's dinner warm as he climbs the corporate ladder. The Matthew Broderick revival in the mid-1990s opened the text by commenting on the cartoonish quality of the women and by deleting potentially offensive material, such as the song "Cinderella, Darling." Neal Simon's *Little Me* (1962) chronicles the misadventures of Belle Poitrine, who sleeps her way to Hollywood celebrity. The musical has been revived twice, both times unsuccessfully. It is difficult to glorify a title character whose career consists of sexually preying on men in any kind of contemporary cultural context. I would prefer not to call these musicals dated, any more than *Cat on a Hot Tin Roof* and its 1950s attitude toward homosexuality is dated. These works are producible, but they must be made relevant to a different cultural moment if audiences are to accept them. Far from being closed, they are unfinished, which is why musicals in revival are often reinvented, rethought, and sometimes rewritten (and the music reworked) to conform to a new audience.

The Privileging of the Integrated Musical

The notion that integrated musicals are closed and autonomous is largely the result of formalistic histories that have privileged authorial intent and assumed the artistic superiority of integration. Before questioning what becomes privileged and what does not, one must address the issue of genres and categories, as well as the problems they raise. Briefly there are at least three genres of pre–Rodgers and Hammerstein musical theatre: musical comedy, the revue, and American operetta. Although these categories tend to bleed into each other, one must acknowledge their differences. According to the accepted paradigm, musical comedies were often star vehicles (for Al Jolson, Eddie Cantor, George M. Cohan, Marilyn Miller, and Ethel Merman, for example) in which songs and comedy routines were devised to fit the specialties and talents of unique performers. The songs were commonly strung together by a thin, frivolous book, filled with topical references and jokes. Though romantically escapist, musical comedies usually took place in the here and now, often in New York, and were filled with the popular music of the day, a peculiar mixture of European-derived music (often influenced by Jewish composers) and African American–influenced jazz that became the vernacular for show music for nearly fifty years.

The New York locale is important to musical comedy. The Cole Porter, Rodgers and Hart, and Irving Berlin musicals of the 1920s and 1930s appealed to an urban audience. Much of the humor involved the out-of-towner, helpless in the face of New York sophistication, or, in such musical comedies as the Gershwins' *Girl Crazy* (1930) that were set outside New York, the Manhattanite who must deal with the hayseeds he inevitably encounters once he crosses the Rubicon or Hudson River. Oddly the humor in American operetta stems from much the same premise. Although operetta, unlike musical comedy, took place in remote, exotic European settings, the comics were often displaced New Yorkers, such as the reporter in *The Desert Song* (1926), lost in a barbarous world outside Manhattan. Even by the 1950s, a show such as *Call Me Madam* (1950), in which Ethel Merman played a mythical U.S. ambassador to a middle-European country, boasts elements of both musical comedy and operetta in its humorous culture clash between the brash, warm-hearted Merman and the crafty middle Europeans of the mythical Lichtenburg.

Musical comedy was fashioned around a book or plot, thus the term "book musical," no matter how slim or frivolous the vehicle. The revue was sometimes fashioned around a unifying theme; for example, Irving Berlin's

As Thousands Cheer (1933) presented a sequence of scenes and songs that reflected the newspaper headlines of the day. At other times, the revue was glorified vaudeville, with no unifying dialogue to link the skits and songs together. A famous example is *The Ziegfeld Follies* (1907–36).[26] Both musical comedy and the revue focused on the performer as cocreator; they did not strive to connect dialogue, song, and dance into a unified whole. On the contrary, despite the presence of a plot, musical comedy was characterized by its roots in vaudeville and the theatricality of its performance style.

American operetta implies a different horizon of expectations. The stories typically concerned European royalty, rather than the average New Yorker. Settings were exotic and varied to provide spectacle. Plots were romantically escapist, but the music had a distinctly European, sometimes specifically Viennese, flavor.

Musicologists frequently maintain that American operetta is often integrated in significant ways. Rather than being a star vehicle, it features a plot with some ballast, usually a sentimental romance based on class distinctions (the prince in love with a commoner, or the reverse). American operettas produced between 1910 and 1930 are also typified by relatively stable scores, without the preponderance of interpolations typical of musical comedy of the period; nevertheless, "alternate" numbers do exist from production to production. Lyrics, particularly of Americanized versions of European operetta, such as *The Merry Widow* (1907), are often drastically altered in content, far beyond the vicissitudes of translation. Finally, operettas are characterized by a musical style that reflects their geographic, ethnic, and social settings.[27] Typical examples are the German drinking song in *The Student Prince* (1924), the "Pontevedrian" social dances in *The Merry Widow*, the exotic "One Flower in Your Garden" in *The Desert Song*, the Neapolitan "Italian Street Song" in *Naughty Marietta* (1910), and the balalaika accompaniment to the Russian torch song "Smoke Gets in Your Eyes" in *Roberta* (1933). *The Merry Widow* even has an integrated dance, the title waltz, which romantically unites Hanna and Danilo.[28]

The standard narrative argues that *Oklahoma!* brought elements of integration, long characteristic of operetta, into a new genre of musical theatre, the "musical play," a marriage between musical comedy and operetta in which lyrics are cut from the same cloth as the `ook. Most historians agree that Rodgers and Hammerstein refined the integration of dialogue, score, and dance. Some of them, however, disagree about when such integration actually began. Many, including Gerald Bordman, have written about the innovation of the Princess Theatre shows. Beginning in 1915 with *Nobody Home,* the Princess musicals, most of which were composed by Jerome Kern with book and lyrics by P. G. Wodehouse and Guy Bolton, featured songs that furthered plot, whereas the characters were "everyday people—neither cartooned clowns nor cardboard lovers."[29]

Those who venerate the groundbreaking nature of the Princess shows fail to say that much of the innovation stemmed from practical considerations. However one feels about the contribution of the Princess shows to the integration of book, song, and dance, it is important to realize they were conceived by Elisabeth Marbury, a literary agent, to fill a small, struggling 299-seat house and were mounted on a seventy-five-hundred-dollar budget, a shoestring even for 1915. *The Ziegfeld Follies of 1915,* by way of comparison, was capitalized at more than twenty times that figure. Consequently the use of a single set per act, the lack of stars, the small cast, and the modest physical production were a product of economic necessity rather than artistic impetus. Even Bordman, an avid champion of the Princess shows, concedes that it was Marbury who publicized the opening of *Nobody Home,* the first of the Princess musicals, as the beginning of something new and important.[30] It is not surprising that this publicity was self-generated, since the stars and spectacle normally thought necessary for enthusiastic reception were missing from the series.

Although many historians credit the Princess shows as the first examples of integration of dialogue, song, and dance, one needs to treat their claim with caution. The original script for *Very Good Eddie* (1915) boasts characters with comic names such as B. Ava Little ("behave a little") and May Anne Ayes ("mayonnaise"). I suppose one needs to define what one means by integration. Although American operetta boasted certain aspects of integration, it is a real stretch to claim that dialogue, lyrics, and music were of one cloth. Similarly, although some historians claim that the Princess series boasted integration of dialogue and song, according to Bill Gile, who directed the Broadway revival of *Very Good Eddie* (1975) for David Merrick, the original production included several interpolations not integral to the text.[31] Moreover, *Nobody Home* interpolated at least six songs by composers other than Kern.[32] The practice of interpolating songs by a variety of composers, common during this period, furnished additional comedy or novelty material, as well as songs that presumably were intended to become popular outside the context of the show. Interpolation then does not support the idea of a seamless integration of song and dialogue, in which music serves to further character or plot, or both.

Throughout the 1920s and 1930s, composers such as Rudolf Friml, Kern, and Rodgers and lyricists such as Hammerstein, Hart, and Otto Harbach perpetuated publicity that their scores were so well integrated with the plot that individual numbers would not be listed. This claim was made in the programs of *Rose-Marie* (1924; Friml and Hammerstein), *Chee-Chee* (1928; Rodgers and Hart); *The Cat and the Fiddle* (1931; Kern and Hammerstein), and *Music in the Air* (1932; Kern and Hammerstein). Why was it of such importance for these men to claim that their scores were integrated, particularly at a time when hit songs were typically written to be extracted from musicals, recorded, and popularized on radio? My hunch is that the American appropriation of the *Gesamtkunstwerk,* in which drama, music, movement, and spectacle were united in one package, gave musicals a highbrow credence they had lacked before. Incorporating middle- or lower-class Americans into mythologized American musical folk plays such as *Oklahoma!* and *Porgy and Bess* (1935) combined highbrow and lowbrow elements into an intriguing Americanization of European high culture. Experiments with integration during the 1920s are subject to speculation and, like the Princess shows, were probably publicity strategies, at least to some degree. For example, one has to doubt the claims of integration by Hammerstein and Friml in *Rose-Marie* when forty-five chorus girls dressed as Indian totem poles performed "Totem Tom-Tom."[33] If this is an integrated number, what does integration mean? The classic model of the integrated American musical for many years was *My Fair Lady* (1956), whose plot and dialogue Alan Jay Lerner unabashedly filched from George Bernard Shaw. *My Fair Lady* is a wonderful musical; it also skillfully Americanizes a much cherished work by a highbrow English playwright.

Hierarchical categories invite hyperbole. As I've suggested, many historians privilege the Rodgers and Hammerstein canon over the work of Rodgers and Hart. Similarly, Stephen Sondheim scholars write hagiographies to his genius while dismissing the works of Jerry Herman. Such difference is a matter of taste. Histories of musical theatre abound with prioritization and privileging of categories. On the one hand, categories and terms must be acknowledged; on the other hand, they often raise more questions than they answer.

Labels such as "integrated," "nonintegrated," "musical comedy," and "operetta" privilege one aspect of a work but deny others. While the original creative team may well have intended integration to some degree, the realities of theatre at different times and in different places intervene and alter the work heavily. What remains often is the title, the basic plot, and certain celebrated songs. Integrated aspects are at times respected and cherished and at other times "improved," updated, or betrayed, depending on one's point of view or one's fondness for the genre in question. All one has to do is watch the Jeanette MacDonald–Nelson Eddy versions of the Victor Herbert, Sigmund Romberg, and Friml operettas on film to realize how drastically Hollywood reenvisioned properties such as *Naughty Marietta, The New Moon* (1928), and *Rose-Marie.* In terms of popularity, these film versions of American operettas may have reached their widest audience by deliberately tinkering with the "integrity" of the original texts. Like musical comedy and operetta, integration and nonintegration are not inherent, stable properties of a work but mutable functions of its changing reception and performance over time.

As popular-culture critic Leslie Fiedler has argued in *The Inadvertent Epic,* once created, a work takes on a life of its own.[34] Harriet Beecher Stowe's novel *Uncle Tom's Cabin* was reworked as one of the most popular melodramas of the nineteenth century. Although George Aiken wrote the most famous adaptation, several other playwrights were responsible for a plethora of stage versions. Stowe's novel eventually found many other incarnations, including an early-twentieth-century musicalization by the Duncan Sisters, vaudeville performers who revived the property and filmed parts of it as late as the 1930s; a sequence in a Shirley Temple film; an episode in one of the *Our Gang* comedies; various film versions; and a Jerome Robbins ballet, "The Small House of Uncle Thomas," in *The King and I* (1951). One of the most famous images associated with the work is Eliza pursued by a pack of bloodhounds as she crosses the ice to freedom. The bloodhounds do not appear in the Stowe novel or in the popular Aiken play; nevertheless, their presence has entered the popular imagination.

Similarly, musicologist Susan McClary has argued that Bizet's *Carmen* (1874) is filled with ambiguities that have made it a "puzzle . . . [that] will pass on, still unresolved, to future generations."[35] Although Bizet, Henri Meilhac, and Ludovic Halévy imploded many of the conventions of comic opera, the work was originally intended for the Opéra-Comique, a venerable French institution that catered to a middle-class audience, whose horizons of expectations did not include a gypsy spitfire who dabbled in prostitution and smuggling, her passive lover, and a final scene in which both the hero and the heroine die violently. By 1875 *Carmen* had opened in Vienna. It was no longer filled with spoken dialogue—a requisite of French comic opera—but outfitted with Ernest Guiraud's recitatives. Whereas the French had attacked Bizet for veering from generic propriety and were concerned that the story's prostitutes and bohemians smacked of the 1871 Paris Commune, the Viennese loved the piece, for it was no longer constrained by the conventions of its original French genre: "Thus the 'Carmen' embraced by the Viennese was not the same 'Carmen' the Parisians had repulsed. In other words, the opera was finally only 'understood' when its premises, its materials, its sources were no longer entirely intelligible."[36]

McClary discusses several twentieth-century productions of the opera, including a 1925 revisionist production in Moscow, in which the heroine is no longer a treacherous, ethnic "other" but a champion of the oppressed proletariat fighting injustice; Oscar Hammerstein II's all-black musical play *Carmen Jones* (1943); a 1984 production at the New York City Opera, in which Carmen appears as a freedom fighter during the Spanish Civil War; and Peter Brook's aforementioned 1981 stripped-down version, in which the conventions Bizet had been forced to acknowledge for the original production at the Opéra-Comique were no longer necessary. Since McClary's book was published, a new musical production, *Carman,* directed and choreographed by Matthew Bourne, has opened in London (2001), as well as the United States. Here the fiery gypsy prostitute has become a bisexual male garage mechanic. The Bourne piece obviously reflects, in part, the male as sex object, a turning the tables on gender roles that reflects attitudes toward gender and sexuality drastically different from the work's genesis in 1874. The piece has become an open text that takes on new meanings depending on its production, reception, and cultural moment.

The same is true of operetta, musical comedy, the nonintegrated musical, and its integrated successor. Again I am not negating the value of genres and categories; I am arguing that despite the original intentions of the author, authentic texts seldom survive from production to production. *Irene* (1919) was a nonintegrated musical comedy; in its 1973 revival, it was reshaped with elements of integration not intended in its original mounting. As we shall see, *Show Boat* has undergone myriad incarnations. Some have stressed aspects of integration, whereas others have emphasized musical comedy or vaudeville conventions. It is valuable to research and preserve aesthetic, formalistic elements of genre. The truth, however, is that any theatrical work takes on a life of its own from production to production. The horizon of expectations for a production of *Carmen* at the Metropolitan Opera in New York is not the same as that for a Peter Brook production at the Vivian Beaumont Theatre. Site of performance, cultural climate, and intended audience are factors that will, for better or worse, question textual authenticity.

Highbrow, Lowbrow, Middlebrow

The privileging of the integrated musical inevitably raises a highbrow-lowbrow argument. The musical seems to combine both lowbrow and highbrow elements. According to Paul Filmer, Val Rimmer, and Dave Walsh, the film musical has inspired several sociocultural studies, while the stage musical has depended on historical accounts of the development of the form and musicological studies: "One reason for this may be the uncomfortable way in which the musical straddles the high/low cultural divide. It is too 'lowbrow' musically and dramatically to interest high-art critics, yet it is too conventional and mundane for culture critics of popular musical form such as jazz and rock."[37]

Andrea Most observes that *South Pacific* (1949), like most of the Rodgers and Hammerstein canon, has been labeled middlebrow: "As the quintessential example of what mid-century critics called 'middlebrow' culture, *South Pacific* sits uncomfortably between the 'low' culture of Tin Pan Alley and the 'high' culture of legitimate theatre and opera."[38] Most argues that *South Pacific* combines lowbrow and highbrow elements in a provocative mix. Certainly this combination was the goal of artists such as Jerome Robbins and Leonard Bernstein, who built on the Rodgers and Hammerstein concept of the integrated musical play that combined popular culture with European notions of high art.

Early in Robbins's career, both he and Bernstein combined highbrow and lowbrow elements in a deliberate stew with *On the Town* (1944), which was based on Robbins's ballet *Fancy Free* (1944). One year after the opening of *On the Town,* Robbins espoused a kind of cultural manifesto that melded the commercial with the classical in an article for the *New York Times Magazine* entitled "Ballet Puts on Dungarees":

> Offering historical and social analysis of theatrical dancing and sounding like one of the left-wing populist critics of his day, Robbins described how ballet was becoming a "people's entertainment." As an elitist, classical art form imported from Europe, ballet was to become accessible to the masses, he argued, by embracing American culture and absorbing popular music and social dances. At the same time, according to Robbins, the traditional American musical as light entertainment was destined to incorporate more serious subject matter and classical aesthetic principles. It was to be a two-pronged revolution, and he placed himself at the vanguard.[39]

Robbins's cultural manifesto anticipates the eclecticism of postmodernism in its deliberate attempt to fuse highbrow and lowbrow and blur the distinctions between the two in a form that is uniquely American. His goal was to apply all that was vital to both highbrow and lowbrow culture and create a totally integrated theatrical experience:

> A choreographer can justifiably look to the ballet as a medium in which he can say pertinent things about ourselves and our world, no less than a playwright or a novelist or a movie scenarist. For its part, the audience will come to expect as much of ballet as it does of a play, a novel, or a film. And as the ballet and the theatre draw closer to each other, an exciting prospect opens in which not only musicals, but theatre pieces with vital ideas will combine drama, dance, and music, to the benefit of all three.[40]

Robbins is preaching a totally integrated theatrical experience, an American *Gesamtkunstwerk,* which mythologizes World War II America, much as Richard Wagner mythologized Germanic culture. Robbins, of course, is building on Hammerstein's similar Americanization of the *Gesamtkunstwerk* in *Oklahoma!,* which he achieved by mythologizing and democratizing homespun American values. By using a European model, Robbins's manifesto becomes provocative and dodges the derogatory connotations of middlebrow. The assumption is that the integrated musical can tackle compelling social problems within a popular vernacular.

Robbins and Bernstein were instrumental in developing something new and interesting with *On the Town,* a mixture of ballet and musical comedy, and with *West Side Story* (1957), a popular-culture retelling of Shakespeare with ballet in an American jazz vernacular. But their goal of an American *Gesamtkunstwerk* lent their musical aspirations a highbrow patina, with Robbins providing the strong, guiding artistic hand that shaped the text and protected its autonomy.[41]

Ironically, contemporary Europeans are attracted to American mass culture: rock, punk, MTV, film, video, even jazz. Where but in France would Jerry Lewis have attracted a highbrow critical following? Americans, on the other hand, have traditionally appropriated what they perceive as highbrow culture from European models. In 1927 Charles Edward Russel theorized that the demise of Theodore Thomas's American Opera Company in the 1880s was the result of the name of the company: "American Opera connoted bad opera. To this day, 'American artist' means, to the average American soul, inferior artist; 'American composer' means inferior composer."[42]

The same has been true of theatre. Americans denigrate their most distinguished playwrights, Eugene O'Neill, Arthur Miller, Tennessee Williams, and Edward Albee, while these same writers are celebrated and widely produced in Europe. Miller had a difficult time securing Broadway productions of his later plays, but he was virtually guaranteed major new productions in London. Albee's newer work has generally been introduced abroad since the 1970s, until his American rediscovery with *Three Tall Women* in the 1990s, which was produced off-Broadway. At the same time, mediocre plays by British writers such as Patrick Marber and David Hare have little trouble finding commercial backing and critical raves in New York.

During the late 1980s columnist Gerald Nachman, in the *San Francisco Chronicle,* questioned why operagoers would tolerate the silliness of *The Barber of Seville,* whereas theatrical producers refuse to revive musicals by Kern, Berlin, Gershwin, and Rodgers and Hart on the basis of their creaky, dated libretti. According to Nachman, if Italian operas had been written by Americans, "[t]hey'd be dismissed as moronic. . . . I realized it must be the American reverence for all things European and our tendency to take for granted all things quintessentially American."[43] As Lawrence Levine notes in response to Nachman's challenge, "Is the idea of a serious comparison of American musicals and opera really so outrageous? Are we certain we would learn so little about opera, musicals, and our own culture from making it?"[44] I think Levine's desire to compare the American musical to opera is valuable, and I intend to take him up on his challenge shortly. The privileging of the serious, integrated musical has skewed the study of the musical and its reflexive relationship with American culture. I am not denigrating the accomplishments of the integrated musical. I am denigrating the tendency to prioritize different genres of musical theatre.

Privileging the Unfinished

Perhaps the best way to deconstruct the privileging of the integrated musical is to question the notion that works in which the author has autonomy are necessarily better than works in which the performer is cocreator. In writing about pre–Rodgers and Hammerstein musicals, historians cite only a handful that they deem worthy of major Broadway revival, including *Show Boat* (1927), *Of Thee I Sing* (1931), *Porgy and Bess* (1935), *Pal Joey* (1940), and *Lady in the Dark* (1941), and these are mostly considered precursors to the integrated musical. The majority of pre–World War II musical comedies are dismissed as star vehicles that often possess glorious scores but are saddled with jerry-built libretti. Until fairly recently, historians and musicologists displayed the same kinds of prejudice toward opera seria, the form of serious opera that thrived during the eighteenth century prior to Christoph Gluck's reforms. These operas depended on the talents (and whims) of individual virtuosi rather than on a finished, revered text. Indeed the texts (both libretti and scores) for opera seria were intended to be incomplete; they were fleshed out by performers, often castrati, who literally were musical cocreators, writing their own ornamentations and interpolating arias to showcase their voices. As such, the genre was dismissed until fairly recently as basically unproducible and unworthy of revival.

During the past forty years, however, musicologists and historians have rediscovered the form, as a generation of countertenors and sopranos have emerged who can cope with the coloratura demands of the music. Whereas opera historians and musicologists of previous generations focused on textual criticism and consequently privileged the work of Gluck and Wagner, "new" musicologists such as Richard Taruskin and Jennifer Brown have rediscovered the excitement and creativity that opera seria can bring to the stage.[45] As historians and musicologists begin to take performance issues, rather than just the text, into consideration when writing about pre–Rodgers and Hammerstein musical theatre, it is likely that a similar phenomenon will occur. It is the incompleteness of these musical comedy vehicles that enabled great entertainers to function as cocreators in ways that would have been impossible with more highly structured texts. I am reminded of a quote from Heywood Broun about Al Jolson: "Jolson can take a song and make it do things its composers did not dream were in it."[46] Certainly the integration of drama and music is a great and worthy accomplishment of the Rodgers and Hammerstein musical play; it is equally worthy to revive nonintegrated shows and create something new based on texts that were never intended to be complete or fixed.

I am *not* arguing that Baroque opera is the grandfather of American musical comedy. That distinction probably belongs to eighteenth-century opera buffa and other national forms of comic opera. These mid-eighteenth-century attempts to present stereotypical caricatures, indigenous forms of comedy, and improvisatory and vernacular theatrical traditions for a nonelitist audience certainly have their parallels with American musicals of the 1920s and 1930s. Furthermore, in its pre-Gluckian, Metastasian form, opera seria, unlike the musicals of the 1920s and 1930s, was an aristocratic enterprise, whose aesthetic rested on vocal beauty and technique. I *am* arguing that in its emphasis on the autonomy of the performer as cocreator and in its veneration of highly skilled and deified virtuosi or "stars," opera seria is an emblematic model from which both sides gain. The nonintegrated musical becomes privileged through its comparison to Handel operas, whereas the latter achieve a new accessibility through comparison to a strand of American popular culture.

To pursue this analogy more fully, it is necessary to examine opera seria and the reforms for which Gluck was responsible. The absolute domination of the aria in pre-Gluckian opera seria presupposed the absolute domination of the singer. The composer furnished the singer with a blueprint; music was not the written score, just as a building is not an architectural blueprint. A successful score depended on the individuality and creativity of the performer; consequently, music was composed to suit the performer's gifts. Indeed, the great Italian singing schools of the eighteenth century encouraged composition as well as performance. Two kinds of improvisation were common. The first, coloratura ornamentation, reached its zenith as arias were given prominence over dramatic action. The second, cadenzas, originated in sixteenth-century solo song and were revived in eighteenth-century opera.[47] Much of the success of the solo arias depended on castrati, perhaps the rock stars of their day, who were most popular between 1650 and 1750. The greatest was perhaps Farinelli (1705–82), the friend of princes and emperors and confidant of two successive Spanish kings. Some cadenzas sung by Farinelli in Geminiano Giacomelli's *Merope* (Venice, 1734) survive and indicate the kind of vocal pyrotechnics that appealed to the public imagination. Added to the virtuosity was a charisma that made Farinelli and other noted castrati the most cherished stars of their generations.[48]

Hand in hand with the domination of performer as cocreator was the phenomenon of pasticcios, a "patchwork comprising arias of several different composers fitted to a new or existing libretto."[49] Two kinds of pasticcio existed. The first included a libretto which was originally musicalized by more than one composer. *Muszio Scevola* (London, 1721), for example, had a first act composed by F. Amadei, a second act by Giovanni Banancini, and a third act by George Frideric Handel. The second kind of pasticcio involved an opera that had traveled from city to city, incorporating new arias into a patchwork musical quilt en route. In the latter case, the libretto might be a collaboration between Pietro Metastasio and Apostolo Zeno, Carlo Goldoni, Silvio Stampiglia, and Lanfranchi Rossi, while the music might include arias by Gluck, Legrenzio Ciampi, Baldessare Galuppi, Giaocchino Cocchi, Gaetano Latilla, and Handel.[50] As Curtis Price, Judith Milhous, and Robert Hume note, the variety of contributors involved in a pasticcio raises the question "Who is in charge?"[51] Increasingly the authority belonged to the singer or, often, as Jennifer Brown has recently established, the impresario.[52] Along with this authority were the abuses that composers and librettists suffered at the hands of these performers. Dr. Charles Burney documents Metastasio, the most prolific and famous of the librettists prior to Gluck's reforms, complaining about these abuses, but even the great Metastasio was powerless to reform a situation to which his own work had contributed so much.[53] Similarly, Handel had to use tact, patience, humor, and threats of violence to curb the more outrageous demands of the singers.

It was Gluck who is credited with the reform of opera seria. During his early career, he had collaborated on seventeen operas with Metastasio. His reputation as a reformer was established when he collaborated with Ranieri de Calzabigi on three operas: *Orfeo et Euridice* (1762), *Alceste* (1767), and *Paride et Elena* (1770). Gluck stated his aesthetic in the preface to the last opera: "He who is concerned with truthfulness must model himself to his subject, and the noblest beauties of harmony and melody become serious faults if they are misplaced."[54] These reforms were based on subordination of music to the dramatic action, plainness of diction, and the importance of orchestration. Gluck's ideas foreshadow Wagner's later reforms, much the way Hammerstein's work with Richard Rodgers set the foundations for Sondheim's later work. Writing of Gluck's arias, Dr. Burney suggests, "It seldom happens that a single air of his operas can be taken out of its niche, and sung singly with much effect: the whole is a chain, of which a detached single link is but of small importance."[55] Certainly this sounds like the groundwork for Wagner's later *Gesamtkunstwerk,* even if Wagner oddly dismissed Gluck: "The famous revolution of Gluck . . . really consisted only in the revolt of the composer against the arbitrariness of the singer."[56] Despite this dismissal, Gluck's influence was considerable. According to musicologist Carl Dahlhaus, at the turn of the nineteenth century, two distinct poles of musical composition existed: Ludwig von Beethoven and Gioacchino Rossini.[57] If Beethoven (in his one opera, *Fidelio,* and, to an extent, elsewhere) was of Gluck's school, Rossini and the bel canto composers were continuing a virtuoso singing style that sprang from opera seria. If the two aesthetics were equal at the beginning of the nineteenth century, by the time of Giuseppe Verdi and Wagner, the Germanic symphonic elements emerged triumphant. Certainly both Verdi and Wagner continued Gluck's reforms. Verdi made it clear that the authority rested in the composer when he insisted on choosing his own librettists and picking his own singers. Wagner wrested even more control by deciding to write his own libretti. But the successful transference of authority from performer to text had begun with Gluck.

If Gluck did much to reassert the authority of composer over performer, the same is true of Oscar Hammerstein II, who is often cast as the hero of post–World War II histories of the American musical. Gerald Mast correctly points out that the singer in a Hammerstein musical play is "a specific character living in a specific place at a specific moment in history. While the voice, the I, of a Gershwin, Hart, or Porter lyric is an undefined surrogate for the lyricist himself, the voice, the I, of a Hammerstein lyric is an Oklahoma rancher, or a nurse from Little Rock, or a Victorian British schoolmarm."[58] Indeed the first three Rodgers and Hammerstein musicals eschewed the idea of star performers; actors were cast to fit the characters, not to sell tickets on the basis of their box office drawing power.[59] Although later Rodgers and Hammerstein musicals did indeed boast star names such as Mary Martin, Ezio Pinza, and Gertrude Lawrence, songs were still fashioned to suit character rather than to exploit a star persona. Hammerstein chose to make the text predominant, not the individual performer. If one were to ask, "Who is in charge?" of a Rodgers and Hammerstein musical, it is clearly the authors. Conversely, if it is impossible to privilege or value pre-Gluckian opera seria without privileging the performer as cocreator, much the same can be said of pre–Rodgers and Hammerstein musical comedy.[60]

If audiences came to opera seria to see what embellishments a virtuoso such as Farinelli might create for a favored aria, Broadway crowds in the 1930s flocked to see Merman and Jimmy Durante ad-lib and clown through chorus after chorus of a number such as "It's All Yours" (Arthur Schwartz, Dorothy Fields) from *Stars in Your Eyes* (1939). The libretti for pre–World War II musical comedy provided excuses for comics to perform star turns and for beloved entertainers to sing great new songs by Cole Porter, Irving Berlin, George Gershwin, and Rodgers and Hart. As Mast points out, often the songs had little to do with the plot; they were not necessarily a reflection of the feelings of the character but expressed emotions comfortable for the performers and songwriters.

To appreciate the kind of star window dressing that musical comedy used to serve, it might be beneficial to look at three early musicals, all produced in 1915. In *Robinson Crusoe, Jr.,* Al Jolson played the chauffeur of a wealthy Long Island magnate who dreams he is Robinson Crusoe; Jolson, of course, becomes his good man Friday. Jolson somehow encountered Spanish dancers, pirates, a goat, a crocodile, and dancing trees while managing to disguise himself as Fatima and sing black spirituals, Stephen Foster melodies, and songs such as "Yaka Hula Hickey Dula" and "Where Did

Robinson Crusoe Go with Friday on Saturday Night?" According to Michael Freedland, the star's biographer, "This was the closest Jolson had yet come to a show with a real plot."[61] Obviously the attraction here was Jolson, both as a clown and as an incomparable singing performer, not the story. Indeed, Jolson was famous for cutting the last scene of a show he appeared in, explaining the plot resolution to the audience and performing his most famous songs in concert, while the rest of the cast stood by and watched.

George M. Cohan's 1915 *Hello, Broadway* was a satiric revue in the tradition of Weber and Fields and their Music Hall productions. Cohan's reputation for fast pacing sprang partly from this production, in which scenes were changed in full view of the audience. Songs were performed not only onstage but in the auditorium itself. During "Down by the Erie," Louise Dresser sang a refrain onstage, after which a boy in the gallery and an older man in one of the boxes continued the song. As these supposed audience members sang, the set was changed to a green-ribboned Erie Canal, on which a chorus dressed in purple velvet rowed gondolas.

Obviously much of this material was presentational, as it was in *The Ziegfeld Follies of 1915*, featuring W. C. Fields, Ed Wynn, Ann Pennington, Mae Murray, George White, Bert Williams, Ina Claire, Justine Johnstone, Bernard Granville, and Leon Erroll. Ina Claire and Bernard Granville introduced "Hello Frisco, Hello," a tribute to the birth of transcontinental phone service. Granville also sang "We'll Build a Little Home in the U.S.A.," addressed to one hundred thousand European refugees from World War I, whereas the most elaborate production number was a red, white, and blue salute to America, led by various star performers who represented the branches of the armed forces.[62] This was the *Follies* that featured chorus girls costumed as months of the calendar, while a tenor serenaded them with Irving Berlin's "A Girl for Each Month of the Year."[63] The 1915 edition also introduced designer Joseph Urban to the *Follies.* Urban used Seurat-like spots of paint, as well as sophisticated layerings and spacklings, to introduce an art nouveau look to the revue. This *Follies* was color-coordinated in shades of blue. The designs were meant to flow in a pattern toward a cumulative effect, which must have driven Urban to distraction when, inevitably, numbers were shifted or cut during tryouts and the Broadway run. Like opera seria, these musicals valued performance rather than a fixed text. It was the clowning, the individual numbers by great performers, and the often sumptuous sets and costumes that drew customers.

Often a number in a musical comedy existed for no logical reason except to provide a star turn. In his autobiography Joshua Logan explains the genesis of "At the Roxy Music Hall," a number in *I Married an Angel* (1938). The show, a romantic fantasy, took place in Budapest, and the song was sung in act 2 during an all-night party:

> The song Rodgers and Hart wrote for the revenge party wasn't about angels, Budapest, banks, parties or anything even remotely connected with the show. It was a wild Larry Hart conceit, "At the Roxy Music Hall," to be sung by Audrey Christie and to be acted out by the whole cast as a takeoff on a Music Hall show. Bewildered and completely at a loss as to how to stage it, I asked them what it had to do with the plot.
>
> Larry began, "Oh, you can't just keep writing about old Budapest all night, so we thought we'd do a takeoff on Radio City—you know, a divertissement. First, we'll have a big symphony orchestra with stages going up and down, then the Radio City male chorus behind Dennis King, a specialty for [Walter] Slezak, Vivienne [Segal] and Audrey [Christie] as Rockettes, the ballet corps for [Vera] Zorina."
>
> "But how do we explain it to the audience?"
>
> Dick [Rodgers] said: "The less you explain, the happier they are. Let's just do it."[64]

Rather than focusing on the integrity of the plot, musicals took pride in their efforts to evade it. The horizon of expectations for a Rodgers and Hart musical allowed for illogical plots and star turns. These were finely crafted divertissements, neither inferior nor superior to later examples of the integrated musical, merely different.

Hart occasionally complained about the abuses of his singers, but since he created numbers specifically geared to show off the talents of his star performers, the shows often encouraged such abuses. Logan recounts an amusing story about Hart attending a rehearsal of "At the Roxy Music Hall." As Audrey Christie began the number, Hart started shouting incomprehensible phrases:

> "Hold the rehearsal. What is it, Larry?"
>
> He kept screaming hoarsely, but I couldn't understand the words.
>
> "Slow down, Larry. Say it a little slower."
>
> Then he said very slowly and carefully, "No now-singers in this show! No now-singers in this show! No now-singers in this show!"
>
> "What are now-singers?"
>
> "*She*'s a now-singer! Did you hear how she began my chorus? It's 'Come with me' and she began, 'Now come with me!' No now-singers!"[65]

The abuses may have been different from those of the castrati and virtuosi two hundred years earlier, but the fight for control was similar.

Although Hart drew the line at Audrey Christie's insertion of the word *now* in a song, he nonetheless realized that audiences came to see star performers and wrote with specific entertainers in mind. For example, the role of Vera in *Pal Joey* was fashioned for Vivienne Segal, whom Hart also cast in the 1943 revival of *A Connecticut Yankee.* He even wrote a new song, "To Keep My Love Alive," to showcase her talents. The struggle for control between author and performer may have existed, but audiences prior to *Oklahoma!* expected that material would be fashioned for a star rather than for a character.

I Married an Angel was produced five years before *Oklahoma!* By that time, scores were generally attributed to a single composer or composer-lyricist team. Between 1910 and 1930, however, interpolated songs were common in Broadway musicals; indeed, the scores were often patchworks, not very different from the kind of pasticcio typical of opera seria. Some shows, like some eighteenth-century operas, were officially composed by more than one writer. For example, *Rosalie* (1927), a Ruritanian fantasy, was composed jointly by George Gershwin and Sigmund Romberg. The reason was expediency. Since both composers were busy with other projects, Ziegfeld had no compunction about dividing the task between them. *Sally* (1920) boasted a score by Jerome Kern but ballet music by Victor Herbert. As late as 1944, Billy Rose augmented Cole Porter's score for *Seven Lively Arts* with a ballet by Igor Stravinsky. Puzzled by Stravinsky's ballet music, Rose wired the composer: "YOUR MUSIC GREAT SUCCESS STOP COULD BE SENSATIONAL SUCCESS IF YOU WOULD AUTHORIZE ROBERT RUSSELL BENNETT RETOUCH ORCHESTRATION STOP BENNETT ORCHESTRATES EVEN THE WORKS OF COLE PORTER." Stravinsky immediately wired back, "SATISFIED WITH GREAT SUCCESS."[66]

A second kind of pasticcio in opera seria involved arias interpolated from city to city and even from performance to performance. Musicals of the second and third decades of the twentieth century often had a similar patchwork of interpolations. For instance, in a typical Al Jolson musical, songs were inserted throughout the run. Although the score for *Bombo* (1921) was officially by Sigmund Romberg, the "hits" were all interpolations that Jolson introduced: "April Showers," by B. G. DeSylva and Louis Silvers; "Toot, Toot, Tootsie!" by Gus Kahn, Ernie Erdman, and Dan Russo; and "California, Here I Come" by DeSylva, Jolson, and Joseph Meyer. "April Showers," the best received on opening night, was not even listed in the program. "California, Here I Come" was not added until *Bombo* left New York for a national tour.[67]

If the composers of opera seria tailored their arias to the virtuosi who embellished them, something similar can be said of writers such as Cole Porter, George Gershwin, and Irving Berlin. Porter, in particular, liked to write with specific performers in mind. Rather than hand Ethel Merman songs for *Anything Goes* (1934) that could be handled by any other performer, he wrote specifically for her voice. According to Merman, "What Cole had done was to analyze my voice and turn out songs which showed off its variety."[68] In 1944 Porter met Delores Gray, then a Broadway novice, at the first rehearsal of *Seven Lively Arts.* He gave her a couplet, which she was to sing in the opening number, that described why she had come to New York. Porter was eager for her reaction to the new material:

> "You made a wonderful impact at the Copa, Miss Gray. I was so happy to learn you were going to be in this show. How do you like the couplet I wrote for you?" "Just fine, thank you very much." He studied her for a few minutes and then said, "Delores, I'd *really* like to know how you like your couplet." She stammered and fussed and finally said, "I have a powerful voice with unusual range, and I'm portraying a singer, but you've written my couplet all on one note." Porter stared momentarily, then said, "You're absolutely right. I'm going home and rewrite it completely." And he did.[69]

Performers expected composers to accommodate their voices and talents.

One of the most demanding was Ethel Merman. Since 1930, composers such as George Gershwin, Irving Berlin, and Cole Porter had written vehicles that catered to her voice and personality. When Gershwin played her the songs he had crafted for her in *Girl Crazy* (1930), her first Broadway show, he solicitously asked the former stenographer from Astoria if there was anything musically that she would like changed.[70] Twenty-six years later, during rehearsals for *Happy Hunting* (1956), a satire based on the much publicized wedding of Grace Kelly to Prince Rainier, one of the two young songwriters corrected Merman's stylistic "improvements." Abe Burrows, the show's director, describes the fallout:

> It seems that Ethel was singing one of the songs in her style, her own great style, and young Dubey, who had his own ideas about how his songs should be sung, had said to her, "Miss Merman, if I wanted the song sung that way, I'd have written it that way." Ethel had apparently

> changed the emphasis of a phrase or something like that. . . . From then Ethel never spoke to him again, and he wasn't permitted to speak to her. Later on, whenever one of the boys wrote a new song for the show, I was the one who had to sing the lyrics to her.[71]

Obviously Merman took no prisoners when it came to fitting the material to suit her style. Perhaps that is the reason she refused to allow producer Leland Hayward to hire Stephen Sondheim as composer for *Gypsy.* She had no objection to Sondheim writing the lyrics but demanded that Jule Styne compose the music, since he knew her voice and would capitalize on its strengths. Famously she changed the rhythm of the triplets in "Everything's Coming Up Roses" and proceeded to sing it incorrectly for the duration of the Broadway run and on the original cast recording. It is almost inconceivable that a performer would make these demands on Sondheim today or on Richard Rodgers during his collaboration with Hammerstein. Interestingly Merman never appeared in a Rodgers and Hammerstein musical. She did star in *Annie Get Your Gun* (1946), which Rodgers and Hammerstein produced, but they declined to write the music. Irving Berlin composed the score with Merman in mind.

Just as Gluck tried to wrest authority away from celebrated virtuosi, Rodgers and Hammerstein did much to dissipate the power and authority of the star performer. As mentioned before, major stars, including Mary Martin, Ezio Pinza, and Gertrude Lawrence, appeared in Rodgers and Hammerstein musicals, and their box office power certainly helped propel shows such as *South Pacific, The King and I,* and *The Sound of Music* (1959) into blockbuster status. Rodgers and Hammerstein, however, were equally big names. Once these musicals became established and the original stars left, each of these three shows continued to run for many years without equally famous name replacements. Moreover, Rodgers was extremely finicky about stars singing his music exactly the way he wrote it. Bill Hayes, a well-known, popular performer by the time he appeared in Rodgers and Hammerstein's *Me and Juliet* (1951), recalls Rodgers's insistence that "No Other Love," the hit song from the show, be sung exactly as written: "To this day, if I sing it, or even just hear it playing in the background of some restaurant I hear Dick Rodgers saying, 'No Bill. It's written eighth-quarter-eighth-quarter-eighth, with the whole note preceded by an exact eighth-note syncopation. . . . Don't linger on the word "love" and then come in on the downbeat. Do it the way I wrote it, thank you.'"[72] Both Rodgers and Sondheim wrote material to suit character, not stars.

The standard narrative, of course, is that with the birth of the integrated musical, authority began to revert to the author rather than to the performer. This is where genres such as "nonintegrated" and "integrated" (not to mention periodicity) become problematic. Musicals displayed elements of both integration and remnants of vaudeville, and the balance between the two often shifted from show to show. *Gypsy,* a star vehicle, was also a well-integrated musical comedy that managed to negotiate elements of the Rodgers and Hammerstein musical play with elements of vaudeville and burlesque. Although *Hello, Dolly!* (1964) was a wonderfully crafted musical comedy with an integrated book and seamless staging by Gower Champion, it relied on a big name descending that staircase at the Harmonia Gardens during the second act as the waiters serenaded her with a title song that had little to do with the character of Dolly Levi. Audiences applauded original star Carol Channing and their memories of her, as they later applauded Ginger Rogers, Martha Raye, Betty Grable, Phyllis Diller, Mary Martin, Pearl Bailey, Ethel Merman, Eve Arden, and Dorothy Lamour.[73]

Harold Prince, whose fame, along with that of Stephen Sondheim, rests with the development of the character-driven musical, turned down the direction of *Hello, Dolly!* He had no interest in material that revolved around a star performer rather than a character: "The 'Hello, Dolly!' number has nothing to do with Dolly Levi. She's a woman who has no money and scrounges around; she's never been to a place as fancy as the Harmonia Gardens, where the number happens. She's heard about it, and she goes there because she's heard about it and wants to have a good time. The way the number is now, you're talking about a woman who has lived her life at '21' [the famous New York nightclub]."[74] Although Prince wanted no part of it, audiences of the time certainly did. The clout in a show such as *Hello, Dolly!* lies with the leading lady. Cannily, producer David Merrick and director-choreographer Gower Champion kept altering the text and score to suit each new Dolly. Martha Raye, a broad physical comic, collided with a horse during the opening number, knocking herself to the ground. Extended dance sequences were added for Ginger Rogers and Betty Grable. Pearl Bailey ad-libbed and was supported by an all-black cast, including jazz great Cab Calloway as an unlikely Horace Vandergelder. Merman, for whom the show was first intended, was the final Dolly. Composer Jerry Herman reinstated two songs he had originally written for her, "World Take Me Back" and "Love Look in My Window," when she joined the cast.

Although most historians assume that by 1964 the nonintegrated musical had been supplanted by the integrated musical, the theatricalist, vaudeville-like elements of the musical-comedy star vehicles of the 1920s, 1930s, and 1940s were very much alive and, as in the abuses of the castrati in opera seria, sometimes produced bitter conflicts about who was in charge, author or performer. A case in point is Harold Prince's production of *Fiddler on the Roof* (1964). Ironically Zero Mostel's performance as Tevye forced Prince to navigate the kinds of problems he had tried to dodge in *Hello, Dolly! Fiddler* was fashioned along the lines of a Rodgers and Hammerstein integrated musical play, which demanded that the text be closed and not subject to the whims of a star performer. After the Broadway opening, the critics were qualified in their approval of the show but ecstatic about Mostel's performance. Even before the show opened, Mostel, who tended to perform in a vaudeville-like style, started interpolating stage business and ad-libs. Director Jerome Robbins and librettist Joseph Stein tried to curb his shenanigans, but to little avail. The shtick would grow from performance to performance. At one point, Mostel accidentally put his arm in a bottle of milk and wrung his sleeve while in the midst of one of his monologues with God. Pleased with the huge laugh he received, Mostel retained the shtick. Over time, the bit grew longer and longer until he wrung his sleeve over the orchestra pit, which, of course, got an even bigger laugh. Breaking the fourth wall by acknowledging the audience foregrounded Mostel's presence as a star comic rather than an actor portraying the character of Tevye.[75] Whereas the text called for Tevye to speak to God, in performance, Mostel, the performer, was carrying on a conversation with the audience.

According to lyricist Sheldon Harnick, "One night in the tavern scene, at the moment when Tevye, while dancing, accidentally bumps into one of the Russians, Zero let out a stream of Yiddish ending with the word 'tuchus.' . . . I was appalled."[76] When I asked Maria Karnilova, who played Golde in the original production, what it was like to work onstage with Mostel, she replied that it was dreadful. Pausing for a moment as if to backtrack, she confirmed that he was a great artist when onstage. Then, shaking her head, she once again reiterated, "It was dreadful."[77] During the dream sequence, in which Tevye tells Golde of the appearance of Fruma-Sarah's ghost, Mostel mugged broadly and burlesqued the scene. The authors and director tried to curb his antics, but he refused their requests. Eventually Robbins had his spotlight turned off, but the star continued to clown in the dark.[78] During the Tony ceremonies, none of the recipients thanked Mostel. When he collected his award, he announced, "Since no one else has thanked me, I will thank me."[79] *Fiddler* was announced best musical at the end of the telecast, but producer Harold Prince, while thanking his investors, neglected to thank his star. According to Karnilova, Mostel's deviation from the script had alienated the company, despite his brilliance in the role. *Fiddler* opened on September 22, 1964. Mostel took a two-week vacation in January 1965 and was replaced by Luther Adler. Originally Mostel had signed a one-year contract, which came up for renewal after nine months. When it was time to renegotiate the contract, his agent demanded a substantial increase in salary. Prince refused, and to the surprise of the Broadway community, Mostel was replaced by Luther Adler, a dubious box office draw for a musical.[80] At the farewell party that followed Mostel's final performance on August 14, 1965, Harnick told Mostel he was sorry that the comic was leaving the show. Mostel replied, "You mean you're sorry to see the grosses fall."[81] Surprisingly the grosses did not fall after Adler replaced Mostel, nor did Adler command a comparable salary. At capacity, profits were actually higher than they had been with Mostel. Instead of a star vehicle, the text of *Fiddler* became the chief "draw." The power reverted from the performer to the property.

The battle for authority has continued ever since. When Danny Kaye starred in Richard Rodgers's *Two by Two* (1970), he tore a ligament in his leg during the run. Released from the hospital, he returned to the production in a wheelchair and, later, on crutches. Since the show had not been well received to begin with, Kaye used his new props to clown and ad-lib, much to Rodgers's displeasure: "Disregarding the text and staging, he turned *Two by Two* into what Rodgers disgustedly termed 'one-by-one vaudeville.'"[82]

The conflict still exists today. In terms of Tony awards, *The Producers* (1999) is the most honored musical in Broadway history. The show's rapturous notices and box office lines were given national publicity, highly unusual in today's world, where such attention is usually reserved for rock concerts, films, and television shows. The assumption was that *The Producers* would sell out for years, possibly competing for all-time long-run champion. Despite elements of integration in the book, score, and choreography, however, *The Producers* is also an old-fashioned star vehicle, crafted for Matthew Broderick and, above all, for Nathan Lane. While Broderick and Lane remained with the show, it was the hottest ticket in New York. After their contracts expired, management replaced Lane with Henry Goodman, a celebrated English actor, who failed to score laughs or sell tickets. Goodman was promptly fired and replaced by Brad Oscar, Lane's understudy. The theory obviously was that since the show had generated so much excitement, once the original stars left, the property itself, along with author Mel Brooks, would generate ticket sales. This has not been the case. Box office receipts plummeted as soon as Lane and Broderick departed. Finally, in 2004, the two original stars briefly resumed their original roles and once again the show was the hottest ticket in New York. Lane and Broderick are slated to film the musical, which is scheduled to be released in 2005. It will be interesting to see which version audiences prefer: Lane and Broderick on film or a substitute cast onstage. Perhaps Lane and Broderick, or two other high-powered names, will be lured to headline the Broadway version. Certainly a Broadway run of four or five years is nothing to sneeze at. On the other hand, today's long-run champions, including *A Chorus Line, Cats,* and *Phantom of the Opera,* run well over fifteen years due to Broadway's spiraling economics. It will be interesting to see how *The Producers* plays out in this context. Another example is *Hairspray* (2002), a star vehicle for Harvey Fierstein. Now that he has left the cast, one wonders about his future replacements and the show's box office longevity. In any case, the question of who is in charge—author or performer as cocreator—is still a source of friction and controversy.

The Problem with Authenticity

Musicologist Richard Taruskin makes a compelling case for reviving Baroque opera.[83] He rebuts the publicity that went hand in hand with the 1920s Handel revival, namely that new productions of opera seria are produced the way they were originally seen and heard. Since opera seria was seldom the same from performance to performance and certainly from city to city, a claim of authenticity seems dubious. Taruskin champions the revival of opera seria; something new is being created that is based on a text that was always incomplete. Other current musicologists, such as Harry Haskell and Jennifer Brown, agree. Brown even champions the revival of pasticcios, since often the arias make sense in the context of the libretto and, more often, they enliven a dull one.[84] Perhaps the revival of opera seria is a reaction against modernism and the tyranny of the composer. Perhaps it springs from the bel canto revival that Maria Callas and Joan Sutherland helped initiate in the 1950s and 1960s. Much of the answer certainly lies in performance.

Just as Taruskin argues that it is impossible to revive opera seria authentically, we cannot revive pre-1943 musicals the way they really were. The libretti (and often the scores) are incomplete, and the stars for whom they were intended as vehicles are long gone. We need to rethink and refashion these musicals to fit new, charismatic performers and to reflect the tastes of a different audience.

The Encores series of concert versions of forgotten musicals, produced annually at City Center in New York, helps to illustrate the problem of locating an authentic text for these older musicals. Encores leads us to believe these musicals are being produced the way they were originally performed. The attitude seems to be that the extant material—the text and score—rather than an unfinished text that needed charismatic performers acting as cocreators, is worth a hearing. This position is about as accurate as the "authentic" Handel revival of the 1920s. Often the texts, to whatever extent they can be reconstructed, are revised. Many of the orchestrations have been lost. Certainly an attempt is made to reconstruct them as accurately as possible, but it is just that, an attempt. It is the forgotten scores that have generated the most publicity and the opportunity for a new audience to be introduced to the glorious songs of past musicals. Often the unfamiliar numbers are those that generate the most applause. There is an excitement and surprise when one sits in a theatre and hears a great song or score for the first time. Despite publicity to the contrary, however, I think what has made the series such a success is not an authentic recreation of these pieces but the chance for gifted performers such as Vanessa Williams, Patti Lupone, Kristin Chenoweth, Donna Murphy, Martin Short, Ann Reinking, Bebe Neuwirth, Brian Stokes Mitchell, Melissa Errico, and Anne Hathaway to find star showcases in a commercial Broadway climate that does not encourage them as frequently as it once did. It is the performer, at least as much as the material, that has helped inject new life into these shows.

In a larger, historiographical sense, the same argument can be applied to texts that have survived intact and that some claim as authentic. It is no easier to revive integrated musicals with authenticity than nonintegrated musicals. If one were to revive *Show Boat,* which basically *does* have an integrated script and score, at least to some degree, which is the authentic text? The 1927 production is markedly different from the 1946 Broadway revival, which was reorchestrated and, as we shall see, contained some alternate musical numbers. The published scripts for both these productions deviate from the 1966 Lincoln Center revival with Barbara Cook and Stephen Douglass, which was again reorchestrated, and that text differs from the 1994 Harold Prince version. To complicate matters, all these texts differ from the 1936 film with Irene Dunne, Helen Morgan, and Alan Jones, which, in turn, is different from the text of the 1951 MGM remake starring Kathryn Grayson, Howard Keel, and Ava Gardner. If these varying texts are not confusing enough, how can we attempt to fix the text from the original 1927 production, since part of it was ad-libbed around star performers?

Show Boat in 1927 was a backstager, a musical comedy about performers, which was reflected in its casting and in its songs and specialities.

Magnolia, Ravenal, Julie, Captain Andy, Frank, and Ellie are all entertainers on the show boat. Indeed, the only important characters who are not performers are Parthy, Queenie, and Joe, although the latter two manage several showstopping turns. The novelty numbers originally written for these performers largely disappeared after the original production. Kim's act 2 specialty in 1927 was a reprise of "Why Do I Love You," in which Norma Terris impersonated show business figures of the day. By 1946 Kim's impersonations were replaced by a character ballad, "Nobody Else But Me." Frank's 1927 dance solo, "Then I Might Fall Back on You," disappeared in 1946, as did Queenie's song and dance turn, "Hey, Feller."

Most important, Captain Andy lost his 1927 act 1 specialty in the 1946 revival, which he originally enacted after two roughnecks interrupted the onstage melodrama "The Parson's Bride." In the original production, Captain Andy stepped in front of the curtain and performed the complete melodrama alone, including a fistfight with himself. This was dream material for a star comedian; indeed, it justified Charles Winninger's name-above-the-title billing. No one today is quite sure exactly what Winninger did or how long the specialty lasted. In subsequent revivals, during the 1950s, 1960s, and 1970s, star comics such as Andy Devine, Mickey Rooney, Joe E. Brown, and Eddie Bracken all inserted their own specialties and ad-libs during "The Parson's Bride." I conducted a production with Van Johnson as Andy in 1981 in which he inserted his own ad-lib version of "The Parson's Bride." Since Johnson was not particularly noted as a clown but was a considerable box office draw, he appropriated Magnolia's 1946 ballad, "Nobody Else But Me," as an up-tempo song to fill out the sequence. In the 1946 Broadway revival, however, Hammerstein cut Andy's star turn completely. Instead of choosing well-known comedians to play Andy and Parthy, Hammerstein cast Ralph Dumke and Ethel Owens, two character actors who were hardly box office names. In effect, Hammerstein trimmed the vaudeville elements from the piece, making *Show Boat* more in line with the integrated post-*Oklahoma!* musical play he was developing with Rodgers. The 1951 MGM film, on the other hand, restored much of the old-fashioned, musical comedy flavor, with stars such as Joe E. Brown playing Andy and Marge and Gower Champion performing Frank and Ellie's vaudeville dance routines. A Lincoln Center revival combined elements of previous productions, as did the Harold Prince version. There *is* no authentic *Show Boat* text, just as there is no authentic text for a Handel opera.

The 1995 Nicholas Hytner revival of *Carousel* and the 1998 revival of *Annie Get Your Gun* are revisionist readings, mounted with a late-twentieth-century critical eye and an effort to make them relevant to a different cultural moment. The *Carousel* revival capitalized on the elements of fantasy inherent in the text to make a contemporary statement about multiculturalism and tolerance. The chorus of New Englanders now included African Americans, Hispanics, and Asian Americans. In fact, Carrie and Nettie were played by African Americans. The color-blind casting gave a new relevance to the musical's endorsement of community. Hytner also confronted the issue of wife abuse, which had previously tended to date the show. In the second act, Billy slaps Louise when she refuses to accept the star that he has stolen for her from Heaven. Julie enters and Billy steps back in the clouds, once more invisible. When Louise asks her mother if it is possible for a man to slap you very hard and not hurt you, Julie nods yes. Hytner had Billy react to this line, at least in the London production, which preceded the Lincoln Center revival. Although he said nothing, he gestured to indicate that this was indeed inappropriate behavior. In the text, the focus is on Julie, who seems to know that Billy has returned. In the revival, the focus was on Billy, who acknowledged that his abuse of Julie was unforgivable. Hytner's multiracial casting and acknowledgment of political correctness did much to make *Carousel* resonate for contemporary audiences.

The text for *Annie Get Your Gun* was also considerably altered in 1998 to meet the needs of political correctness. A juvenile-soubrette subplot involved an interracial romance between a young Native American in love with a white member of the Wild West show, a romance that Annie encourages. Frank Butler's ode to male cockiness, "I'm a Bad, Bad Man" was cut as sexist, and "I'm an Indian Too" was excised as racist. The show's climax was changed as well. Instead of trying to win Frank by deliberately conceding the final shooting match to him, Annie made sure that both conceded to each other. Rather than the woman taking second place to the man, both acknowledged the equality of the sexes. The text was obviously altered but altered from what? How much came from the original 1946 production, which involved a subplot with a juvenile and soubrette whose names were identical to those of characters in the 1998 subplot, Tommy and Winnie? What material was lifted from the 1957 television version with Mary Martin and John Raitt? How much of the text and orchestration remained from the 1966 Lincoln Center revival that starred Ethel Merman and injected a feminist element to Annie's character with the addition of "Old Fashioned Wedding"? Did anything remain of the Los Angeles Civic Light Opera version staged by Gower Champion for Debbie Reynolds? There is no stable text for this Irving Berlin musical.

If texts do not remain stable, neither, of course, do performances. In the 1998 *Annie Get Your Gun* revival, Bernadette Peters did not play Ethel Merman; she created her own concept of the role on the basis of her unique gifts and talents. Even more than Mary Martin in the national company and 1957 television version, Peters emphasized the character's innate softness. It was clear from the beginning that Annie was the kind of pink and white woman Frank was seeking all along; she just had to learn how to express her femininity. Whereas Merman's Annie was all invincible tomboy, Peters's interpretation stressed the character's vulnerability in understated versions of "They Say It's Wonderful," "Moonshine Lullaby," and "I Got Lost in His Arms." Merman's Annie was gloriously All About Annie; Peters made it a love story. Similarly, when Peters recreated Mama Rose in Sam Mendes's 2003 *Gypsy* revival, she played the character as if she were a grown-up version of Baby June; her Rose looked as if she could have been a child star. Merman, on the other hand, was a big noise, both monstrous and hilarious. Her outrageousness provided the humor that made this archetypal stage mother palatable. Merman's Annie and Mama Rose are perhaps her two most famous roles. Rather than try to slay an indomitable ghost, Peters made new choices that forced audiences to see both shows with fresh eyes. The result was a new *Annie Get Your Gun* and a new *Gypsy.*

Are any texts, stripped of performance, reception, and their cultural moment of production, authentic? It is the gaps and absences, not to mention the excitement of trying to fill them, that create a memorable, new theatrical experience.

2

◆ ◆ ◆ ◆ ◆ ◆ ◆

The Star as Cocreator: Performing Jewishness During the Melting Pot

Although nonintegrated musical comedy and the revue have generally been historicized as old-fashioned fluff that served as window dressing for stars, the very openness of these vehicles, which, like vaudeville, relied on the participation of performer as cocreator, encouraged some of the greatest Jewish comics and entertainers of melting-pot America to adopt numerous racial, ethnic, and gendered disguises not only within the musical as a whole but also within a given scene or song. The structural looseness of these vehicles helped promote a theatricalist, presentational mode of performance from these stars, most of whom had received their training in vaudeville or burlesque. Audiences delighted in a star comic's bamboozlement of other onstage characters, most typically the straight white male, whom the ethnoracial comic inevitably outwitted. In reality, Jewish performers from 1910 to as late as the mid-1960s helped destabilize fixed notions of racialized and gendered Otherness by performing identity as a comic construct rather than as a racial inheritance or biological fact.[1]

This chapter celebrates the entertainers and comics whose performances of Jewishness in musical comedies during the melting-pot era helped audiences realize that the Jewish experience offered insights into the predicaments not only of Jews but also of other immigrant or marginalized groups as well. In *Making Americans,* Andrea Most argues that the writers of many of the most successful musicals from the 1930s through the 1960s were Jews trying to find their proper place as Americans; consequently, she sees the Broadway musical as a story of American-Jewish assimilation.[2] More than the writers, I am fascinated by the performance of Jewishness during these melting-pot years by stars such as Eddie Cantor, Al Jolson, Fanny Brice, Sophie Tucker, Ed Wynn, and Groucho Marx. Their varied assimilationist strategies to achieve success on Broadway did much not only to mainstream Jewishness but also to assuage the tensions of other immigrants anxious about fitting into the white melting pot. In effect, they helped redefine American identity. Rather than labeling their star vehicles as old-fashioned according to formalistic criteria, I argue that nonintegrated musical comedy, never meant to be fixed or closed in the first place, was at least as potent (and often more subversive) than the historically privileged integrated musicals that have supplanted them.

Since Jews historically were masters at adapting to change, Jewish comics served as guides who provided valuable knowledge and insights into the traumas of uprooting. In *The Haunted Smile,* Laurence J. Epstein theorizes about the contributions of Jewish comics to American identity:

> A model was thus established for Jewish comedians. When Americans felt uprooted—which they did often in the century—they found in Jewish comedians people who could simultaneously help them laugh at and therefore control that feeling but also, based on their history, be emotional pioneers, guides to the new frontiers of American life. A new humor was needed, and new people who had actually undergone comparable experiences were needed to perform their humor. The Jews were among those who could fill that need.[3]

Jewish performers, in particular, soon became adept at providing comic nostrums to a wide variety of anxieties about American identity, including perceptions about class, race, ethnicity, and gender.

For example, Bert Lahr was a master at ridiculing class, social pretensions, and traditional notions of masculinity. In *Two on the Aisle* (1951), Lahr played an assortment of characters that commented on perceived ideas about gender, including a frightened astronaut, a dim-witted professional baseball player who brags about booze and broads as he is being interviewed for a children's program, and a German-accented Queen Victoria ("I am a kveen").[4] In *Life Begins at 8:40* (1934), Lahr and Ray Bolger played two Frenchmen hopelessly in love with the same woman, portrayed by Luella Gear. Both men wear Inverness capes over their formal evening attire and are about to jump into the Seine. Gear rushes in, claims that she has just seen Noel Coward's *Design for Living,* a play about a sophisticated ménage à trois, and announces that they can all live happily together. The two men kiss, discover to their astonishment that they no longer need a woman, and throw Gear into the Seine.[5] Lahr's final Broadway appearance, in *Foxy* (1964), a musical version of *Volpone,* saw him masquerading as a British lord, complete with violet walking suit, deerstalker hat, and yellow leggings with black buttons, as he remembers sailing on either the Firth of Forth or the Forth of Firth.[6] As late as 1962, Sid Caesar similarly ridiculed essentialist notions of masculinity and class when he performed all seven lovers of Belle Poitrine, a fictionalized film siren, in *Little Me,* including sixteen-year-old Noble Eggleston, the richest boy in Venezuela, Illinois (who is so smart he goes to both Harvard and Yale to become a legal doctor); crusty eighty-eight-year-old banker Pinchley; Val du Val, a French entertainer who fakes his tap dancing; Fred Poitrine, a nerdish, nearsighted sad sack hopelessly going off to fight in World War I; and the suspiciously Jewish-sounding Prince Cherney, the expiring King of Rosenzweig, who performs a frenetic Russian peasant dance atop his deathbed as he bids farewell to his subjects.

If impersonation and disguise were part of these performers' comic strategies, tragically this fluidity of identity did not apply to the African American, whose racialized Otherness remained fixed. Unlike the off-white Western European immigrant, including the Italians, the Irish, and the Germans, the African American was unable to transcend perceived notions of identity if for no other reason than that she or he often was not allowed to appear on stage with white performers at all. Much has already been written about minstrelsy and blackface. Certainly the contribution of the African American to the development of the Broadway musical, beginning with shows such as *Clorindy* (1898), deserves more detailed exploration, particularly in relation to perceived notions of American identity. What strategies did African Americans employ to negotiate the performance of race? How was fluidity of identity limited for these performers? How did African American actors react to, let alone endure, blackface? How did black and white audiences receive African American performers? Were audiences primarily concerned with affirming whiteness or perpetuating the idea of blackness? These are crucial questions, but the answers would comprise a book in itself.[7]

This chapter then details the fluid strategies Jewish performers negotiated to subvert stable notions of Anglo-American identity, including appropriation of African American and Native American identity. It celebrates the performer as cocreator, since audiences did not flock to see a particular show (text) but rather stars such as Cantor or Jolson as long as they were willing to remain with whatever vehicle showcased their talents. Since the story of performing Jewishness involves blackface, stereotyping, and melting-pot perceptions about American identity, one needs to consider the ethnoracial apparatus necessary for understanding these performance strategies, including connotations of the term *melting pot,* racial appropriation, and stereotypical perceptions of Jewishness.

Performance Strategies During the Melting Pot

The idea of an American melting pot can be traced back as far as Crèvecoeur, an eighteenth-century French immigrant, who described a new country "where individuals of nations are melted into a new race of men."[8] In 1831 Alexis de Tocqueville, another Frenchman, observed American identity with wonder: "Imagine, my dear friend, if you can, a society formed of all the nations of the world . . . people having different languages, beliefs, opinions: in a word, a society without roots, without memories, without prejudices, without routines, without common ideas, without a national character. . . . What serves as the link among such diverse elements? What makes all of this into one people?"[9] If Tocqueville was puzzled about what unified such a diverse population, Ralph Waldo Emerson, later in the century, described a new race of diverse peoples who would eventually constitute America, suggesting both Crèvecoeur and Tocqueville's notion that American identity is ever-changing and fluid.[10] Herman Melville agreed that the American was constantly reinventing himself: "We are not a nation, so much as a world. . . . Our ancestry is lost in the universal paternity. . . . On this Western Hemisphere all tribes and people are forming into one federated whole."[11] Crèvecoeur, Tocqueville, Emerson, and Melville agreed that being American meant abandoning one's past and celebrating an exciting if unknown future identity.

Israel Zangwill popularized the term *melting pot* in his 1908 play of that title.[12] Believing that American identity is inevitably dynamic and in flux, he described a nation teaming with a multiplicity of races and ethnicities living together, sharing customs, intermingling, and inevitably intermarrying. Looking out toward New York Harbor from the roof of a settlement house, David Quixano, the Russian-Jewish protagonist of Zangwill's play, celebrates the dynamism of a nation that will eventually produce, through intermarriage, a new, if unpredictable, race of Americans: "It is the fire of

God round His Crucible. There she lies, the great Melting pot. Listen! Can't you hear the roaring and the bubbling? There gapes her mouth . . . the harbor, where a thousand mammoth feeders come from the ends of the world to pour in their human freight. Ah, what a stirring and a seething! Celt and Latin, Slav and Teutonic, Greek and Syrian—black and yellow."[13] Note that Zangwill is all-inclusive in terms of ethnoracial groups, although as Harley Erdman points out, he tends to minimize the importance of the controllers of the great Crucible—the Anglo-American power structure.[14]

The unpredictability of Zangwill's great Crucible, with its racial and ethnic bleeding over, was unacceptable to many. Fearing the idea of the hyphenated American, Theodore Roosevelt advocated the abandonment of past loyalties. The logical solution to massive European immigration was to whiten ethnoracial groups so that they could be controlled. The new immigrants challenged nativist attempts to define an American type, which according to the "science" of eugenics involved being blond, blue-eyed, and Anglo-Saxon.[15] Roosevelt had previously scolded Anglo-Saxon women for allowing "native stock to be outbred by inferior immigrants"; he feared "race suicide."[16] These anxieties were legitimized by scientists who developed theories of eugenics—breeding for a better humanity—and scientific racism. Madison Grant's influential *Passing of the Great Race* (1916) popularized the notion developed by William Z. Ripley and Daniel Brinton that there were three or four major European races: superior Nordics of northwestern Europe to inferior southern and eastern races of Alpines, Mediterraneans, and, worst of all, the Jew.[17] For Grant, the idea of mixing races was anathema: "The cross between any of the three European races and a Jew is a Jew."[18] As long as one had a single drop of Jewish blood, one was contaminated.

By the second decade of the twentieth century, Woodrow Wilson and Henry Ford were instrumental in creating a new, distorted, but widely accepted version of Zangwill's melting pot, one that lasted well into the 1960s. In this version, the melting pot was a process of anglicization, or "whiteness," in which racial exclusionism prevailed. Perhaps the ultimate version of this white melting occurred in January 1914, when Henry Ford insisted that all immigrant workers who wanted to partake in the profit-sharing plan of the Ford Motor Company had to enroll in the Ford English School. Like Roosevelt and Wilson, Ford was adamant that immigrants who wanted to be assimilated had to prove their patriotism by their willingness to abandon all past ties. He set up commencement exercises for his school in a large auditorium:

> On the stage in front of a model of an immigrant ship stood a huge pot, seven and a half feet high and fifteen feet in diameter. The graduating members of the class, dressed in clothes representative of the nations from which they had come and carrying the types of luggage they had brought with them when they first arrived in the United States, marched down the gangplank from the ship and disappeared into the pot. Six of their teachers then stirred the pot with ten-foot-long ladles. When the pot began to "boil over," the workers emerged, according to an eyewitness, "dressed in their best American clothes and waving American flags."[19]

Ford's version of the American melting pot was more palatable to Anglo-Americans than Zangwill's far more sophisticated, unpredictable notion of a new American race dynamically reinventing itself. Moreover, the threat to the Anglo power structure was temporarily curbed by the Johnson-Reed Immigration Act of 1924, which ended massive European (and Jewish) immigration to America, an act that would have tragic repercussions during the Holocaust, when Jewish victims of Nazism were refused entry into the United States. In 1923 Lewis Gannett commented on the conjoining of the melting pot with Anglo conformity: "Anglo-Saxon Americans have small interest in the 'melting pot' except as a phrase. They do not want to be fused with other races, traditions, and cultures. If they talk of the melting pot, they mean by it a process in which the differences of the immigrant races will be carried away like scum, leaving only pure ore of their own traits."[20] With the Johnson-Reed Immigration Act, as Erdman notes, "both racialism and the melting pot then devised paradigms for preserving American purity, one by separating out impurities, the other by melting them away."[21] The hegemonic solution to Jewish or other undesirable immigration seemed to be to either stop it or to turn the immigrants white.

Not all European immigrants found this notion flattering. As early as 1915, Horace Kallen countered the notion of the melting pot by coining the term *cultural pluralism,* which anticipated multiculturalism by sixty years.[22] By 1924 Kallen, a champion of the hyphenated American, suggested a different metaphor for a diverse society as a reaction to the new immigration laws and the new connotation of the melting pot as white. He argued that America was a symphony, with each diverse ethnicity blending its tonalities into a glorious harmony. Rather than an act of will, Judaism became a function of inheritance. According to Kallen, one can change one's dress, customs, and clothing, but one can never change one's grandfather.[23] This innateness of Judaism implied a racial dynamic that precluded "whitening." If Jews were an ethnic group, they could assimilate by will and desire; however, if Judaism implied a biological racial legacy, the Jew could not abandon his past and was necessarily excluded from assimilation. Sadly Kallen ignored the African American in his theory, which dealt only with European ethnoracial groups, although W. E. B. Du Bois later applied Kallen's theories to African American identity.[24]

During the melting-pot years, the choice for the immigrant Jew was difficult. If he subscribed to the Henry Ford melting-pot theory, he could achieve limited assimilation through desire and will. At the same time, he did not necessarily want to abandon his heritage. If he clung to Kallen's "cultural pluralism," he was, by implication, racialized, which excluded him from being "whitened" and from the privileged world of the Anglo majority. This is precisely the conflict the Al Jolson character negotiates in *The Jazz Singer* (1927), in which Jakie Rabinowitz is torn between becoming an American vaudeville performer in blackface and clinging to his Jewish heritage by replacing his father as cantor in the synagogue.

This conflict between assimilation and racialized identity was common before World War II. Although ethnicity has been used to describe the cultural heritage of Europeans, whereas race has been used for everyone else's heritage during the latter part of the twentieth century, the two terms were virtually interchangeable between 1910 and 1940.[25] According to Karen Brodkin, America regarded immigrant European workers as something other than white—as biologically different—before the Holocaust.[26] Moreover, Brodkin argues that despite the desire of many Jews to assimilate into the melting pot, cultural pluralism was both attractive and valued, since it cemented a sense of community, within which different versions of Jewish identity could coexist.[27] Jews were often careful, even secretive, about exposing their heritage to outsiders. As Andrea Most argues, the Jewish immigrant had a split consciousness, an awareness that one behaved in a certain fashion with fellow Jews and in a different fashion with non-Jews.[28] For the Jew or other European working-class immigrant, success meant outwitting the gentile. For Most, theatre was, in part, a "metaphor for the presentation of self in everyday life."[29]

It was during this climate that Jews, as well as other immigrants, were faced with several questions. What constituted an American, particularly during the era between the two world wars? How did European immigrants, especially the Jew, negotiate the thin line between ethnicity and race? How were women encouraged to perform gender, whiteness, and class in an America that still believed in turn-of-the-century eugenics and "scientific" racism?[30] To what extent did race, ethnicity, and gender, affect acculturation? Jewish comics confronted these questions through playful, self-conscious theatricality in an era when American identity was volatile and subject to multiple interpretations. Jews, particularly those in show business, resisted racial exclusionism, which was not the ticket to financial success or social mobility. At the same time, they also wanted to retain their Jewish heritage, which did not conform with Anglo assimilation. As a result, the Jewish performer often played both sides against the middle, devising a variety of strategies to maintain his or her ethnoracial identity while gaining limited assimilation (being whitened) through success in show business.

Mocking the society they wished to enter, the Marx Brothers were perhaps most subversive in their anarchic approach to assimilation. Although all four were Jewish, each had his own immigrant persona. Groucho was the Jewish con man, the upstart, the outsider always smarter and more facile with language than his gentile superiors, including the pompous, obtuse grande dame usually played by Margaret Dumont. Whether playing a statesman, a real estate developer, a college president, or some other authority figure, he was always the outsider trying to finagle his way in, either by outwitting the powers-that-be or by trying to seduce a beautiful gentile girl, usually to no avail. His impersonations, including that of Captain Spaulding, African explorer and "schnorer," in *Animal Crackers* (1928), were characterized by the incongruity between his nouveau status or position (his mask) and the wisecracking, leering manner that exposed his fraudulence and invariably gave him away. In *I'll Say She Is* (1924), Groucho donned a plethora of disguises, including those of a trial lawyer, Napoleon, and Cinderella at the ball, all the while manically pacing and chomping on his ever-present cigar.[31] Each of these disguises enabled him to overturn authority, whether the legal justice system, the French government, or the fairy-tale morality that justice is rewarded and evil punished.

Harpo, on the other hand, was the archetypal new American immigrant, childlike in his incapacity to speak. Like so many new immigrants to America, he found ways of making himself understood without conversing in the language of his new country. In a classic routine that the brothers repeated for years, Harpo tried to hide from Groucho. Breaking a mirror, he pretended he was Groucho's reflection, imitating the latter's every move only to be foiled at the last minute. As Lawrence Epstein observes, "The scene made exquisite psychological sense to an immigrant audience. Harpo was trying to hide by imitating someone else, just as many immigrants and their children believed they had to hide their true selves to imitate Americans."[32] Chico underscored his own outsider status by performing an Italian immigrant, smart, cunning, and practical despite speaking in stereotypical broken English as he peddled fish, peanuts, and tootsy-fruitsy ice cream. Of the four, only Zeppo, basically the straight man or juvenile of the team, usually had a love interest. He was also the only brother to assume a nonimmigrant persona, presumably someone with whom gentile audiences could identify, at least to some degree. The bungling brothers usually tried to bail him out of some plot complication.[33] Ironically Zeppo had no need for a stage disguise, although the persona itself was a mask for this Jewish performer. The impersonations of the other brothers confirmed a deeper truth that resonated with immigrant audiences of various backgrounds. To assimilate, an immigrant often was forced to play someone at odds with his true identity. Without a mask, he was constantly, if comically, in danger of being exposed.

Assimilation strategies for Jewish performers during the melting pot varied widely. Jewish performers such as Sophie Tucker, Eddie Cantor, Milton Berle, and Fanny Brice refused to make jokes that reinforced hurtful anti-Semitic stereotypes. Their humor came from self-mockery. Barbara Grossman argues that Brice created cartoons using Yiddishisms and a heavy dialect as a comic contrast to the characters that she played. Whether Brice caricatured Nijinsky, Becky at the ballet, or stripper Sally Rand balancing two ostrich feathers in a fan dance, her Yiddish accent commented on the incongruity of her impersonation. Often this commentary was explicit, with sly winks and gestures to the audience.[34] In "I Was a Floradora Baby," which Brice performed in *The Ziegfeld Follies of 1920,* she laments her being the only member of the famous *Floradora* sextette who failed to marry a millionaire stage-door Johnny. Instead, she settled twenty years earlier for Jewish Abie, with whom she shares a cold-water flat on Delancey Street in New York's Lower East Side with five children and a sixth on the way. If she poked fun at high culture and stuffiness, she nonetheless encouraged immigrant audiences to identify with her Jewishness: "It was all right to get a laugh because they were laughing at me as much as at themselves."[35]

Brice was also respectful of other ethnoracial groups in her characterizations. She almost lost her first Broadway part in *The Ziegfeld Follies of 1910* after an argument with producer–theatre owner Abe Erlanger. Rehearsing her big ballad, "Lovie Joe," Brice impersonated, without blackface, an African American woman crazy about her black lover.[36] Brice sang the song in a Negro dialect, which offended Erlanger, not for the politically correct reasons of today's audiences but because Erlanger thought Negro dialect too lowbrow for his audiences. Brice refused to change her rendition: "I live on 128th Street. It's on the edge of Harlem. No Negro would pronounce those words the way you did. I can't sing them any other way."[37] Brice stood her ground and expected to be fired after the out-of-town opening, which she described with relish:

> I was sheathed in a white satin gown that fitted like a silk stocking—that was the fashion then. When the signal came for my appearance it wasn't a stage I was on—it was a magic carpet! After about eight encores of "Lovie Joe," the audience was still so enchanted with me that I decided they should have all I had.
>
> I was painfully thin and my dress fitted like a vise. The last roar that met my ears came when I pulled my skirt up over my knees and then, peering down on legs that looked like two slats, put my hand over my eyes in one despairing gesture and stalked off.
>
> As I left the stage, Erlanger was standing in the wings. He had his straw hat in his hands, the rim broken. He was beaming as he held it out to me.
>
> "See. I broke this applauding you."[38]

The use of the mask here is complex. On one hand, Brice respectfully impersonated an African American woman in love with her man; on the other hand, she distanced herself from the characterization to make fun of herself as a Jewish woman too homely to be able to hold *any* man. Just as the Marx Brothers carried their personae from show to show, Brice was known for self-mockery, whether through deflating her attempts at high culture with incongruous, heavy Jewish inflections or ridiculing her own gawkiness and lack of sex appeal.

The great musical theatre stars, like vaudevillians, generally carried their personae along from show to show. The 1920s predated the time when American acting training would be almost uniformly based on the Stanislavsky system. This transition did not occur until the 1950s and 1960s, with the fame and notoriety of the Actors Studio; even then, stars such as Ethel Merman retained their personae from show to show. Certainly in the 1920s, 1930s, and 1940s, musical theatre actors did not inhabit their roles; they performed them. As Ann Douglas observes, "The goal onstage and off was less to be oneself than to pick and play oneself."[39] Perhaps this goal reflected a New

York society characterized by Damon Runyon's assertion: "I know everyone. No one is close to me, remember that."[40] One might know another's chosen self-presentation, but not the real self. An actor on the musical stage maintained a certain distance from his role; his task was to perform rather than to be the character in nonintegrated musicals.

It should be no surprise that comics such as the Marx Brothers and Brice played with an assortment of ethnoracial disguises. Appropriation of identity was a key assimilationist strategy for Jewish performers during the melting-pot period. Indeed, both Ann Douglas and Eric Lott argue that theft among races, ethnicities, and genders defines American popular culture, of which the musical may be the crowning achievement.[41] Beginning with minstrelsy, Douglas points out that the idea of whites playing blacks, blacks playing whites playing blacks, and men playing women involved a dynamic of doubling and double doubling that carries over into vaudeville and the American musical: "Minstrelsy put the fooling techniques of black culture, the 'puttin' on ole massa' routines of mimicry and role-playing developed in the days of slavery, at the heart of American entertainment. Blacks imitating and fooling whites, whites imitating and stealing from blacks, blacks reappropriating and transforming what has been stolen, whites making yet another foray on black styles, and on and on: this is American popular culture."[42] The nonintegrated musical, with its roots in minstrelsy and, later, vaudeville, encouraged appropriation.

It is easy to find evidence to support Douglas's theory. In the 1830s, T. D. Rice supposedly appropriated "Jump Jim Crow" from a black stable hand. By 1920 Ethel Waters was called the ebony Nora Bayes. Al Jolson stole his famous line "You ain't heard nothing yet" from the black vaudevillian Joe Britton, while Ted Lewis appropriated his trademark "Is everybody happy?" from black minstrel Ernest Hogan. Men stole from women, as women did from men. When Jolson interpolated "You Made Me Love You" into *Honeymoon Express* (1913), he famously dropped to one knee, while he stretched his arms heavenward to sing "Gimme gimme what I cry for." He stole the bit from Blossom Seeley, who had used it the previous year when she performed "Toddlin' the Todalo" in *A Night with the Pierrots* at the Winter Garden.[43] Later, Judy Garland, during her concert years, appropriated Jolson's trademark runway and much of his repertoire. George Gershwin appropriated black jazz and Jewish-black syncopation at Carnegie Hall with "Rhapsody in Blue," whereas he incorporated Gullah spirituals in *Porgy and Bess*. At the same time, Cole Porter, a WASP, confessed that his show tunes were really Jewish music. In the 1950s and 1960s, Elvis Presley sang black gospel. For at least the first six decades of the twentieth century, American popular culture relied on appropriation.

Appropriation, however, lends itself to charges of racism. If a white performs black identity, as in Jewish or Irish blackface, the appropriation threatens to essentialize the African American. Racial or ethnic stereotypes are rarely appropriated in the politically correct environment that reigns in 2005. An African American performing caricatured black identity is justified because the possibility exists, hopefully, that there is irony in the stereotypical performance. Unfortunately this is often not the case. The depiction of African Americans in gangster rap and rock videos as pimps and whores and the stereotyping visible in black situation comedies on television are incredibly racist, a point that Spike Lee makes in the film *Bamboozled* (2000). Michael Bronski, on the other hand, argues that in the 1920s, Jewish blackface was an expression of outsider status through identification with the black persona; or, conversely, blackface was a way to prove whiteness by the performer distancing himself from a race that could never be white.[44]

Indeed, blackface, from 1830s minstrelsy until its decline in the 1930s, is seen as a way that Jewish and Irish performers ascended by masquerading as a more despised minority.[45] According to Michael Rogin, it became an assimilation strategy that essentialized African Americans and reinforced their humiliation. Stephen J. Whitfield, on the other hand, argues that blackface was a strategy that Jewish and other minority performers used to achieve American nationality rather than racial transcendence: "The allure of blackface was that through its artifice such entertainers could separate themselves from the Old World. What was at stake was not their race but their nationality. By walking and talking like Negroes, Jewish performers could transform themselves and the masses whom they represented, from outcasts into Americans."[46] Although both of these theories were undoubtedly true for many Jewish performers, they seem counterintuitive to an entertainer such as Eddie Cantor, who invariably spoke with a thick Yiddish accent when he appeared in blackface. In this case, despite Rogin's theory, it was clear that once he rubbed off the burnt cork, he was not white but Jewish. Similarly, in contradiction to Whitfield, he was hardly divorcing himself from the old world by walking and talking like an American. Sadly, Jewish performers—or any performers—during the late nineteenth century and early years of the twentieth century had to deal with the convention of blackface if they wanted to enter the world of show business. It is difficult to theorize that all Jewish, Irish, or ethnic Americans who donned burnt cork had the same motivation unless that motivation was to succeed in their chosen profession. Jewish stars honed their own performance styles and strategies of reconciling blackface with Jewish assimilation. With the exception of Jolson, who clung to the blackface persona he had learned to rely on since his days with Lew Dockstader's minstrel troupe, many Jewish performers who engaged in blackface, such as Cantor and Sophie Tucker, eagerly shed burnt cork as soon as they were able.

Certainly blackface presented a challenge for Jewish entertainers who performed for a diverse audience just as it had for black performers during the late nineteenth century. African Americans who appeared in minstrelsy entertained a multiple spectatorship during the same performance: white American Protestants; western and eastern European working-class immigrants; African Americans, often physically segregated from the whites in the audience; and women from a variety of ethnic and racial backgrounds and classes. According to Roger Abrahams, black performers "operated out of a kind of double consciousness, knowing that they are called upon to present an image which will be interpreted as exotic to the outside world and not to the blacks in the audience."[47] The dynamic was incredibly complex. A black performer imitated a white man in blackface performing a black man or sometimes a black woman for an ethnically and racially diverse audience. For David Krasner, "This double consciousness [performing for blacks and whites simultaneously] in black theatre indicated multiple layers of racial, gendered, and cultural interrelationships."[48]

Similarly, during the 1927 theatre season, the peak season in Broadway history, when there were more shows produced and more active theatres than at any other time, the audience was no less complex or fragmented. Although opening nights typically catered to the carriage trade, most audiences consisted of a variety of ethnicities and classes.[49] The star performer, by necessity, had to collaborate with his role to create a persona that could be mainstreamed to a heterogeneous crowd.

For a Jewish performer, blackface implied dancing for the white folk while simultaneously showing marginalized ethnics within the audience that the clever servant could best his master. At the same time, the Jewish performer who donned burnt cork, such as Jolson, distanced himself from the African American, whom his blackface seemed to essentialize, whereas other Jewish performers who played Yiddish or Indian in blackface, such as Cantor, never attempted to play black. The dynamic was similarly complex in terms of gender. The effeminate hypochondriac obviously read differently to male and female spectators and to straight and gay spectators.

Jewish entertainers also had to please Anglo-American audiences if they wished to achieve popular and financial success. In a carnivalesque twist, the WASP element of the audience came in for their share of ridicule, which managed to flatter them while flattening them. The aesthetic was a bit like the Feast of Fools, at once both transgressive and conservative. The Anglo melting pot was still controlled by a white hegemony, which also comprised many of the ticket buyers. The goal of appropriation of race, ethnicity, and gender was acculturation, not the displacement of the power structure. In this sense, the performances were conservative. At the same time, the strategy of transcending fixed notions of race, ethnicity, and gender enabled Jewish performers to take pride in their ethnoracial heritage and win the admiration of Jewish audience members. Sophie Tucker sang "My Yiddishe Momma" well into the 1950s, despite her reputation as the "last of the red-hot mommas," whereas Al Jolson was as well known for his recordings of "Kol Nidre" and "Cantor on the Sabbath" as he was for some of his black-face "Mammy" numbers. Intuitively, other immigrant groups probably viewed these performances of songs that delineated the Jewish experience as metaphors for their own attempts to retain elements of their pasts while they tried to assimilate into the melting pot.

A challenge that stars obviously had to face was finding a way to provide something for everyone. Material had to be at once ribald and chaste in an effort to embrace various groups within the same house.[50] The working class had to be satisfied as well as the respectable and the fashionable. According to Richard Butsch, "No simple answer can describe the diverse audiences."[51] In vaudeville, where musical comedy stars such as Eugene and Willie Howard, Bert Lahr, Al Jolson, and Eddie Cantor learned their craft, the Keith-Orpheum circuit stressed playing to multiple spectatorships within the large, big-time houses, so that "things must not be keyed too high, nor too low."[52] Performers learned how to maximize audience response. According to Alison Kibler, vaudeville slang institutionalized this goal: "'Riot' described a successful act; an audience 'killed' an act, or it 'died,' getting no reaction from the audience; an act 'drew blood,' meaning enthusiastic applause."[53]

Since performers depended on their ability to control these diverse audiences, coding was encouraged in vaudeville and later was applied to musical comedy. The Keith-Orpheum circuit was known as the Sunday school circuit; management insisted on clean language to encourage women and children to attend. Peter Bailey argues that coding and double entendres enabled stars to circumvent the house rules and be clean and risqué at the same time: "In vaudeville, transgressions of managerial policy, with complicity between performers and audiences, were often of the nature of sexual innuendoes. The shift in control and content produced a version of 'knowingness' between them and a means to maintain the balance performers depended upon."[54] In her autobiography, Sophie Tucker recounts fighting with executives of the Keith-Orpheum circuit about double entendres in her act. According to Tucker, she was a big enough draw that she could do what she wanted—and what she wanted was to control her diverse audiences.[55]

Another kind of coding existing with the Marx Brothers in *The Cocoanuts* (1925), although given their propensity for ad-libs, it is not clear whether the coding was part of the Broadway show or was added for the 1928 film version. Certainly the film boasts more veiled Yiddish slang and allusions than any other Marx Brothers vehicle. For example, Groucho encourages Harpo and Chico to sign a hotel register, assuring them that everything will be A.K., rather than okay. *A.K.* is an abbreviation of a Yiddish expression, *alter kocker,* that means "old shit," a joke presumably accessible only to Jewish audiences. Similarly, Chico cheers another character on with the words, "Bravo Galitzianer," a reference to a Jew from Galicia, which indicated someone with the demeanor of a Polish prince. A final example of coding in *The Cocoanuts* involves Groucho informing Chico that levees abound along the river. Chico concludes that the river must be a Jewish neighborhood, something New Yorkers accustomed to the Jewish name "Levy" would readily comprehend. Groucho replies that he'll pass over that, a fairly obvious reference to the Jewish holiday Passover. In any Marx Brothers vehicle, Groucho's wisecracks were so fast and furious, it was virtually impossible to digest them all in one sitting. These coded Jewish references probably tickled Jewish audiences and presumably went above the heads of others.[56]

Jewish comic Ed Wynn's star persona itself involved coding. Billing himself as "the perfect fool," he performed with a fully American accent, although he drew on a Jewish character type from Yiddish folklore, the fool of Chelm. A typical story about the amiable, befuddled denizens of Chelm involves the rabbi who visited the town prison. Since all the prisoners claimed to be innocent, the rabbi proposed to the town leaders that Chelm should have two prisons: one for the guilty and one for the innocent. Another story from Yiddish folklore describes a fool with a heavy burden on his back. A stranger with a horse and cart stops, gives the fool a ride, and observes that the passenger has not dislodged his burden onto the cart. When confronted, the fool answers that the horse has enough trouble carrying two passengers. If he removed the load from his back and placed it on the cart, the horse would then have more to carry.[57]

This is very much the kind of humor on which Wynn based his comic routines, which typically involved silly inventions, such as an eleven-foot, four-and-a-half-inch pole intended for those who could not touch anything with a ten-foot pole.[58] In Rodgers and Hart's *Simple Simon* (1930), Wynn invented a painless mousetrap. Since it had no entrance, the mouse could not be hurt. Wynn also rode across the stage in the Rodgers and Hart musical on a bicycle equipped with a piano, which he played while peddling.[59] Epstein explains Wynn's appeal to Jewish audiences: "It is crucial to note that the Chelm characters, like Wynn's fool, were seen as foolish but were liked for it. The audience is led to understand that but for the gift of common sense, they, too might be fools."[60] Perhaps even more to the point, Jews were not alone in mythologizing a town as the home of innocent and self-delusional people. The idea of the perfect fool resonated with many immigrant cultures, each of whom had their own version of Chelm: Kampen for the Dutch, Cuneo for the Italians, and Schildburg for the Germans.[61] Wynn's coded persona embodied a compassion for all outsiders, even the silly and slightly simple-minded.

Performing Jewishness

According to Will Rogers, "No Christian ever made good at the Winter Garden."[62] Presumably Rogers is pinpointing the Jews here, since the Irish, the Italians, and most other Western and Eastern European immigrants were Christians. Why were Jews in particular so successful as musical theatre performers? Italians had the same emotional catch in their singing; however, with notable exceptions such as Jimmy Durante, their fame centered in the opera house and in the nightclub, not in the musical. Certainly the Irish had made their presence known in musical theatre during the late nineteenth century. Harrigan and Hart played with disguises and masks as early as 1878 in their *Mulligan Guard* series. Harrigan was straight man to Hart's often drag or blackface persona. Their musicals underscored tensions between marginalized Americans, specifically between Irish and African Americans, and between the upper and lower classes. By the turn of the century, the most celebrated star of musical comedy was George M. Cohan, whose musicals focused on the patriotic pride of Irish assimilation.

The Irish, however, were among the first of the hordes of European immigrants to be assimilated. By 1919 even Florenz Ziegfeld characterizes them as American rather than as a marginalized group. In "Picking Out

Pretty Girls for the Stage," he notes that "there are more types of beauty among strictly American girls," and the one nationality he singles out for praise are Irish women, because they often have "nice eyes, a good nose, pretty hair, and an expressive mouth."[63] Linda Mizejewski observes that Ziegfeld is categorizing Irish women as Americans rather than as an immigrant group, whereas Martha Banta hypothesizes that the Irish were the immigrant group that could assimilate most easily into nativist American thinking: "[The Irish were] at least imaginatively assimilable . . . these young Irish women were Northern European, Caucasian, and Christian, after all. . . . It was all the others—the Indians, Negroes, Mediterraneans, Asians, Slavs, and Jews—who could not be conceived of as being Americans."[64] By 1920 the need to transcend perceived notions of identity for the Irish was considerably less than for the Jew. Once assimilation occurs, one doesn't want to be reminded of a marginalized status.

Whereas the Irish had made great strides at assimilation in New York by the turn of the century, Jewish immigration from central and eastern Europe was soaring. By 1910, 1.25 million Jews inhabited New York City; 92 percent belonged to families in the lowest socioeconomic class.[65] Many of these Jews had come from nations in which they were often the least accepted marginalized group, much like African Americans in the United States. Writing of the Jewish affinity for the stage in France during the nineteenth century, Rachel M. Brownstein theorizes that both Jews and actors were transgressive; neither group comprised respectable members of society.[66] American Jews discovered opportunities in show business, be it vaudeville, minstrelsy, or musical comedy, that did not exist for them elsewhere. A similar situation existed for African Americans. According to Thomas L. Riis, census statistics verify that by 1910 there were more actors and musicians among African Americans than members of any other professional employment category.[67] It is not surprising that American Jewish immigrants would seek the stage and identify with the minstrel persona. The musical theatre welcomed them far more openly than American society as a whole.

Although many Jewish performers used a variety of onstage ethnoracial disguises while simultaneously making their Jewishness clear, other entertainers were less open about performing their Jewish identity. In the first decade of the twentieth century, Ziegfeld's first wife, Anna Held, promoted herself as a Parisian music hall performer, chic, glamorous, and sexually knowing. She even managed to incorporate a new category, the "Parisian Coon Song," which she performed without burnt cork but with a chorus of blackfaced minstrel chorus boys. What Held avoided publicizing was that she was Jewish and had been born in Warsaw. Before her success in Parisian cabarets, she worked extensively in Yiddish theatre, both in Paris and in London, where she performed with Jacob Adler's company. Held promoted her French identity and subverted her lower-class, ethnic background. By 1907, when Ziegfeld "defined" the American girl in the first edition of his *Follies,* she looked like Anna Held. In fact, the showgirls were labeled "The Anna Held Girls." One did not have to be upper-class or of a particular race or ethnicity to be the quintessence of beauty and sophistication; one merely had to "perform."

This is not unlike the kind of transcendence of class and ethnicity achieved by Jewish actresses, such as Rachel and Sarah Bernhardt in Paris, that Andrea Dworkin describes in *Scapegoat.* Like Anna Held, Rachel was able to use the stage as a means of "passing": "Her talent, her style, subverted both French xenophobia and Jew-hate. Regarding the first, 'Rachel was so good at passing for a young girl of good family. . . . In effect, her play implied that manners, Frenchness itself, might be acquired, that a foreigner could get herself up to be absolutely *comme il faut,* as it were *plus française que les Françaises,* and breach the wall of French high society and undermine it.'"[68] Perhaps Bernhardt's performance of "passing" was even greater, since her mother was a Jewish courtesan. She transcended not only ethnicity and class but also gender, through her acclaimed trouser roles. From 1896 to 1900, French anti-Semitism had raged around Dreyfus, a Jewish army officer unjustly convicted of treason. Although the government finally pardoned Dreyfus in 1900, the nation was torn between Dreyfusards and anti-Dreyfusards. Bernhardt's own Jewishness had long been reviled in the French press with cartoons that ridiculed her long nose, stringy hair, avarice, and eroticism, all of which suggested stereotypical anti-Semitic prejudice. Bravely she not only supported Dreyfus but also, during this period, played three princes who fought social injustice: Lorenzaccio (1896), Hamlet (1899), and L'Aiglon (1900). Her triumph in *L'Aiglon,* in which she played the son of Napoleon, was astounding in that a Jewish woman was able to market herself as the spirit of France, unifying both camps in a patriotic celebration of the principles of the French Revolution while defying race and gender.

In America Cantor and Jolson were not playing whiteness, nor were Jewish female comic entertainers such as Fanny Brice and Sophie Tucker. To understand the dynamic that made these performers so successful, it is important to acknowledge that ethnicity and gender (not to mention class) are often inextricable. Laura Doyle argues that "hierarchies of race and gender require one another as co-originating and codependent forms of oppression rather than merely parallel, compounded, or intersecting forms."[69] Building on Doyle's assumption, one can say that Jewish men have a long history of being *perceived* as effeminate and sexually degenerate. The emotionalism of speech, the singsong vocal mannerisms, the flailing hand gestures, and the Hassidic dress, including the long gabardine gown, all stereotypically feminized the male Jew.

Indeed Shakespearean scholars such as James Shapiro have pointed out that the anti-Semitic depiction of Shylock in *The Merchant of Venice* has much to do with the practice of circumcision, which during the Middle Ages was somehow interpreted by gentiles as implying a kind of male Jewish menstruation. Shapiro claims many gentiles believed that loss of blood produced a vampirism that incited Jews to ritual murder of gentile children.[70] Marjorie Garber agrees with Shapiro that circumcision was perceived to mean that the Jewish man was less masculine than his gentile counterpart and that this effeminacy was responsible for the association of the male Jew with a perverse sexual identity.[71] According to Sander Gilman, circumcision, the act of making a Jew a Jew, was equated with castration.[72] Along these lines Andrea Dworkin chronicles the belief that Londoners assumed Jack the Ripper was Jewish during his brief reign of terror and that racial vampirism caused him to feed off prostitutes.[73] Wilhelm Fliess theorized that the nose was a primary signifier of sexual neurosis; a "suspiciously" shaped nose was a sign of excessive masturbation. Fliess consequently performed operations to normalize suspicious noses and relieve neurotic symptoms. Large noses were perceived to be characteristic of Jewishness, which again supports the notion that Jews were perceived to be sexually perverse.[74]

Another feminizing aspect of Jewish culture involves the intellectualism of the Jewish man. Masculinity in the Jewish culture is defined by the Talmudic scholar, not by the warrior, the typical role model in most other Western European cultures. Jewish veneration of the intellectual over the physical can be perceived as a sign of masculine weakness. For H. L. Mencken, pre-Israeli Jewish men chose to manipulate their enemies intellectually rather than to confront them physically, which further linked them with women.[75] Responding to the dichotomy between Jewish intellectualism and the Aryan concept of the virile warrior, the Zionist Max Nordau demanded during the second Jewish Congress in 1898 that all Jewish males become muscle Jews rather than coffeehouse Jews. According to Dworkin, when Israel became a state, Zionists wanted to remake the Jew into the Hebrew, replacing intellectualism with a more militant, virile notion of masculinity:

> While many Zionists wanted to turn Jews into peasant-farmers, the father of military Zionism, Zeev Jabotinsky, wanted to turn Jews into soldiers, "Because the Yid is ugly, sickly, and lacks decorum, we shall endow the ideal image of the Hebrew with masculine beauty. The Yid is trodden upon and easily frightened and, therefore, the Hebrew ought to be proud and independent. The Yid is despised by all and therefore the Hebrew ought to charm all. The Yid has accepted submission and, therefore, the Hebrew ought to learn to command. The Yid wants to conceal his identity from strangers and therefore, the Hebrew should look the world in the eye and declare: I am a Hebrew." This is an extraordinary expression of Jewish self-hate.[76]

Jabotinsky's suggested mandate for the metamorphosis of the Jew into the militant Hebrew sounds remarkably like gay rights activists in the early 1970s recycling outward gay identity into the superbutch leather queen and gym clones so much in evidence today. Indeed, gay icons, including Garland, Streisand, Merman, and Channing, ironically seem to embody Jabotinsky's suggested traits for the new Hebrew warrior; they are proud and independent, commanding, and forthright, and irresistibly charming.

In line with the perception that the Jewish male is effeminate, Dworkin cites Otto Weininger's *Sex and Character,* published after the author's suicide in 1903, as a remarkably influential (at the time) argument that all Jewish men were essentially women. Although, as Marjorie Garber points out, Weininger's book seems deranged and incredibly racist today, it was well received when it was read by Jews such as Sigmund Freud and feminists such as Charlotte Perkins Gilman. The Jew, according to Weininger, was a sign of the increasing effeminacy of the age.[77] Arguing that race and gender are interlocked, Carl Jung supported Weininger's thesis about Jewish effeminacy: "The Jews have this in common with women; being physically weaker, they have to aim at the chinks in the armor of their adversary."[78] Dworkin builds on Jung's comparison of Jews and women: "Contempt for Jews is warranted because contempt for women is normative; both Jews and women have been locked in at night, Jews in ghettos, women in houses. Because like women, Jews have not fought back, the men are taken to be biologically deviant in having none of the violent pride that distinguishes men from women."[79] The personae of the male star comics of the nonintegrated musical, many of whom either were Jews or performed Jewishness, fed into these sociological perceptions of the effeminate Jew. Their use of blackface itself was emasculating, turning the African American into a sexless caricature rather than a potent, sexually threatening male. By blacking up and incorporating Yiddish vocal inflections, Jewish comics linked their ethnicity with the emasculated African American figure of minstrelsy. At the same time, these comics exploited the intellectualism of the Jew. They subverted the power of the Anglo majority through disguise and cunning. Ultimately they triumphed through their wit and intelligence rather than through brute force or Anglo hegemonic notions of physical power.

This playfulness with Anglo virility was particularly transgressive during the 1920s. While Ziegfeld marketed a formula for what the American woman should look like, the huge immigrant population threatened the perceived WASP image of the American male. Tans and sunlamps were popular by 1925, marking a growing negroization of Manhattan culture. Dark Latino screen lovers, such as Valentino with his flashing eyes, flamboyant gestures, heavy eye shadow, and slave bracelets, posed a threat to the more traditional Anglo-American ideal of stalwart, square masculinity. The negotiation of gender was complex. Jewish male star comics reassured WASP audiences that they were no threat to American masculinity; yet by playing the racialized and gendered Other and by inevitably outwitting the onstage Anglo-American male, they were suggesting that previously fixed notions of identity were radically subject to change.

Cantor

As I've suggested, the negotiation between ethnicity and race for the Jew was particularly topical during the 1920s, due to the Johnson immigration act and prejudice against the hyphenated American. Resisting racial exclusionism while managing to cling to one's Jewish heritage is illustrated by Eddie Cantor's performance in his most famous vehicle, *Whoopee!* (1928), which survives in a Samuel Goldwyn film adaptation (1930), supervised by Ziegfeld and presumably close to the original Broadway production.

Whoopee! finds Cantor playing Henry Williams, an effeminate WASP hypochondriac who inexplicably speaks with a Yiddish inflection. Henry's nurse, played by Ethel Shutta, tells him of her love, but he seems more interested in the half-naked physique of Wanenis, an American Indian whose race precludes marriage to Sally Morgan, the white girl whom he loves. The plot is contrived and silly, an excuse for Cantor's clowning, singing, and ultimate donning of blackface. Trying to save Sally from marriage to Sheriff Bob Wells, Henry runs off with her. The nurse misconstrues

Henry's relationship with Sally and thus finds opportunities to smack him around and manhandle him. The butch, aggressive Shutta character finally is united with Henry/Cantor at the conclusion of the film, while Wanenis is reunited with his beloved Sally when he discovers that he is not really an Indian, but of white parentage.

Although Henry is ostensibly a WASP, it is clear that Cantor is performing a Jewish man. Note the following dialogue between Wanenis and Cantor's Henry Williams:

> *Wanenis*: I studied the ways of your race—I went to your schools!
> *Henry*: An Indian in a Hebrew school? Tell me, how did you get along?[80]

Like Fanny Brice, who had to learn Yiddish phrases from Jewish comics, Cantor was not well versed in Yiddish when he first went on the stage but performed with a Jewish vocal inflection. At one point he impersonates an Indian chief; later he plays an Indian in a red union suit. Although assuming the character of an Indian, he still speaks with a Jewish inflection.

At the end of act 1, he bursts out of a gas oven that explodes, a convenient excuse for him to emerge in blackface. Ethan Mordden describes this remarkable sequence, which served as justification for Cantor to interpolate a variety of songs in blackface: "Evading a posse, Cantor slips into an oven. 'Look over the ranch,' the sheriff snarls to his men. 'Don't let a white man get by you.' The oven explodes and Cantor pops out in his minstrel make-up. He gets by. Claiming to be a 'singing waiter,' he proves his stuff in a spot left blank for interpolations."[81] The key here is the sheriff's demand that no white man escape. This is a complicated moment, since Cantor bests the authority figure by appearing in blackface, a comic reversal of the traditional perception, at the time, of white superiority. Borrowing from minstrelsy, Cantor's blackface persona is the trickster. During the nineteenth century the blackface trickster was outwardly subservient but invariably was more intelligent and clever than his white master. The dynamic is similar to the wily servant in Plautus's comedies. Cantor uses blackface as a strategy to subvert the all-American, virile idea of the white Western hero.

The other fascinating aspect of Cantor's blackface in *Whoopee!* is that he does not "play" black but continues to incorporate his Jewish vocal inflections in his blackface scenes. Contrary to late-twentieth-century show business mythology, the Jewish (or Irish) blackface comic did not necessarily sound black despite the grotesque physical exaggerations and stereotypes that blackface promoted. Douglas Gilbert notes that from the 1880s onward there existed a significant tradition of blackface performers who donned burnt cork but made no attempt at Negro dialect or impersonation, including Lew Dockstader, Leopold and Bunnell, Frazer and Allen, Carroll and Nealey, Keating and Sands, Smith and Byrne, and Bryant and Saville. These were blackface entertainers rather than Negro impersonators.[82] Interviewed by jazz critic Gary Giddins, Bob Hope, who performed a blackface act in vaudeville, confirms Gilbert's assertion: "In those days, you did blackface but you downplayed the minstrel aspect."[83]

In an article entitled "The Vaudeville Theatre" written in 1899, Edwin Royle stresses that blackface did not necessarily mean the performer sounded black or played black in any but the most obvious physical sense: "This unique and original world has its conventions, too, quite as hard and fast as elsewhere. . . . The comedian will black his face, though he never makes the slightest pretense to negro characterization."[84] Royle's quote invites questioning. Jolson often used a southern dialect, which in blackface implied playing black; he also used other identities and ethnicities. Cantor, at least on film, plays every identity but black while donning burnt cork, the most prominent being Jewish. George M. Cohan, an Irishman, also played blackface not only early in his career but also as late as 1933 in the film *The Phantom President.* Rather than using black characterization, however, he clung to his own Irish ethnicity and Yankee-Doodle-Dandy performing style. Various Jewish and ethnic performers appropriated the use of blackface for their own purposes, which sometimes did include black characterization. Despite much literature on the subject and a plethora of theories by scholars such as Michael Rogin, Eric Lott, and Noel Ignatiev, it is difficult to make any hard and fast rules about a stage convention that was so prevalent and that was used in so many different ways by such a wide variety of performers.

Again it is hard to know how much of Cantor's blackface persona was convention and how much was Cantor. Goldman stresses the closeness of his relationship with the black star Bert Williams, who was Cantor's mentor when he first worked for Ziegfeld. Williams reportedly instructed Cantor in the correct use of blackface during the run of *The Ziegfeld Follies of 1917* and encouraged him not to be too broad. Instead of being threatened by Cantor, who was the only other blackface comic in that edition of the *Follies,* Williams did his best to encourage Cantor to perform with as much dignity as possible, under undignified circumstances, and still get laughs.[85]

Cantor's Henry Williams was characterized not only by his use of blackface and disguise but by his performance of effeminacy. As the shy hypochondriac, Cantor played with gender to such a degree that Herbert Goldman, his biographer, argues that the character borders on homosexuality.[86] At one point Henry compares his "operation" scars with those of another male character. The scars, of course, appear to be around the genitalia, an obvious reference to circumcision, so the two are forced to peer down each other's pants. Eventually they wind up entwined on the floor. It is clear, however, that Cantor is ambivalent, since he seems genuinely appreciative of the Ziegfeld beauties on display during the next scene. The gender dynamic here is complex. Cantor's character is like an adolescent boy who has not committed himself sexually. He is homosexual in his admiration of strong, physically attractive men such as Wanenis, whom he unabashedly ogles. He is also smitten with women. Goldman comments on this contradiction: "Cantor, in his stage work, seemed to play both ends against the middle, suggesting a borderline homosexual at one moment and rolling his eyes in a genuine appreciation of the Ziegfeld beauties in the next. His character's effeminacy seemed part of a presexual youth's sexual awakening—a young man uncertain of his sexual orientation but with a definite susceptibility to the charms of beautiful women."[87] The shy, effeminate persona was maintained throughout Cantor's career, although the Yiddishisms disappeared when he abandoned Broadway and became an American institution through his films for Samuel Goldwyn.

Today *Whoopee!* serves as a model for appropriation as well as the impossibility of separating gender, ethnicity, race, and class. Virtually all the characters, save one, play complex, topsy-turvy identities. Shutta's nurse is man-hungry yet relentlessly butch. Her pursuit of Cantor's sexually ambivalent Henry is in itself a turn on conventional gender relations, though with roots in earlier works, such as *The Mikado*'s Katisha and other man-hungry females in the Gilbert and Sullivan repertoire. Wanenis is sexually attractive, virile, and Indian but, to his surprise, realizes by the film's end that his Indian identity has really been a performance, since his parents were both white. Sheriff Bob is a brave authoritarian WASP figure, until Cantor's blackface persona exposes him as a thief and a coward. The showgirls, ostensibly Indian, transform themselves with headdresses and ostrich plumes into glamorous Goldwyn Girls. Like Wanenis, race has been a performance. If they dress white and perform white, they can be white.

The sole character without a topsy-turvy identity is Sally, the ingenue, who appropriates no racial, ethnic, or gendered characteristics except whiteness, which is, of course, a racial construct by itself. Hilary Harris and Kate Davy argue that whiteness gives women access to respectability.[88] According to

Richard Dyer, the construction of whiteness for women provokes anxiety about sexuality. It is the white woman's responsibility to reproduce her race; however, the sexual act of reproduction paradoxically is a disturbance to her "refinement" and "racial purity."[89] The plot of *Whoopee!,* such as it is, hinges on this anxiety. Transgressively, Sally is in love with the Indian Wanenis rather than with white Sheriff Bob. In fact, most of Cantor's antics are aimed at the plot's concern with whom Sally should wed. Since Wanenis is revealed to be of white parentage, the final scene oddly and comically reconfirms the hegemonic notion of whom proper (white) American girls should marry. What is striking is the contrast between Sally and the comic insanity of the rest of the production, as well as Sally's identification with the glorified showgirls. As Linda Mizejewski observes, "Situated among the more playful masquerades and ethnic/racial disguises of *Whoopee!* is the Glorified American Girl as a 'genuine' article, a real boundary of 'Americanization,' that could make possible a liminal space for Cantor's clowning."[90] Cantor not only bests dim-witted straight white men such as Sheriff Bob but also provides ironic commentary for the glorified showgirls, who serve as embodiments of the ideal Nordic-American beauty. In fact, the Goldwyn Girls in the film (or the Ziegfeld Girls onstage) are really clones of Sally. While Cantor sings the title song, he is surrounded by forty showgirls who pose flirtatiously as bridesmaids. The lyrics of the song are comic; they chronicle the collapse of a marriage due to excessive extramarital "whoopee." The showgirls seem blithely ignorant of the meaning of the words. Their refusal to respond to the racy lyrics confirms prevailing notions of white female purity and refinement and only contributes to Cantor's outrageousness. At the same time, as Mizejewski notes, their deadpan obliviousness to Cantor's number confirms that whiteness is also a performance, to be treated with a mixture of respect and humor. If the glorified American girl is revered and stable, her respectability and innocence are springboards for the antic humor that surrounds her.

Jolson

Like Cantor, Jolson played Jewishness, appropriated a variety of ethnoracial identities, and performed ambiguous, if not ambivalent, gender. Both performers used blackface interspersed with Yiddishisms, and both used performance styles from the minstrel tradition. Although Jolson's "Mammy" songs justifiably are regarded today as racist, he also used blackface to consolidate Jewish identification with the African American. Jolson often sustained his Jewish American identity while in blackface, occasionally singing in cantorial tones to emphasize the similarities between these marginalized groups. I do not mean to overstate my case. Certainly he exploited the minstrel traditions of rolling eyes and tasteless grotesqueries as well. But the blackface dynamic in films such as *Big Boy* (1930) and *The Jazz Singer* (1927) is complex and worthy of further study.

In *Vera Violetta* (1911), Jolson introduced the character of Gus—a blackface version of the Pseudolus of Roman comedy—which would be his persona in most of his Winter Garden musicals and which was as closely identified with the Jolson persona as Lorelei Lee was with Carol Channing or Peter Pan with Mary Martin. Like Cantor's Henry Williams, Gus was the trickster from minstrelsy, the black underdog who lived by his wits and was always far more clever than his master. Eddie Anderson famously recreated a variation on the character years later on radio and television as Rochester, Jack Benny's man Friday. Gus was a constant in Jolson's book musicals, but the character was a mélange of racial and ethnic appropriation. Jolson is best known today as a singer who worked in blackface; it is important to realize that he was also known as a comic who confided in and joked with audiences in the guise of his Gus persona and who, like Cantor, often played a variety of ethnicities within blackface. Jolson's blackface persona was always dynamic and changeable. In his shows he managed to combine Gus with a Venetian gondolier, Robinson Crusoe's Man Friday, Inbad the Porter to Sinbad, and Bombo, Christopher Columbus's black navigator.

Like Cantor, Jolson also played with gender. If Cantor was sexually ambivalent, Jolson was sexually ambiguous and more knowing; his nickname was "the black Peter Pan of the Winter Garden."[91] He curried favor with the straight men of the audience by ridiculing effeminacy: "Jolson often touched his listeners while speaking. He also pinched cheeks and occasionally kissed other men. Onstage his work was filled with sly references to homosexuality: suggestive moistening of the lips, risque use of the behind and hips, and what was then known as a 'nance walk.'"[92] A typical Jolson reference to homosexuality occurs in *Wonder Bar*, a 1934 film version of his 1931 stage musical. Jolson plays Al Wonder, the owner of a Parisian nightclub. The role allows him to interject a variety of wisecracks and nightclub performance numbers as he unravels a rather complex, seedy assortment of romantic entanglements concerning others. Indeed the role is a kind of "whiteface" Gus. At one point, Jolson, as emcee, performs in front of the bandstand. He notices a handsome man asking a dancing couple whether he can cut in. The couple agrees, and the man proceeds to dance with the male partner, while the woman stomps off the dance floor. Jolson crows, "Boys will be boys."[93]

Jolson's comment in *Wonder Bar* may simply have been meant to exploit the "pansy" craze prevalent in midtown Manhattan when the show was produced in 1931 but that had become unpopular by the film's release in 1934. On the other hand, Jolson's onstage ribbing of homosexual men may have been influenced by his offstage sexual preferences. He was a tortured character in real life, the victim of several unhappy marriages. According to Ann Douglas, his cruelty and sadism involved urinating on people, which he thought was funny.[94] Rumors abounded that Jolson was bisexual. Herbert Goldman recounts a story about Jolson and Harry Richman, another vaudeville and musical comedy star of the 1920s, who was also rumored to be bisexual. He and Jolson, once close friends, had a falling out and Richman remained bitter. After Jolson's death, Richman ran into Pearl Goldberg Sieben, who had worshiped Jolson. According to Goldman, Richman's conversation was brief: "'I lived with your boyfriend,' he whispered in her ear. The remark startled Sieben, who had already heard rumors of Jolson's possible bisexuality."[95] Whatever his offstage sexual preferences may have been, however, the nance jokes and ribbing of homosexual men persisted throughout Jolson's career.

Whereas Cantor capitalized on his effeminacy and seeming inability to decide between men and women onstage, he made it clear throughout his career that he was a devoted family man and father of five daughters. To further promote his offstage masculinity, he even staged a mock boxing match with pugilist Jack Dempsey as a comic publicity stunt. Jolson adopted an onstage persona that was basically asexual, despite the sexual double entendres and jokes about homosexuality. He enabled his young "master" to marry the girl of his dreams or he exposed women with questionable financial or sexual motives, but as Gus, he was never in a position to be the romantic lead. When he left Broadway to become a film star, Jolson mistakenly often played romantic roles, in which he was never comfortable.

Jolson's only film appearance as Gus is in *Big Boy,* which is unique in his film canon, since as far as one can tell, it is pretty much a duplicate of his 1925 Broadway vehicle of the same title. Because it contextualizes blackface through the Gus character, *Big Boy* gives a close approximation of Jolson's pre–*Jazz Singer* stage style.

In the movie, Gus, the blackface stable boy on a southern plantation, rides Big Boy, a champion horse, in the Derby. A group of crooks try to discredit him and replace him with an English jockey, a foppish dandy. The plot borrows heavily from George M. Cohan's *Little Johnny Jones* (1904). The script, as such, is an excuse for Jolson's wisecracks and clowning. For instance, Leslie, the English jockey, snottily announces, "The more I read the less I know," to which Gus replies, "You must be well read."[96] Later, the jockey mutters condescendingly to Gus, "My word, what a lovely tan. Just been to Palm Beach?" Gus replies, "No, I was to a funeral and I had to wear all black."[97]

The film then reverts to a flashback of the plantation before the Civil War. We see white southern aristocrats on the plantation porch, the women among them twirling parasols. Jolson, in blackface as Gus, is in the front yard with the other slaves. The scene is typical of the minstrel plantation setting, supposedly nostalgic for the old South and the gentle lifestyle that nurtured the stereotypically loyal slave. What is startling here is Jolson's choice of song, the African American spiritual, "Let My People Go," which he sings in a Jewish cantorial tenor. The lyrical references to "smite Pharaoh" and "Go down, Moses" are obvious references to Jewish slavery and Jolson's own racial and ethnic heritage. There is no vestige of black dialect here. In the context of the plantation setting, the antislavery message is both clear and emotionally stirring, although tasteless to an early-twenty-first-century critical eye. This performance is not just minstrelsy but a deliberate yoking of African American and Jewish culture.

After the gospel number, Big John Bagby is introduced, obviously a take-off on Simon Legree. The villainous Bagby, a racist bully, taunts Gus: "Remind me to horsewhip you at 6 p.m. tonight." Gus replies, "Remind me to be away from here at quarter past five."[98] The lecherous Bagby kidnaps the fiancée of Gus's master. As Bagby rides off with the woman, Gus chases him on horseback, eventually roping and lassoing him—a kind of blackface Tom Mix–Gene Autry. In this scenario, it is the blackface slave who rescues the fair damsel, not her wealthy white fiancé.

The scene shifts back to the 1920s. Gus's young master, like his pre–Civil War incarnation, is weak and passive. He has been bribed by a bunch of crooks to throw the Derby. The master interrogates Gus:

> "Am I your boss?"
> "You're my boss."
> "Have I common sense?"
> "You're my boss."[99]

The message is clear: the black servant is morally, ethically, and physically superior to his white master. Through a series of plot convolutions, Gus punishes the crooks, exposes the wicked, licentious wife of one of the villains, restores the honor of his young if unworthy master, and rides Big Boy to glory in the Derby. Although he engages in several wisecracks about pansies, Gus is not romantically involved with a woman. He enables his master to be reunited with his fiancée, but his great love in the film is Big Boy, the Derby winner. Sexually he is prepubescent. Interspersed through all this, of course, are several Jolson showstoppers, all performed in blackface. During one, "Hooray for You," Jolson navigates the first two verses in English and sings the third in French. As in "Let My People Go," he constantly traverses boundaries of fixed identity.

Jolson's most famous film role, Jakie Rabinowitz in *The Jazz Singer,* is far removed from his Gus persona on Broadway, although it closely mirrors events in Jolson's own life. Jakie is the son of a cantor, who leaves his Lower East Side home to become a blackface ragtime and jazz singer. He explains to his father that the music of the synagogue is like jazz, except that jazz can reach more people. Jakie's explanation is dismissed by his father, who wants him to be a cantor. At the climax of the film, Jakie is backstage in blackface, waiting to go on for his big break, when his mother appears to tell him that his father is dying. Should he return to the synagogue and sing "Kol Nidre" to please his father or sing ragtime and accomplish his dream of stardom? While his mother pleads with him to replace his father at the synagogue, Jakie's split loyalties and desires are maximized as his gentile girlfriend, a chorus girl, hovers sympathetically in the background. Blackface works both in conjunction with and in opposition to Jakie's Jewishness. Jakie has two identities: his blackface or American identity, which feeds into his ambition to be a jazz singer, and his obligations to maintain his Jewish heritage. The conflict was controversial in 1927. Subscribing to the white melting-pot aesthetic meant assimilation at the price of de-Judaization. Miraculously, Jakie manages to appear at the synagogue and affirm his Jewish heritage, while later appearing onstage in blackface. His successful stage appearance makes him a star and guarantees his assimilation. In effect, the film attempts to meld the idea of the melting pot with cultural pluralism, admittedly a difficult union. Although Jolson is not playing the trickster persona, he still performs a complicated and flexible version of American identity by negotiating the gap between ethnicity, with its promise of assimilation, and racial Otherness, with its inherent separation from the center of the Anglo hegemonic power structure. The chasm between possible assimilation and exclusionism defines Jolson's character in the film and reflects the unstable notion of Jewish identity during a cultural moment still stinging from the Johnson immigration act of 1924. Like other ethnicities and races, Jews were subject to familial pressures as well as societal pressures that set rules about assimilation and Americanization. Justifiably these marginalized groups were confused about their unstable position both within their own cultural heritage and within the larger framework of American society, which at the time still clung to discriminatory hiring practices and ethnoracial quotas.

Jolson's blackface persona in *The Jazz Singer* arguably plays with gender as well as race. Whereas Jack Robin (Jakie Rabinowitz's Americanized stage name) is self-confident and aggressive in whiteface, blackface, in Michael Rogin's view, renders him childlike: "In a decade when Jewish aggression was feared and blacks [were] kept securely in their place, and when white collegians considered blacks less aggressive than Jews, the black mask of deference enforced on one pariah group covered the ambition attributed to the other."[100] Rather than playing Gus the trickster, Jolson plays Peter Pan in *The Jazz Singer.* He yearns for his Jewish home and family as Jakie Rabinowitz but also wants the never-never land of a career in mainstream show business as Jack Robin. Singing "Mammy" in blackface onstage, he manages to win Mary, his gentile girlfriend, while avoiding alienation from his adoring Jewish mother. As Peter Pan, Jolson negotiates the two attitudes that divided the American Jew between the two world wars: the yearning for ethnic assimilation in an Anglo power structure and the fear of becoming essentialized as racialized Other by clinging to one's heritage. He constantly slips between both worlds, his identity self-consciously theatrical and blurred.

Unfortunately for his post–*Jazz Singer* film career, Jolson was lost without burnt cork. As radio and motion pictures replaced Broadway as mass entertainment, the ethnic-racial dichotomy posed by blackface wore thin in movie palaces outside New York and other major urban areas filled with ethnic audiences. Jolson continued to make films during the 1930s but was unable to find an on-screen persona that would justify his continued use of blackface. Whereas Cantor's burnt cork number in *Whoopee!* is appropriate to his trickster persona, we are left with snatches of Jolson performing various songs in blackface on celluloid without the context of his Gus persona or the ethnic-racial dichotomy of his role as Jakie Rabinowitz. Jolson was also cursed with a sentimental streak, which he exhibited in treacly songs like "Sonny Boy" and a string of sappy films that only demonstrated that Jolson's gifts were not those of a romantic lead. He tried to secure starring roles in both *The Green Pastures* and *Porgy and Bess,* but happily for posterity, he failed. He also performed some of the most tasteless blackface numbers in Hollywood history, including the notorious "Heaven on a Mule" sequence from *Wonder Bar,* in which he cavorts with Uncle Toms shooting craps as well as with dancing watermelons, fried chickens, pork chops, and possum trees. This sequence, by itself, is enough to permanently tarnish his reputation. Watching the later film *Rose of Washington Square* (1939), in which he recreates numbers like "California Here I Come," "Avalon," "Rock-a-bye Your Baby with a Dixie Melody," and "April Showers," one admires his boundless energy, but the blackface, without the Gus persona, is off-putting, to say the least.

When we think of Jolson and Cantor today, it is often their singing styles that come to mind. Never much of a serious actor, Jolson had a comedic genius that was virtually lost on celluloid, and what remains is his song stylization. Similarly, Cantor's impersonators focused on his singing style, aping his rolling eyes, outstretched palms, high tenor voice, and busy, mincing dance steps; these were the most easily identifiable aspects of his film persona. Ann Douglas suggests that cooler film crooners like Bing Crosby and Ross Colombo replaced the hard-sell ethnic emotionalism of Jolson and Cantor once talking films were established. Douglas blames Jolson's decline on technology. Once talking pictures and radio became popular, she argues, Jolson's performance style became doomed, since he was by nature a stage performer:

> The crooner's subtle nuances of phrasing and casually natural pronunciation were made possible by the invention of the electric microphone in 1925 . . . and their fame was tied to the new sound media of radio and talking pictures; they marked the beginning of a shift from live to canned entertainment. The crooners personified an ultra-sophisticated, upper-crust cool, an intimate yet bland sexuality, very different from the tears-and-laughter-drenched raw craving of Jolson's belt-it-out style. Live performers of Jolson's generation had to project, even shout, their songs by putting the energy of their entire bodies into their performance; "all upper-cuts" is the way Ethel Waters described Jolson's delivery. . . . The crooners gave listeners their voices in place of their bodies; they cleaned up black and Jewish sexuality from the WASP or would-be WASP middle-class mainstream audience.[101]

Douglas is surely correct in asserting that Jolson and Cantor were replaced by more physically economical male singers—the models being Crosby and later Frank Sinatra. Still, if male singing styles changed because of the technology of film and the microphone, how can one explain the phenomenon of Elvis Presley in the 1950s, who shot to fame on television because he performed with his body, not just with his voice? Presley, like Jolson, was a consummate live performer. If Jolson was kinetic in his minstrel routines, Presley's pelvic gyrations were considered salacious when he first appeared on *The Ed Sullivan Show.* Here was a white male singer who did not perform economically but sang as though he were performing black gospel and moved with an abandon and physicality that was foreign to white male singers of his time.

One could make the case that male singing styles changed during the early 1930s not because of technology but because ethnicity, race, and gender threatened the concept and image of the American male. With the rise of the Latin lover, the Jewish musical star, the new icons of the Harlem Renaissance, and the flapper with bobbed hair, American identity during the 1920s was in a constant state of flux. In such a fluid mix, one group had to remain stable. Women and African Americans had always been perceived as inferior, as had Jews. In fact, one of the truisms of minstrelsy was the persistent effort to ridicule women's desire to wear pants, both figuratively and literally. Throughout the nineteenth century, minstrelsy was antiabolitionist and anti–women's rights.[102] Women, as long as they were not ingenues, could perform with an ethnic style; they were hopelessly marginalized anyway. It was the male who became more stabilized in the early 1930s to counter the threat to WASP masculinity.

Jolson's singing style was in fact inherited by women, from Judy Garland on-screen to Ethel Merman onstage. The reliance on a mixture of Jewish and black growling chest tones became known as "belting." Not only did it not disappear from the stage, but it remained intact on film. Garland was Jolson's spiritual heir. Her vocal style was characterized by the same ethnic throbbing, the spastic, flailing hands, the slurred speech, the impossibly busy little dance steps between lyrics and between choruses, and the over-the-top emotional flamboyance. Trained in vaudeville, Garland consciously modeled her concert persona after Jolson. The jacket cover publicity on the recording of her Carnegie Hall concert (1961) calculatedly compares her performance style to Jolson's. Many of her famous songs either had been introduced or had been popularized by Jolson, including "When You're Smiling," "After You've Gone," "For Me and My Gal," "Swanee," "Mammy," "April Showers," "Rock-a-Bye Your Baby with a Dixie Melody," "Among My Souvenirs," and "Chicago." Like Jolson, Garland used a runway during her concerts; the runway enabled both performers to establish an intimate rapport with their audiences, despite the vastness of their performing spaces. Both had enormous sincerity, a keen sense of comedy, and a kinetic performing style. A singing style that had begun to be considered overly theatrical and overemotionalized for the man was now viewed as revered for the woman. It is ironic that Garland was imitated by a generation of drag queens, who in effect modeled themselves after a Jewish blackface minstrel entertainer who frequently derided gay men.

Beyond Multiculturalism: Back to Zangwill

American identity has always been volatile and continues to be. In "Beyond the Melting Pot," William A. Henry predicted that by 2056 the average U.S. resident "will trace his descent to Africa, Asia, the Hispanic world, Arabia, almost anywhere but white Europe."[103] The 2000 census has generated much discussion about a new generation of Americans with multiracial parents who were unable to identify themselves as belonging to one race.[104] In a diverse society, is it not logical that various groups will share their cultures, intermarry, and eventually forge a new and unpredictable race of Americans, dynamically reinventing themselves? How different is this observation from Zangwill's original notion of the melting pot, not to mention the observations of Crèvecoeur, Tocqueville, Emerson, and Melville? Ironically, Zangwill's melting pot, in which *American* signifies a process of becoming, may well play itself out differently in a multiracial society, where whiteness may not be hegemonic in the future.

The last quarter of the twentieth century saw a decline in musical comedy and a rise in the serious, integrated musical. This transition is not surprising, since the playfulness and theatricality that were strategies of musical comedy performers during the melting-pot years seemed racist to a diverse, multicultural society that frowns on ethnoracial appropriation. Mel Brooks's blockbuster *The Producers,* the saga of Jewish tricksters Bialystock and Bloom, may have reversed the trend, however. Brooks understands the older conventions of musical comedy that exploited ethnic, racial, and gendered appropriation. If musicals are products of their cultural moments, does the success of *The Producers* herald a cultural change or a throwback to an older tradition?

It will be fascinating if we move from multiculturalism to a new version of Zangwill's notion of American identity: unpredictable, ever-changing, and dynamic—a process of becoming through diverse cultures that bleed into each other and form a new, multiracial nation. I would like to see musicals embrace hip-hop performance artists such as Danny Hoch, who promotes his own, contemporary version of ethnoracial, gendered appropriation of identity. His impersonations would be well suited to the playfulness and transgressiveness of the form. Hoch's roster of impersonations includes a white teenager whose goal is to become a black gangster rapper, a cop who antagonizes a light-skinned Bronx street vendor because the vendor's race defies categorization and is not obvious from his skin color, and a Puerto Rican on crutches who enthusiastically brags about his dancing abilities. Hoch appropriates Brooklyn Polish, Jamaican patois, Bronx Dominican Spanish, and Queens Trinidadian English. His purpose is not to make fun of gender, race, or class but to reflect a new, multiracial society that puzzles the white hegemony. Add music to this playful aesthetic, and perhaps once again, musical theatre will reflect dynamic issues that are relevant to contemporary society through subversive strategies of performing identity.

In 2005, with a new generation of Americans of multiracial descent and the dawning realization that America may not be ruled forever by a white patriarchy, America may well be grappling with another vision of identity. Holland Cotter suggests the seeds of change in an article in the *New York Times* on July 29, 2001, entitled "Beyond Multiculturalism: A Way to a New Freedom in Art."[105] If the center cannot hold, it is time to redefine the center. That redefinition is heading toward an ever-changing social dynamic among gendered, racial, and ethnic groups to redefine public culture. A crucial question has always been whether American identity can successfully negotiate the thin line between race and ethnicity. As William A. Henry III observed in 1990, "For whites, American heritage is a source of pride; for people of color, it is more likely to evoke anger and sometimes shame. The place where hope is shared is in the future."[106]

Harrigan *(left)* and Hart in an undated cabinet card from *Ireland vs. Italy.* Courtesy of the Museum of the City of New York.

Anna Held, Florenz Ziegfeld's wife and the epitome of French glamour, who hid her Jewish roots in the Yiddish theatre (undated, ca. 1906). Photo courtesy of the Museum of the City of New York, the E. B. Marks Collection.

The great African American performer Bert Williams in his last musical, *Under the Bamboo Tree* (1921). Williams mentored Eddie Cantor in the use of blackface, which may be one of the reasons Cantor seldom played black but adopted Jewish and Indian personae when he donned burnt cork.
Photo courtesy of the Shubert Archive.

Jack Dempsey *(left)* and Eddie Cantor in an undated mock boxing match. Photo courtesy of the Shubert Archive.

Eddie Cantor in his first Winter Garden Show, *Broadway Brevities* (1929). Photo courtesy of the Shubert Archive.

Al Jolson with a bucket of worms and two showgirls in *Bombo* (1921). Photo courtesy of the Shubert Archive.

Al Jolson and an "Indian" chorus of white showgirls in *Bombo.* Jolson is about to buy Manhattan Island for twenty-four dollars. Photo courtesy of the Shubert Archive.

The "In Dahomey" number from the original production of *Show Boat* (1927).
Photo courtesy of the Rodgers and Hammerstein Organization.

Charles Winninger, the original Captain Andy, performing his ad-lib comic star turn in "The Parson's Bride," the onstage melodrama in the original production of *Show Boat.* Notice the perspective of the onstage setting, designed by the great Joseph Urban.
Photo courtesy of the Rodgers and Hammerstein Organization.

Bert Lahr *(left)*, Luella Gear, and Ray Bolger in *Life Begins at 8:40* (1934). In this sketch Gear announces she has just seen Noel Coward's *Design for Living* and all three can live happily together in a ménage à trois. Lahr and Bolger decide to dump her in the Seine.
Photo by De Bellis courtesy of the Museum of the City of New York.

June Havoc *(right)* as Gladys Bumps and an unidentified tenor singing "Flower Garden of My Heart," one of the funniest (and tackiest) burlesques of a *Ziegfeld Follies* number, as the girls of Chez Joey parade through a huge heart. The show is *Pal Joey* (1940).
Photo courtesy of the Rodgers and Hammerstein Organization.

LIZA

The circus dream sequence from *Lady in the Dark* (1941), with Gertrude Lawrence and Victor Mature *(far left)* and Danny Kaye *(far right)*. Photo by Vandamm Studio courtesy of the Museum of the City of New York, gift of the photographer.

Ethel Merman *(left)* and Paula Laurence appearing as Indian squaws in Cole Porter's *Something for the Boys* (1943) for no logical reason except to stop the show with "By the Mississississinewah." Photo courtesy of the Billy Rose Theatre Collection, The New York Public Library for the Performing Arts, Astor, Lennox and Tilden Foundations.

The original sheet music cover for *Oklahoma!* (1943).
Photo courtesy of the Rodgers and Hammerstein Organization.

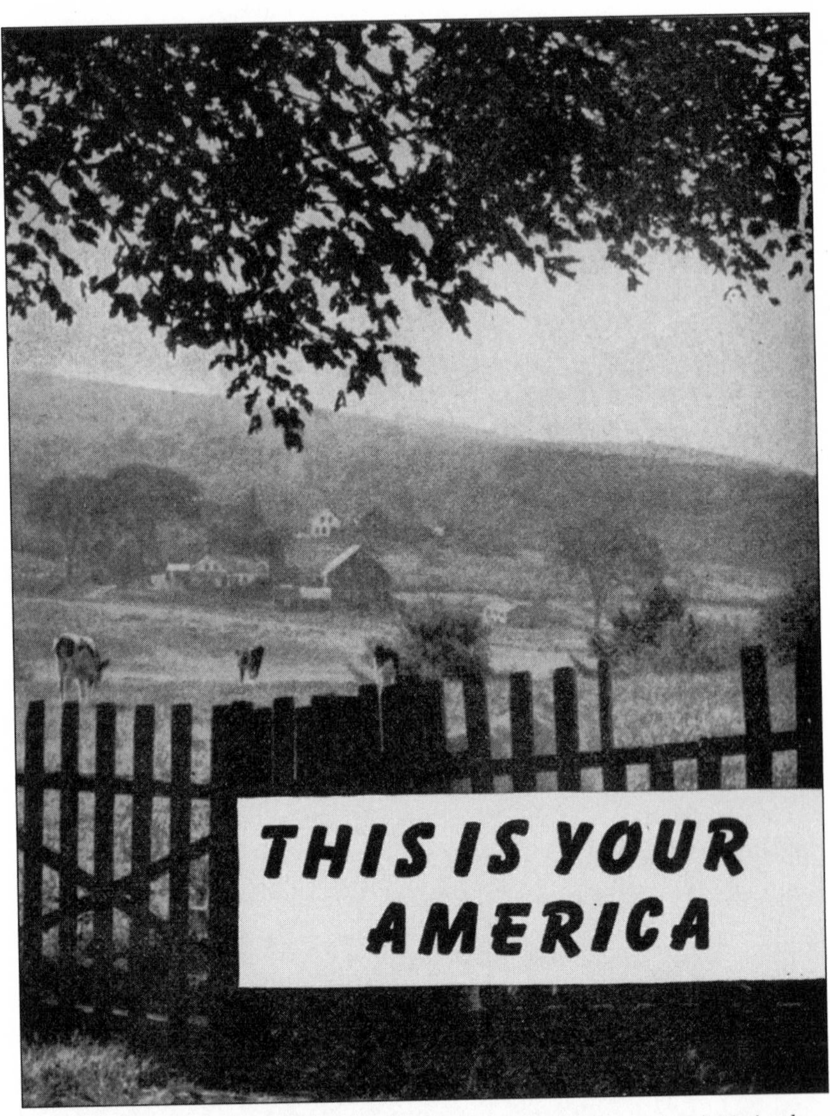

The cover of the PAC-CIO pamphlet "This Is Your America" (summer 1943). Notice the resemblance to the original *Oklahoma!* sheet music cover, published the previous March.
Photo courtesy of the George Meany Memorial Archives (archives of the AFL-CIO).

The surrey finale in *Oklahoma!* From left to right around the surrey are Lee Dixon (Will Parker), Celeste Holm (Ado Annie), Alfred Drake (Curly), Joan Roberts (Laurey), Joseph Buloff (Ali Hakim) kneeling, and Betty Garde (Aunt Eller), along with other members of the original cast. Photo courtesy of the Rodgers and Hammerstein Organization.

Joseph Buloff (Ali Hakim) peddling his wares to *(from left to right)* Joan Roberts, Betty Garde, and Celeste Holm in *Oklahoma!* Photo courtesy of the Rodgers and Hammerstein Organization.

EXTRA! EXTRA!
JOSEPH TAYLOR, JR.
BORN
JOSEPH TAYLOR

The opening sequence of Rodgers and Hammerstein's *Allegro* (1947), in which Joe Taylor Jr. is born. Notice the absence of scenery and the huge cyclorama on which images were projected. The Greek chorus is on the left. Photo courtesy of the Rodgers and Hammerstein Organization.

The children's dance, staged by Agnes de Mille, in *Allegro*.
Photo courtesy of the Rodgers and Hammerstein Organization.

Ezio Pinza singing "Some Enchanted Evening" to Mary Martin in *South Pacific* (1949). Stage directions notwithstanding, the embrace is steamy. Photo courtesy of the Rodgers and Hammerstein Organization.

Bette Midler *(center)* singing "Matchmaker" in *Fiddler on the Roof* (1964) on Broadway. She joined the show as a replacement. Photo courtesy of the Billy Rose Theatre Collection, The New York Public Library for the Performing Arts, Astor, Lenox, and Tilden Foundations.

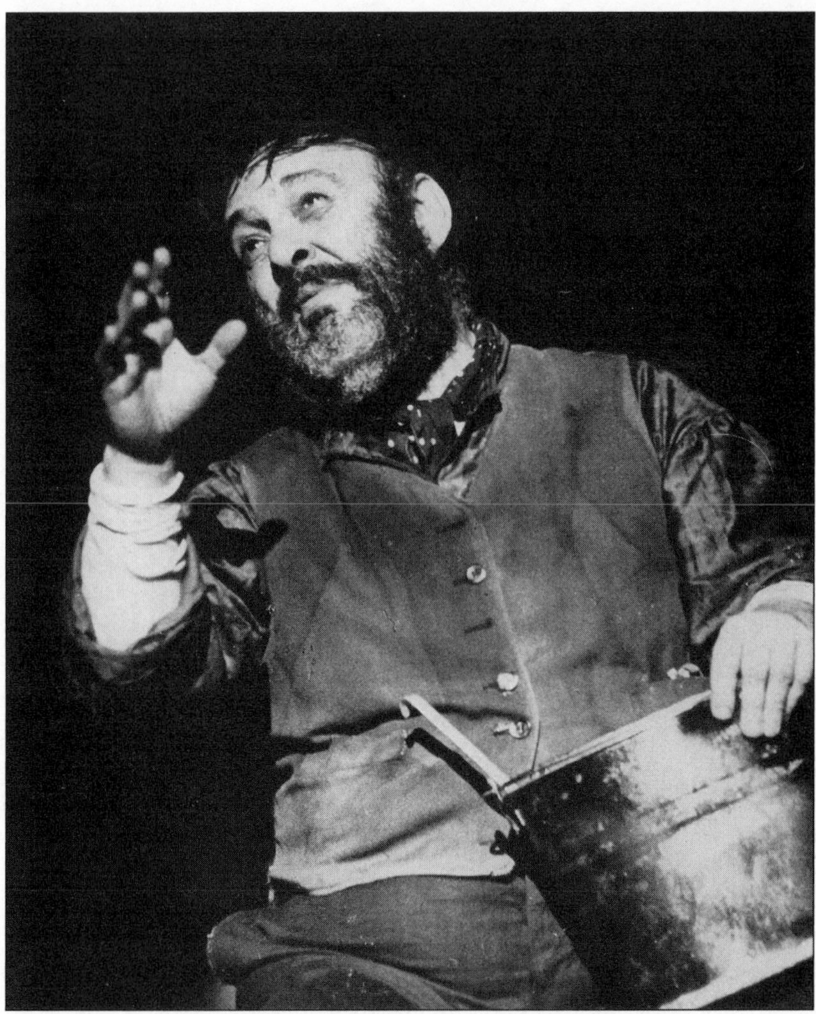

The great Zero Mostel as Tevye in *Fiddler on the Roof.* Photo courtesy of the Billy Rose Theatre Collection, The New York Public Library for the Performing Arts, Astor, Lenox, and Tilden Foundations.

Is she or isn't she? Katharine Hepburn as Chanel supervising her models in *Coco* (1969).
Photo courtesy of the Museum of the City of New York. Zodiak Photographers, Joseph Abeles and Sy Friedman.

Dean Jones and Susan Browning singing "Barcelona" in *Company* (1970). Photo courtesy of the Billy Rose Theatre Collection, The New York Public Library for the Performing Arts, Astor, Lenox, and Tilden Foundations.

Larry Kert, who replaced Dean Jones as Bobby in *Company.* Photo courtesy of the Billy Rose Theatre Collection, The New York Public Library for the Performing Arts, Astor, Lenox, and Tilden Foundations.

Lauren Bacall and the boys having fun at a gay bar in *Applause* (1970). Photo courtesy of the Museum of the City of New York, gift of Bill Doll and Co.

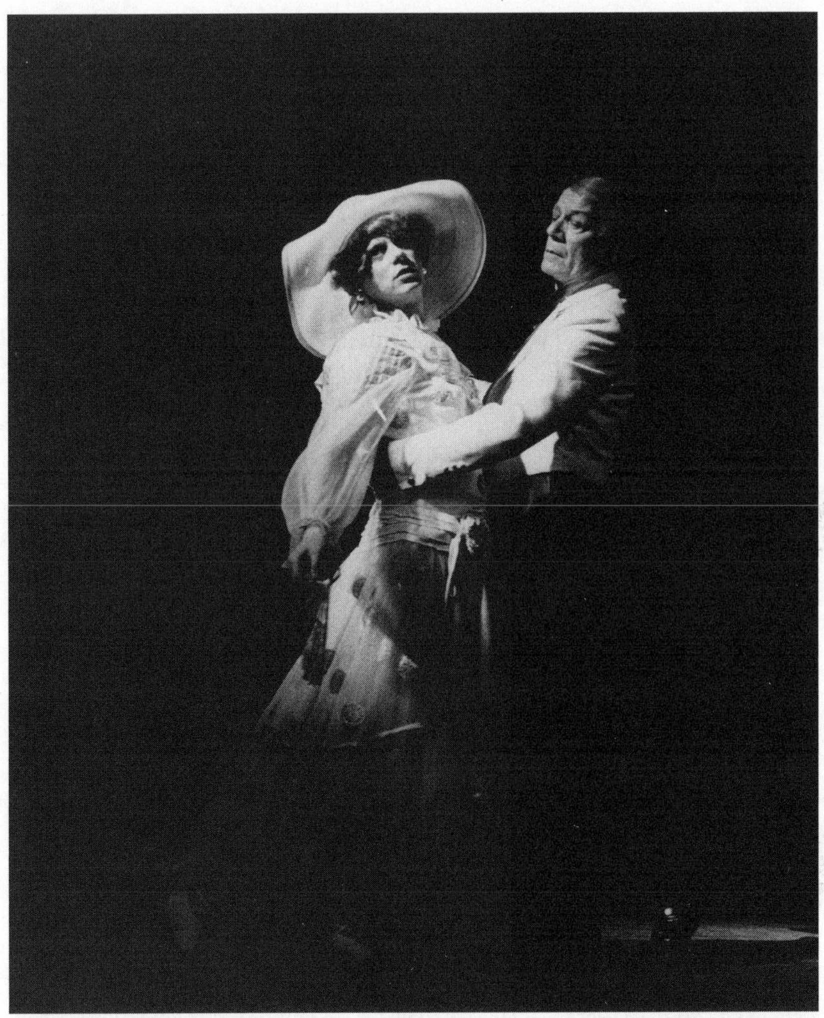

The incomparable Robert Morse as Daphne with Cyril Ritchard as Osgood in *Sugar* (1972). Photo courtesy of the Museum of the City of New York.

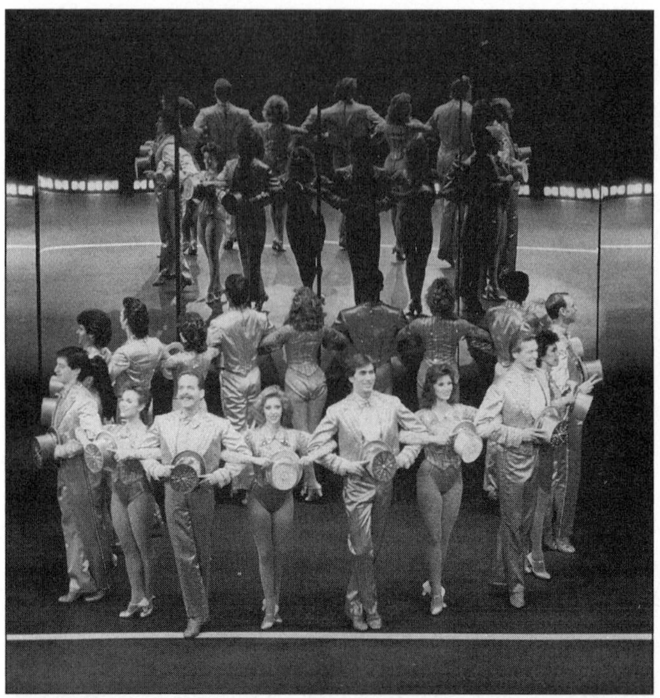

The "One" finale in *A Chorus Line.* Photo: © Martha Swope; courtesy of the Billy Rose Theatre Collection, The New York Public Library for the Performing Arts, Astor, Lenox, and Tilden Foundations.

Hugh Jackman as Peter Allen in *The Boy from Oz* (2003), one of the great male song-and-dance star turns. Photo courtesy of Joan Marcus.

3

◆ ◆ ◆ ◆ ◆ ◆ ◆

Unfinished Business

The case for the openness of musicals may be proved partially by showing the ways in which such works are constantly reinvented as products of their sociocultural moments. It is naive to study the text without paying equal attention to the material conditions in which the text was created, mounted, and received. These conditions include not only the historical moment of production, which obviously predicates the ways in which audiences are inclined to read a theatrical presentation, but also the impact the complex, collaborative process of staging a musical has on the text.

The standard trajectory has been that the integrated musical is a linear outgrowth from the Hammerstein model, beginning with *Show Boat,* refined with the Rodgers and Hammerstein canon (1943–59), and taken to new heights by Hammerstein's protégé, Stephen Sondheim, after which the musical often "dies." As noted earlier, Gerald Mast casts Hammerstein as the hero in the development of the form.[1] According to Foster Hirsch, "The Rodgers and Hammerstein musical plays invited variation and further experiment, as the careers of the ambitious inheritors Hal Prince and Stephen Sondheim have happily demonstrated."[2] Sondheim credits his mentor with creating songs for character rather than performer: "Oscar taught me how to construct a song like a one-act play, which is what he always did, in essence, and how to use songs to strengthen character and theme rather than to provide easy breaks for the audience."[3] According to Harold Prince, Hammerstein's book for *South Pacific* was the inspiration for Prince's future collaboration with Sondheim.[4] For Ethan Mordden, Rodgers and Hammerstein laid the foundation for the American musical to supersede popular culture and to "confront its audience" as a work of art, a statement that pretty much summarizes the formalistic agenda of most musical theatre narratives.[5]

Each of these historians implies that the development of the integrated musical is a direct offshoot of Hammerstein's work. Whereas Hammerstein's contribution to the form is unquestionable, musicals are characteristically eclectic. Rather than reinvent the wheel, Hammerstein himself combined influences of realism, romanticism, and melodrama. The Gershwin and Weill experiments in the 1930s followed a different path, owing much to Gilbert and Sullivan, epic theatre, expressionism, and political satire, whereas the Prince-Sondheim concept musicals of the 1970s borrowed from sources as varied as Meyerhold, Piscator, Kabuki, Ziegfeld, and Ringling Brothers. If Sondheim is a protégé of Hammerstein, he is also a descendant of Brecht and Pirandello. Part of the fluidity and vitality of the form involves borrowing from everything.

Broadway musicals have been a strand of American popular, if not mass, culture for well over a hundred years. It is simplistic to argue that the form is the linear outgrowth of one mind, even if that mind belonged to as fertile a figure as Oscar Hammerstein. The development of the integrated musical reflects the text's negotiation with the prevailing sociocultural zeitgeist as well as with prevailing theatrical conventions. In looking at musicals throughout the decades it will become apparent that many have become inadvertent epics, at times very different from the intentions of their authors, as cultural zeitgeist, performance, and audience reception embellish or alter the written word or score. Since they are necessarily works-in-process, open to a variety of influences, musicals are indeed unfinished business.

The Influence of American Realism in the 1920s

If *Show Boat* (Hammerstein, Kern) is generally regarded as the first "serious" musical, it is not accidental that it was produced in 1927. Although realism dates back to Ibsen and the last third of the nineteenth century, at least on the Continent, American realism, as a viable commercial force, began to flower in the 1920s and was concurrent with realistic aspects of serious musicals during the same decade. Before framing *Show Boat* in the context of American realism of the 1920s, however, one must qualify the term. American plays that were regarded as realistic in the 1920s tended to mix elements of European realism with older, more familiar conventions of romanticism and melodrama. Hammerstein similarly mixed genres with the musical. He tackled serious issues and social problems, psychologized his characters, focused on the bourgeoisie, and emphasized settings and musical leitmotifs that evoked determinism, all of which were characteristic of realism. At the same time, he borrowed freely from romanticism, melodrama, and vaudeville to sugarcoat his serious content and social determinism.

The emergence of American realism was the result of several factors: the rise of the Independent Theatre movement in America, particularly in New York with the birth of the Provincetown Players and the Washington Square Players in 1915; the enshrining of Eugene O'Neill as America's most important and successful realistic playwright with the production of *Beyond the Horizon* in 1920; America's exposure to Chekhov and the Moscow Art Theatre through American tours by that theatre in 1923 and 1924; and the artistic and financial prominence of the Theatre Guild, a commercial offshoot of the aforementioned Washington Square Players, which produced acclaimed star-studded productions of Shaw and Ibsen as well as other Continental playwrights.[6] Indeed, in 1928 Eva Le Gallienne and Blanche Yurka starred in two rival Broadway productions of *Hedda Gabler.* While farces, melodramas, operettas, and urban musical comedies were still commercially popular, clearly a revolution toward American realism was occurring, with productions of such plays as O'Neill's *Anna Christie* (1921) and *Desire under the Elms* (1924), John Colton and Clemence Randolph's *Rain* (1922), Maxwell Anderson and Laurence Stallings' *What Price Glory* (1926), Phillip Dunning and George Abbott's *Broadway* (1926), and Elmer Rice's *Street Scene* (1929), which Kurt Weill later adapted for the musical stage.

Many of these examples of American social realism from the 1920s also exhibited heavy elements of melodrama, a combination that Oscar Hammerstein adapted to his musical libretti in the 1920s. Much of what we consider early American realism does not seem terribly realistic today. Critics William Dean Howells and Henry James had been pioneering the cause of realism since the end of the nineteenth century, long before the visits of the Moscow Art Theatre to America. In the 1879–80 season, Steele Mackaye's *Hazel Kirk* was considered a landmark of American realism, basically because Mackaye dispensed with the standard melodramatic villain. By the turn of the century, Howells had praised the earlier work of musical theatre writer Edward Harrigan, the author of *The Mulligan Guard's*

Ball, as pioneering. As Brenda Murphy notes, "Howells praised Harrigan for creating ethnic types—Irish, German, Italian, and black—that rang true. But his plots were the hackneyed structures of comedy, and if his characters represented some particular ethnic type on the surface, they represented some conventional comic type at bottom."[7] Howells went so far as to compare Harrigan's reforms of melodrama to Carlo Goldoni's reforms of commedia dell'arte.[8] Early-twentieth-century playwrights such as David Belasco, Clyde Fitch, and Edward (Ned) Sheldon managed to combine elements of realism with decidedly melodramatic plots. Sheldon is a particularly important figure, since he was a strong influence on librettist-lyricist Dorothy Donnelly, who later influenced Oscar Hammerstein.

As a playwright, Donnelly collaborated with Sheldon on *The Proud Princess* (1923), a romance about an oil heiress and an organ grinder, which closed out of town. Eventually they reworked the script into a libretto for an operetta, *My Princess* (1927), which dealt with the same odd romantic coupling. This was the first libretto with a contemporary setting that Donnelly had written. Although the piece was not successful, the *Boston Globe* praised the libretto for its elements of realism: "To an extent rare in musical comedy, the situations and characters are drawn from typical American life. There is a well knit plot, sufficient to make a play without the music."[9] Lorraine Arnal McLean, Donnelly's biographer, argues that Donnelly paved the way for Hammerstein's work and set in motion the groundwork for the development of the serious musical.[10]

Donnelly's other libretti, namely those for *The Student Prince* (1924) and *Blossom Time* (1921), two of the most successful operettas of the 1920s, tended to reflect many of the romantic conventions one associates with a Sheldon play. These libretti also foreshadow the work of Hammerstein, not only in *Show Boat* but also in *Rose-Marie* and *The Desert Song,* as well as his later collaboration with Richard Rodgers. Both Donnelly libretti are sentimentalized love stories: *Blossom Time* deals with Franz Schubert's unrequited love for the fictive "Mitzi," whereas *The Student Prince,* based on the 1902 play, *Old Heidelberg,* revolves around the bittersweet love of a mittel-European prince and a barmaid. Donnelly used many of the conventions that Hammerstein later developed and perfected. Like Hammerstein, her libretti always had comic relief, though critics of the time found comic characters such as Lutz in *The Student Prince* less than hilarious and carped about Donnelly's sense of humor. Just as Hammerstein would do later, Donnelly fashioned libretti that highlighted a principal romance, usually supported by a subplot.

Despite clinging to these conventions, Donnelly added an element of realism to the unhappy endings of both operettas. She fought the Shuberts, producers of *The Student Prince,* who objected to the separation of the principal lovers at the end of the play. Similarly, in *Blossom Time,* Franz Schubert dies, his love for Mitzi unrequited. Gerald Bordman comments on the fatalism of *The Student Prince* ending: "The saddened but essentially rebellious lovers accept the social dictates of their world. The heroine is not discovered to have royal blood, nor is there any hint that future generations will resolve their woes. There is, instead, a touch of fatalism rare in pieces of the period."[11] Donnelly's characters, however, tend to be one-dimensional, and her plots sentimentalized and overromanticized. Her comic characters and novelty songs usually stop the plot cold rather than develop the story or further character. It took Hammerstein to perfect the symbiosis of comedy and character, eventually trimming unnecessary operetta and musical comedy conventions while making plot, song, and dance part of an organic whole.

Episodic in structure, *Show Boat*'s story revolves around Magnolia's journey toward independence. By the play's end, she has survived the desertion of her husband, Ravenal, raised her daughter, Kim, and maneuvered a career as a Broadway star. At the end of the play, Kim's emergence as a 1920s flapper and a star in her own right reinforces Hammerstein's celebration of female independence. Magnolia and Kim's successful fight for autonomy is contrasted with the luckless mulatta, Julie, who is left destitute and alcoholic. Women's struggle for equality had been a presence in realist theatre at least as far back as Ibsen. By the time *Show Boat* was produced, the issue was reflective of a decade in which American women had won the right to vote.

In terms of realism, Hammerstein manages to psychologize several of the principals. Andy and Parthy act as foils to Ravenal and Magnolia. The irresponsible Ravenal is mirrored in the unreliably ebullient Captain Andy, whereas the latter's wife, the prim, schoolmarmish Parthy, instills the drive and desire in Magnolia to succeed at her career. According to Ann Douglas, the conflict between the New England Victorian matriarch, who exhibited "that atavistic yearning for a bad time if a bad time is possible," and the New York modern, who championed the "lighthearted, streetwise, and more or less secular popular and mass arts as America's chosen means of self expression" was endemic to the decade.[12] Although no "New York moderns" exist in *Show Boat,* Ravenal and Andy bear more than passing resemblance to Douglas's description. Neither Andy nor Parthy is a model of correct behavior. Both exhibit undesirable extremes. Andy is irresponsible; Parthy, shrewish. Ravenal's love for the high life, to which Andy is more than sympathetic, is blasphemy to Parthy's New England Victorianism; yet it is Magnolia who manages to negotiate a middle road between them.

Although serious in content, *Show Boat* nevertheless trimmed much of the realism from Edna Ferber's source novel. Julie is no longer a prostitute; she becomes an alcoholic saloon singer deserted by her husband. Many of the characters who had died or disappeared throughout Ferber's epic tale were illogically reunited at the musical's happy ending. As Oscar Wilde's Miss Prism pontificates, "The good end happily, the bad unhappily. That is what fiction means."[13] Prism could well be writing about an Oscar Hammerstein libretto. The relationship of Magnolia and Ravenal is mirrored in two subplots. One revolves around the squabbling, comic dancers Frank and Ellie; the other, as noted earlier, focuses on the antagonism between Captain Andy and Parthy. This episodic structure was typical of Hammerstein's libretti for the next thirty years. Through mirroring subplots, Hammerstein is able to mix genres, supplying comic relief to serious, at times tragic, situations. Hammerstein likewise dispenses with unity of time and place, providing his designer with opportunities for exotic settings and colorful costumes.

Joseph Urban's designs, uncharacteristically (for him) following pictorial illusionism, emanated from the realistic-melodramatic plays of David Belasco, Clyde Fitch, and Ned Sheldon, in which a set in effect became the environmental antagonist, a force against which the characters were destined to struggle.[14] The curtain rose on an onstage levee, which eventually served as dock for the *Cotton Blossom*. In a later scene, the auditorium for the show boat, including main floor and balconies, revealed onstage spectators engrossed by the show within a show. During the second act, Urban recreated the magic of the 1893 Chicago World's Fair.[15] These settings frame the presentational numbers performed on the boat and at the fair. Other settings, such as the boardinghouse in Chicago, stress deterministic environment. We see the poverty and hopelessness Magnolia must overcome when we find her in a cheap rooming house as she learns of Ravenal's desertion. Throughout the play, the dock on the levee returns, as Joe and the stevedores reprise their anthem to determinism, "Old Man River."

Despite *Show Boat*'s serious subject matter, Hammerstein softened the harshness of the story with older theatrical conventions. He cast Tess Gardella, an Italian actress and the original Aunt Jemima, to play Queenie in blackface, a popular theatrical convention of the period that few would have questioned. Period songs, included to establish an authentic nostalgia, were blended with Kern's magnificent score to frame the story in what is, in effect, a backstager, another popular musical comedy convention of the 1920s. Indeed the 1920s was the decade of the backstage musical, beginning with *Irene* (1919) and ending with *Sweet Adeline* (1929). Often musicals were fashioned around the title character, a woman who journeys from rags to riches and becomes a musical theatre star. Marilyn Miller had made something of a specialty of this subgenre by 1927, particularly with *Sally* (1920) and *Sunny* (1925), the first Hammerstein-Kern collaboration.

By definition, a backstager must be theatricalist. Presentational numbers are not realistic except in the literal sense—they mimic real performance situations. A surprising number of songs in the original *Show Boat* score exist as part of the show-within-a-show convention, performed onstage or in rehearsal: "*Cotton Blossom,*" "Life upon the Wicked Stage," the reprise of "Can't Help Loving That Man," "I Might Fall Back on You," "Hey Feller," and "Bill," as well as non-Kern standards such as "Goodby My Lady Love" and "After the Ball." The finales of each act adhere strictly to both operetta and musical comedy conventions of the day by reprising several songs and linking the reprises with a recitative that includes new musical and lyrical material that furthers the story. As I mentioned earlier, Hammerstein himself reenvisioned this material for the 1946 Broadway revival, eliminating many of the vaudeville conventions, including some of the presentational numbers, while stressing aspects of integration, which by then he had begun to perfect with such shows as *Oklahoma!, Carousel* (1945), and *Carmen Jones* (1943).

Show Boat's plot, of course, revolves around racism, most notably in the bloodletting scene, where Steve swallows a drop of Julie's blood to prevent their being banished from the show boat for miscegenation. The unjust treatment of African Americans borrows from realistic folk plays of the era, including Paul Green's *In Abraham's Bosom* (1926) and Dubose and Dorothy Heyward's *Porgy* (1927), the latter of which opened just three months prior to the Kern-Hammerstein musical. Moreover, *Show Boat*'s theme of miscegenation was timely during this decade of the Harlem Renaissance. For Ann Douglas, the 1920s saw the collaboration of whites and African Americans in an ethnically mixed society in New York that brought African American art and culture into the mainstream.[16]

One year before *Show Boat,* Arthur Hopkins had produced an uncompromising musical that explored the theme of miscegenation. *Deep River* (1926) was written by Laurence Stallings, a coauthor with Maxwell Anderson of *What Price Glory,* one of the notable examples of American realism of the 1920s. Set in New Orleans in 1835, the musical involves Muguette, a quadroon, who becomes mistress to Brusard, a Creole, who has murdered three men and thrown over his former mistress. Muguette falls in love with Hazard, a visiting Kentuckian, whose brother is in turn murdered by Brusard. Muguette runs off to engage in a voodoo seance in the Place Congo and to pray for Hazard's love. Finally, Hazard kills Brusard in a duel but returns to Kentucky, leaving Muguette in New Orleans, where she is prey to another unscrupulous Creole suitor.

Whereas *Show Boat* tackled elements of realism while simultaneously interjecting conventions of romanticism, operetta, and musical comedy, Stallings's libretto was strewn with complex character relationships and was devoid of comic relief or subplot. The voodoo scene at the Place Congo was performed with virtually no dialogue and probably was difficult for audiences of the time to assimilate, whereas a comparable scene from *Show Boat,* the "In Dahomey" number, was performed at the Chicago World's Fair amid colorful sets and Zulu costumes that, at best, patronized the African American. Franke Harling, who had previously written a rather highbrow version of Keats's "The Eve of St. Agnes," commissioned by the Chicago Opera, wrote the music for *Deep River.* Like the libretto, the score was uncompromising in its integrity and apparently quite beautiful. But without a degree of pandering to musical comedy conventions of the day, producer Hopkins was unable to find an audience for *Deep River.* Despite excellent reviews from critic Burns Mantle, among others, the musical play closed within four weeks.[17]

Golden Dawn (1927) opened less than a month before *Show Boat,* became a significant commercial success, and was later turned into a Hollywood musical. Like *Show Boat, Golden Dawn* had a book and lyrics by Oscar Hammerstein II, although in this case Otto Harbach was coauthor. Unlike *Show Boat,* however, it reads as though it predates *Uncle Tom's Cabin.* Produced by Arthur Hammerstein (Oscar's uncle) and codirected by Reginald Hammerstein (Oscar's brother), the musical featured a score by Emmerich Kalman, Herbert Stothart, and Robert Stolz and sets by Joseph Urban. This Viennese-flavored operetta, incongruously set in Dutch East Africa, seems, incredibly enough, to be the musical stepsister to O'Neill's *The Emperor Jones* (1920). Dawn, a voluptuous blonde beauty in a sari, has been raised in her African village to believe she is a native princess, her whiteness a gift from the gods. She falls in love with Steve Allen, a British prisoner of war, but their romance runs into grave difficulty when the evil black overseer, Shep Keyes, does everything in his power to keep Dawn for himself. When

Dawn rejects Keyes, he turns the village against her, blaming her for a drought that has destroyed the crops. Keyes menaces Dawn in "The Whip Song," which electrified audiences in 1927 as the evil brute cracked his whip and threatened her with what was then unspeakable sexual sadism. He is finally silenced when the village chieftain admits that Dawn is really of white European parentage and not "black" after all. Dreading his comeuppance, Keyes shrieks for mercy as he is led away for punishment.[18]

If this story were not preposterous enough, Keyes was played by Robert Chisholm, a white actor in blackface. The African villagers also performed in blackface, while the score by Kalman and Stothart was basically cut from the same cloth as Lehar's *The Merry Widow* minus the Hungarian local color. Writing of the film version, Richard Barrios marvels at its racism and bad taste:

> Poor Vivienne Segal, forced to wear a blonde wig, skimpy sarong, and leopard skin while trilling a gay waltz called "My Bwana"; . . . Alice Gentle as Dawn's vindictive mother Mooda [actually her African stepmother] . . . with her fervent rendition of "Africa Smiles No More"; . . . and above all, Noah Beery. Perhaps Otto Harbach saw *The Emperor Jones,* ate heavily, fell asleep, and had unthinkably bad dreams. Little else can account for Beery's role and performance as Shep Keyes, the self-crowned tyrant who terrorizes the Africans, antagonizes the British, and pants for Dawn. Wearing badly applied dark makeup, sporting a Kingfish-like accent, stomping about and cracking his whip as he growls the sadomasochistic "Whip Song"—he is utterly spectacular, in a way as to make orthodox notions of bad acting, even in operetta, wilt in comparison.[19]

Barrios seems to blame Harbach for the eccentric inanity of the libretto, but Oscar Hammerstein is billed as co-librettist. It is difficult to fathom how Hammerstein's libretti and lyrics, not to mention his take on racism, could vary so widely between two shows produced within a month of each other. Perhaps the difference in approach is the result of his collaboration with Harbach on the libretto, although Hammerstein alone is responsible for the racist lyrics to "The Whip Song." Perhaps some of the disparity between these two Hammerstein musicals can be attributed to the good taste of Florenz Ziegfeld, *Show Boat*'s producer.

Hammerstein followed *Show Boat* with *Rainbow* (1928), a musical about the California gold rush, written in collaboration with librettist Laurence Stallings (of *Deep River*) and composer Vincent Youmans. *Rainbow* shared

Show Boat's sprawling, slice-of-Americana romanticism as well as its epic sweep but, like *Deep River,* lacked the latter's crowd-pleasing, backstager, musical comedy conventions. Hammerstein's characters were spinoffs from *Show Boat:* a gambler as the male protagonist, a humorous, irascible muleteer, somewhat reminiscent of Captain Andy, and a tragic supporting role that conceivably could have been played by *Show Boat*'s original Julie, Helen Morgan.

The original production illustrates the complex relationship between text and performance as well as the minefields authors often negotiate with a new musical-in-process. During the tryout engagements in Philadelphia and Baltimore, critics hailed *Rainbow* as potentially another *Show Boat.* Though reviewers agreed that the show was flawed, their notices praised Stallings's dialogue as gritty and raw and Youmans's score as innovative and operatic. The rehearsal period and out-of-town engagements, however, were wars. Producer Philip Goodman battled with the equally temperamental Youmans. Eventually Goodman fired director John Harwood and replaced him with Hammerstein, who cut songs that performers found too difficult to sing, revised the sprawling book, and made major cast changes.[20] Torch singer Libby Holman, whom Harwood had originally passed by, learned that the role of Lotta was being recast in Philadelphia. Apparently the original Lotta had trouble learning her lines. "She dances with a broken heart and sings like a goddamn canary" invariably became "She sings with a broken heart and dances like a goddamn canary."[21] Holman met Hammerstein and Youmans in Philadelphia, where they requested she hum something to show her unique vocal style. Apparently Holman kept humming as Youmans noodled on a piano trying to accommodate her low vocal range. Soon composer and lyricist had fashioned "I Want a Man" specifically to suit her growling alto and sensual delivery, whereupon Holman was hired.[22]

Despite Hammerstein's last-minute changes, the show was still overlong and unwieldy. Its opening night become a legendary disaster. Hard hats were tearing up the street in front of the Gallo Theatre, so ushers herded first-nighters through a side entrance. The combination of the sidewalk blasting in front and the vibrations created by the crosstown elevated trains on the Eighth Avenue side of the theatre was so overwhelming that the backdrops began to shake. Overlong to begin with, the show was paralyzed by interminable set changes, one of which lasted more than half an hour, forcing conductor Max Steiner to vamp everything but "Dixie." By the time audiences returned from intermission, it was after eleven o'clock. To make matters worse, Fanny, the onstage mule, defecated copiously downstage center during a production number, and featured dancer Louise Brown was forced to navigate around the mess. The show's pivotal love scene was enervated, since it followed this hilarious fiasco.[23] Although the following morning New York critics were forced to acknowledge the musical had elements of greatness, the mechanical failures and performance mishaps doomed the production. *Rainbow* lasted twenty-eight performances.

Although the horrific opening night performance may have been unique, *Rainbow*'s turbulent preopening history is not unusual for new musicals-in-process. Broadway shows typically undergo major renovations once text and score are tested by performance and reception before a live audience. The result is often baffling and inexplicable, even to those intimately involved with the production. I remember working on a new musical in which a ribald production number set in a whorehouse during rehearsals metamorphosed into a hushed choral hymn set in a convent during the Detroit tryout. Once a show is on its feet, songs that seemed to work in rehearsal often suddenly fall flat and have to be replaced. The substitution of a new song necessitates reexamination of what precedes and follows it; consequently another scene or song may have to be altered as a result of the initial change. As William Goldman observes, "Out of town, it's a constant wild race: changing, trying like hell to fix and patch and forget what you said the show was about back before rehearsal; under the gun you go with what works. And slowly, without anyone knowing it at first, the whole giant structure begins to change direction."[24] I suppose an apt metaphor involves patching a sinking canoe with bubble gum; the object is survival. It is naive to suppose that texts are sacrosanct and end up onstage exactly as written. When the authors prevail, as Rodgers and Hammerstein did for so many years, it is because they are the most powerful members of the production team and are skillful enough as practitioners not to lose sight of their initial direction. Such is not the case in a typical star vehicle or in a Jerome Robbins, Bob Fosse, or Gower Champion show. Commercial musicals are vast machines with huge production staffs, large casts, desperate producers, and combative egos. It is easy to veer from the author's initial vision when huge amounts of money, artistic reputations, and egos are at stake, which is just one of the reasons why musicals are collaborative works-in-process subject to great subversion in the way their texts eventually are performed.

Deviation from the Hammerstein Model

If Hammerstein was the dominant force behind the book musical in the 1920s, he spent most of the 1930s in virtual hibernation, licking his wounds from a long string of failures after successes early in the decade with *Music in the Air* and *The Cat and the Fiddle.* Rather than moving forward in a linear fashion, "serious musicals" during the 1930s were characterized by experiments with the form, including political satires, the Gershwins' transformation of grand opera into an American sung-through folk opera with *Porgy and Bess* (1935), and Kurt Weill's musical attempts to Americanize epic theatre.

This changing horizon of expectations for musical theatre audiences reflects trends in both the nonmusical theatre and the cultural zeitgeist. Certainly realism continued to blossom in the nonmusical theatre during the 1930s. This was, after all, the period of the Group Theatre, Clifford Odets, and the WPA. At the same time, many of the most commercially successful playwrights of the decade were satirists and farceurs, including George S. Kaufman, Morrie Ryskind, and Moss Hart, all of whom played a major role in musical theatre. In *The American Stage and the Great Depression,* Mark Fearnow argues that farce was the leading form in the nonmusical Broadway theatre of the 1930s, since it afforded Depression audiences the opportunity to rebel against authority.[25] The anarchy provoked by comics such as the Marx Brothers on film was a strong statement of freedom for audiences who increasingly feared domestic social collapse and the growth of fascism in Europe. The 1930s zeitgeist was to laugh at the chaos and danger constantly lurking around the corner. The subject matter was certainly serious; the treatment, however, was farcical rather than realistic and often involved fantasy. As Albert Bermel notes, "Farce deals with the unreal, with the worst one can dream or dread. Farce is cruel, often brutal, even murderous."[26]

Fearnow argues that farce captures chaos by placing characters in dangerous situations within a ridiculous, grotesque universe. Whereas these situations would provoke commiseration within melodrama or realism, their dreamlike context within farce provokes laughter.[27] For Fearnow, *Hellzapoppin* (1938), a musical revue, has a serious undertone; it furnishes an evening of attacks on authority that validates Eric Bentley's notion that farce is "hostility enjoying itself."[28] The opening sequence highlights a filmed newsreel with Hitler speaking in Yiddish dialect, Mussolini in heavy Negro dialect, and Roosevelt talking gibberish. Sirens, cannons, and guns constantly erupt, while workmen, supposedly making repairs, climb over the seats of audience members, simultaneously terrorizing them and eliciting their laughter. As Fearnow stresses, "Every violence was possible without risk. Beatings, murder, suicide, attacks on every kind of authority were carried out in a context of fun."[29] The context of the fun was often metatheatrical and Pirandellian, but the subversion of authority was constant.

Kaufman, Ryskind, Moss Hart, and the Gershwins experimented radically with musical theatre conventions. Just as Hammerstein had diluted realistic subject matter through older conventions of romantic theatre and melodrama, the authors of these political satires filtered their attacks on fascism, big business, unemployment, and bungling governmental bureaucracy through farce and Gilbert and Sullivan topsy-turvydom. Unlike Hammerstein, Kaufman had a strong distaste for romance and sentimentality. Though hard-boiled, ironic, and topical, Kaufman was in no sense a revolutionary; if he criticized the status quo, he was usually, if not always, careful to temper his acerbity so as not to offend the commercial audiences on which he relied.

Kaufman collaborated with Morrie Ryskind on the libretto for *Strike Up the Band,* a satire of politics, capitalism, and warmongering. The quintessential musical dependent on its cultural moment, *Band,* originally mounted in 1927, closed during its out-of-town Philadelphia engagement. The libretto detailed the repercussions of the Swiss protesting an American tax on their cheese. Manufacturer Horace J. Fletcher persuades the United States to declare war on Switzerland. He promises to finance it if the United States agrees to name it the Horace J. Fletcher Memorial War. Despite many plot convolutions, the war becomes hugely profitable, not only for the United States but also for Swiss hoteliers housing idle American troops. At the final curtain, the United States and Russia prepare to go to war over Russian objections to an American import tax on caviar.[30] Although critically praised, audiences were disinterested in an uncompromising indictment of American materialism and capitalistic corruption, particularly during the economic boom year of 1927. By 1930 the stock market had crashed and those Americans who could afford a ticket to a Broadway show were perhaps more cynical about politics, economics, and growing instability abroad. Ryskind revised Kaufman's text to soften its social bite. Rather than encourage a World War over Swiss cheese, as in 1927, Fletcher, the American businessman-fascist, urged war over seemingly more frivolous Swiss chocolate. To further sugarcoat the social commentary, Ryskind's final curtain, rather than predicting a war with Russia, revealed that the whole story had been a dream. To help ensure the commercial appeal of the 1930 version, the great comic team of Clark and McCullough were recruited as stars. The result was an impressive six-month Broadway run during the Depression.

The score for *Strike Up the Band* was the work of the brothers Gershwin. Whereas Oscar Hammerstein had been reared on Viennese operetta and contributed the libretti or lyrics, or both, for some of the most successful American operettas based on the Viennese model (*The Desert Song, Rose Marie, The New Moon,* to name but three), the Gershwins modeled their satirical musicals after the work of Gilbert and Sullivan, who in turn borrowed from Offenbach's French operettas of the 1860s.

Both French and English operetta models featured music that was melodic, varietal, satirical, and representative of the popular music of the day. Librettists Meilhac and Halévy, in France, as well as Gilbert, in England, foregrounded topsy-turvy plots, ingenious rhymes, witty lyrics, and peculiar, even bizarre characters. The difference between Offenbach's libretti and those of Gilbert was mostly due to the cultural prejudices of their local audiences: the French were eager for bawdy, sometimes vulgar situations and jokes, whereas the English were considerably more subdued. Richard Traubner quotes a 1906 speech in which Gilbert explained the differences between the Offenbach model and his own:

> We set out with the determination to prove that these elements [those of French operetta] were not essential to the success of humorous opera. We resolved that our plots, however ridiculous, should be coherent, that our dialogue should be void of offence; on artistic principles, no man should play a woman's part and no woman a man's. Finally, we agreed that no lady of the company should be required to wear a dress that she could not wear with absolute propriety at a private fancy ball.[31]

Whereas Viennese operettas tended to have illogical plots, Gilbert's plots (like those of the Offenbach libretti) were coherent in their own topsy-turvydom. The settings for Viennese operetta tended to be exotic and glamorous; those for Gilbert's libretti often echoed the England of his day. Even when the team grew more exotic in *The Mikado,* an effort was ostensibly made to capture Japanese culture accurately and truly, although, ironically, more than a hundred years later, critics and scholars tend to regard these efforts at cultural accuracy as not only erroneous but also patronizing and insulting.

If the Savoyard scores inevitably included catchy Victorian music hall numbers, *Strike Up the Band* included several songs that went on to hit-parade status, including the title song; "The Man I Love," which was cut from the final production; and "I've Got a Crush on You." Musically, however, the score was more sophisticated than those of the musicals and operettas to which New York theatregoers had grown accustomed. Although extended finalettos were well within operetta convention and had been used by Kern in *Show Boat,* the Gershwins' experiments included complex choral numbers that commented ironically on plot and character.

The musical satires of Kaufman, Ryskind, and the Gershwins would be echoed by E. Y. Harburg's satirical musicals, including *Hooray for What?* (1938), a political spoof on the armaments race; *Finian's Rainbow* (1947), a satire on racism; and *Flahooley* (1951), a satire on McCarthyism; as well as musicals like Irving Berlin's *Call Me Madam* (1950), *Li'l Abner* (1956), and the Abe Burrows–Frank Loesser *How to Succeed in Business Without Really Trying* (1961). The innovative use of the chorus to comment on the action and characters, also characteristic of Weill's experiments with epic theatre in the 1930s, was not fully replicated until the Brechtian irony of the Sondheim-Prince concept musicals of the 1970s, although an exception is the innovative *Allegro* (1947), which uses a Greek chorus, though without the humor and irony that Kaufman, Ryskind, and the Gershwins were able to muster.

Of Thee I Sing (1931), the second of the Gershwin musical satires of the 1930s, was even more successful than *Strike Up the Band.* Here Kaufman and Ryskind limited their social commentary to politics and good-naturedly spoofed American political institutions. Again, the seriousness of the message was lightened by a refusal to engage in specific, personal political attacks. Wintergreen, the presidential candidate, runs on a campaign that celebrates love, corn muffins, and kissing babies, while Alexander Throttlebottom, the vice president, is all but invisible to his colleagues—a comment on the ceremonial role of most holders of that office (Richard Cheney excepted). The social commentary earned the librettists the first Pulitzer Prize accorded to a musical. The score followed many of the conventions of the Gilbert and Sullivan operettas, again with complex ensembles and finalettos. According to Richard Traubner, Diana Devereaux, the jilted winner of the beauty contest, "functions as a modern Broadway equivalent of the Katisha-type spinsters in Gilbert and Sullivan."[32] To guarantee hit-parade status, the Gershwins included tunes such as the title song, "Who Cares," and "Love Is Sweeping the Country." The satire was also commercialized by the antics of beloved milquetoast comic Victor Moore as Throttlebottom.

During the 1952 election year, Kaufman persuaded Ryskind to revise the libretto for a revival. Whereas the original version had been good-natured and generalized in its satire, the revival had more specific contemporary targets. Jokes were updated to poke fun at President Truman and perennial presidential candidate Harold Stassen. Reviewers also criticized the revisionist tempi applied to some of the Gershwin score. Jack Carson and Paul Hartman, playing Wintergreen and Throttlebottom, also were judged inferior to original stars William Gaxton and Moore.[33] Whereas Burns Mantle and John Gassner hailed the 1931 production as a "devastatingly complete revelation of the American scene," critics in 1952 found the show dated and it closed after a brief run.[34] As so often happens, the reputation of a musical is often as good as its last production. Perhaps *Of Thee I Sing* is dated. On the other hand, it is also likely that the sociocultural climate in 1952 was wrong for a revival. The postwar economic boom, combined with the height of McCarthyism, was not conducive for political satire. Timing, for musicals, is everything.

Let 'Em Eat Cake, produced in 1933, was the last political musical Kaufman worked on with the Gershwins. In this Kaufman-Ryskind sequel to *Of Thee I Sing,* Wintergreen becomes a blue-shirted Fascist. Having failed in his reelection bid, Wintergreen decides to overthrow the American government. His wife, Mary, makes blue shirts for his followers and saves Throttlebottom from the guillotine. Finally, the coup d'état is settled by a baseball game between the Supreme Court and the League of Nations. Here, the standard conventions of the musical are pushed too far. The tone of *Let 'Em Eat Cake* was acrid and bitter, substituting a cynical prediction of American fascism for the love plot that framed *Of Thee I Sing.* Audiences confronted by the cost of unemployment, economic peril, and encroaching fascism (Hitler had become the chancellor of Germany six months earlier) were not assuaged by an unconventional score and the lack of a conventional love story. The show was a failure.

Despite his celebrated observation that satire is what closes on Saturday night, Kaufman nevertheless persisted with the genre he had done so much to develop. He directed Irving Berlin's *Face the Music* (1932), which sardonically commented on the scandal-ridden Tammany Hall administration of Mayor Jimmy Walker, and wrote the libretto with Moss Hart for Rodgers and Hart's *I'd Rather Be Right* (1937), in which George M. Cohan played FDR, the first incumbent American president to be the subject of a book musical. Both shows were topical and very much products of their time. Cole Porter and librettists Sam and Bella Spewack also tried their hand at a satirical musical, *Leave It to Me* (1938), but the text had to be altered during its run to avoid being dated. When *Leave It to Me* opened, America was on friendly terms with the USSR; indeed, during the first-act finale an actor playing Joseph Stalin performed a dance in Red Square. By the time the show went on tour a year later, Hitler and Stalin were allies. The Stalin character was written out of the play, and a program note denied any resemblance to current events.[35]

The spate of 1930s musical satires waned after *Leave It to Me.* Occasionally an offshoot appeared, such as *Louisiana Purchase* (1940), a veiled satire on Huey Long's influence on Louisiana politics. The Irving Berlin score provided several tunes that became popular on the radio, including "It's a Lovely Day Tomorrow," an appropriate theme for a nation potentially menaced by the Nazi terror machine. By the time America entered World War II, audiences were not keen to see their country denigrated or ridiculed. Patriotism and nostalgia for the past were more reasonable positions, particularly as America became entrenched in battle. When American soldiers returned home in 1945, the economy was booming and a mood of optimism had replaced the grim fears that fascism, the Depression, and looming war had brought to the previous decade.

Gershwin and Weill: Folk Opera, Expressionism, and Epic Theatre

If the Gershwins borrowed heavily from the operettas of Gilbert and Sullivan in writing their political satires, they also pushed the Broadway musical in a new direction with *Porgy and Bess* (1935), which incorporated the conventions of grand opera into a new genre, the American folk opera. Certainly, *Porgy and Bess* derives from nonmusical black folk plays of the time, including the previously mentioned *In Abraham's Bosom* by Paul Green, a realistic look at the troubled life of the black son of a mixed-race marriage; *The Field God* (1927), also by Green; and, of course, the Heywards' source play, *Porgy,* which follows much the same storyline as the musical. The genre would later include DuBose Heyward's gritty *Mamba's Daughters* (1939), an Ethel Waters vehicle, which told the grim tale of Hagar, a generous-hearted black woman, who endures imprisonment, abuse, and betrayal only to sacrifice herself to protect her daughter.

Director Rouben Mamoulian, who had staged the nonmusical *Porgy* eight years earlier, used the gritty, poverty-stricken Catfish Row setting to establish the impossible social and economic obstacles with which the principals of *Porgy and Bess* were forced to grapple. The setting of the grimy courtyard of Catfish Row, the characters trapped in a shanty during a South Carolina hurricane, the onstage rape of Bess at the picnic, and Crown's murder were uncharacteristically naturalistic for a musical. The deterministic setting of Catfish Row was reinforced by the street cries of its vendors:

the Honey Man, the Crab Man, and the Strawberry Woman. Borrowing from Gullah spirituals, Gershwin composed a wake, "Porgy's Prayer," as well as "My Man's Gone Now." The piece ended with the crippled Porgy ready to ride his goat cart from South Carolina to New York to find Bess as he sings the gallantly foolish "I'm on My Way." Although Dorothy Heyward maintained that the ending, which she had suggested to her husband, was intended to be pathetic, audiences invariably interpreted Porgy's final odyssey, accompanied by Gershwin's gospel-influenced music, as uplifting.[36] Eliminating spoken dialogue and substituting sung recitatives, the score contained not only Gershwin songs that could be extracted from the plot with popular success but also complex, extended passages more suitable to opera. As a result, the original production defied neat categorization. It pleased neither opera lovers nor theatregoers, although the theatre critics were kinder than the music critics were on opening night. The original New York production ran 124 performances, lost its fifty-thousand-dollar investment, and proved to be the last work George Gershwin would compose for Broadway.

Like *Show Boat* and *Strike Up the Band, Porgy* has a production history that denies a stable text. Subsequent mountings have drastically altered the text and structure of the score in accordance with popular tastes of the times. Producer Cheryl Crawford first revived the show in 1942. Convinced that the original recitatives had contributed to *Porgy*'s initial failure, she substituted spoken dialogue and streamlined the cast and orchestra to make the show financially viable. Critics, including Richard Watts Jr. and Walcott Gibbs, hailed the new version as a classic, while music critic Virgil Thomson, who had panned the original production, now reversed his verdict and declared *Porgy* a work that "America might well be proud to honor and happy to love."[37] At least part of the praise resulted from *Porgy*'s increased accessibility. Without the recitatives characteristic of grand opera, it played more like a musical.

The enormous success of *Porgy*'s first European production, which debuted at the Danish Royal Opera on March 23, 1943, with an all-white cast, owed much to the political zeitgeist of occupied Denmark during World War II. The gestapo, incensed that an American work was being performed at a state opera house, threatened to bomb the theatre if *Porgy* was not excised from the repertoire. Soon the opera became a symbol of resistance, so much so that when Nazi radio broadcasts propagandized their victories, the Danish underground frequently interrupted with a recording of "It Ain't Necessarily So."[38]

Another metamorphosis of the text occurred during the 1952 international tour, funded by the State Department, that starred Leontyne Price, William Warfield, and Cab Calloway. Director Robert Breen altered the three-act structure of the opera into a first act of four scenes and a second act of six, again closer to the standard structure of a Broadway musical. Stagecraft had changed considerably since 1935, and scenery changes could now be accomplished swiftly. With only one intermission and fewer stage waits, Breen was able to both accelerate the tempo of the piece and restore material cut from the original production, including the "Buzzard Song," "Roll Them Bones," and "I Ain't Got No Shame." Breen also restored some of the Gershwin recitatives that he thought worked, although he also added new spoken dialogue from the Heywards' novel. The production won international acclaim, eventually playing Leningrad, Moscow, and, eventually, the Ziegfeld Theatre in New York.

Samuel Goldwyn's film version (1959), directed by Otto Preminger, continued to reshape the text and score. Critics attacked the performances of Sydney Poitier and Dorothy Dandridge as synthetic, since their voices were dubbed by Robert McFerrin and Adele Addison. Even more damning was the effect of the burgeoning civil rights movement on the piece. During film production, Little Rock, Arkansas, became fodder for headlines as the national guard blocked black students from entering a segregated school. Once the film was released, many southern theatre owners banned blacks from segregated film houses showing the film. In retaliation, African American and civil rights organizations picketed the theatres. Finally, Goldwyn, claiming he did not want to acerbate racial tensions, withdrew the movie from distribution in the South. The depiction of African Americans in *Porgy,* always fairly controversial even among black cast members in the original production, exploded once the film was released. According to playwright Lorraine Hansberry, "We object to roles which consistently depict our women as wicked and our men as weak. We do not want to see six-foot Sydney Poitier on his knees crying for a slit-skirted wench. We do not want the wench to be beautiful Dorothy Dandridge who sniffs 'happy dust' and drinks liquor from a bottle at the rim of an alley crap game. We do not like to see our intelligent stars reduced to the level of Catfish Row when they have already risen to the heights of La Scala."[39] The film failed at the box office. At the insistence of the Gershwin estate, it has all but disappeared, available for viewing at the Library of Congress by appointment only.

Almost twenty years later, the reaction to the Houston Grand Opera production during America's bicentennial was considerably different. Outspoken star Clamma Dale defended the portrayal of African Americans in the piece, citing Bess as a black woman whose priority is survival and the physically brutal Crown as signifying the strength with which black men have been valued. According to Dale, "The era of fist-shaking honky-calling is over."[40] By 1985 *Porgy* was enshrined at New York's Metropolitan Opera House in a production that restored much of the original material and that augmented the huge cast and large orchestra. Finally *Porgy* was free of the expectations of the Broadway musical; Met audiences gladly accepted it as perhaps the most beloved of American operas.

Porgy's production history is that of an inadvertent epic, embracing and shedding aspects of grand opera and the more conventional Broadway musical, as well as confronting inconstant public attitudes toward racism and the depiction of African Americans by white writers. Rather than a closed text, the 1935 Broadway version is but one chapter in a long, sociocultural, musical chronicle that often has subverted the creators' original intentions.

Somewhere between the Gershwins' experiments with political satire and grand opera, Kurt Weill, newly transplanted to the United States, was exerting a powerful, if different, influence on the Broadway musical by mixing his German-Jewish theatrical background with his enthusiasm for American popular musical idioms. Though often satirical, Weill's musicals were rooted in German expressionism and epic theatre rather than the American farce of Kaufman, Hart, and Ryskind. Having worked with librettists such as Bertolt Brecht and Georg Kaiser in Germany, Weill was to search for distinguished American dramatists with whom he could collaborate as he built on his European past and simultaneously assimilated his work into a viable commercial structure for America.

The first Weill musical to reach Broadway was a translation of Brecht's *Threepenny Opera* (1928 in Berlin; 1933 in New York) by Gifford Cochran and Jerrold Krimsky. Flaunting its own brand of topsy-turvydom, *Threepenny* attacked the avarice and corruption of capitalism. Based on John Gay's *Beggar's Opera* (1728), Brecht set his libretto in Victorian London, a historicization of the decaying Weimar Republic. Foster Hirsch describes the sardonic thrust of the piece: "Telling stories of thieves, beggars, whores, capitalist sharks, criminals who act like businessmen and businessmen who act like criminals, and unholy alliances between religious and criminal 'gangs' and between the law and the underworld, Brecht and Weill used music and lyrics to support their satiric themes."[41] Brecht even borrowed a Euripidean deus ex machina, in which Queen Victoria spares Mack the Knife's life and grants him a castle. In accordance with his theory of alienation, Brecht wanted the songs to comment on the action rather than to further plot or to define character. Instead of identifying with his character, the Brechtian actor distanced himself from his role as he interrupted the action to provide ironic musical commentary in such numbers as "The Instead of Song" "Ballad of the Easy Life," and "Song of Dependency."

Although the Gershwins also used music as commentary in their political satires, the philosophy was more didactic and the tone considerably more acerbic in *Threepenny.* Whereas Kaufman wrote to amuse a commercial audience, Brecht was out to destroy hegemonic "culinary" theatre. Weill's musical style was eclectic. He blended modern jazz idioms with Victorian patter songs and spoofed not only the conventions of nineteenth-century operetta but also those of grand opera, as in the dueling divas of "The Jealousy Duet." The finales of the first two acts are unique in that they contain only one song apiece and are not scored for the chorus. As Brecht instructed, the title of each finale was projected on a banner in the 1933 Broadway production while the principals approached the audience not in character but as ironic commentators. In contrast, the finale of the last act was a parody of operetta conventions, as the chorus heralded the appearance of the Queen's riding messenger.[42] Although American socialism had its proponents during the height of the Depression, the Marxism of the piece seemed not only incongruous but also politically threatening on the Broadway musical stage when *Threepenny* first opened. In fact, the *New York Post*'s Richard Lockridge derided it as "sugar-coated communism."[43]

On March 10, 1954, a year after the controversial conviction and execution of Julius and Ethel Rosenberg, an off-Broadway revival opened at the Theatre de Lys to mixed reviews. The show repaid its capitalization within six weeks but was forced to close because another production had been booked into the theatre. By the time it reopened on September 20, 1955, the televised Army-McCarthy hearings had permanently tarnished Senator Joseph McCarthy's reputation. What was sugar-coated communism in a different cultural moment now took on a different, bitterly ironic tone for liberal off-Broadway audiences enraged by the self-serving McCarthy and his years of red-baiting. Just as the *Chicago* revival would later profit from the O. J. Simpson trial, the 1955 *Threepenny* profited from McCarthy's downfall. Incredibly, *Threepenny* ran for six years, finally closing in 1961 after setting a long-run record for a New York musical. Despite other major New York revivals in 1977 and 1989, no other American production of *Threepenny* or, for that matter, any other Weill work has matched its impact.

After *Threepenny,* Weill's Americanization of epic theatre began with *The Eternal Road* (1935), on which he collaborated with playwright Franz Werfel and director Max Reinhardt. Intended as a protest against Nazi persecution of the Jews, *Road* was an ambitious, panoramic retelling of the suffering of the Jewish people. Later in the decade, Weill collaborated with distinguished playwright Maxwell Anderson on *Knickerbocker Holiday* (1937), a period piece about Peter Stuyvesant, the tyrannical governor of old New York. The script portrayed Stuyvesant as a despot who abolishes most of the freedoms of the town. A veiled allegory about growing government interference from Washington, *Knickerbocker Holiday* warned Americans that the fascism then enfolding Europe was also a threat to the United States.

Eager for success, Weill knew that the piece desperately needed a bravura star performance. Since Stuyvesant was a comparatively small role, attracting a major name would be difficult. Director Josh Logan contacted Walter Huston, who seemed enthusiastic about the challenge of singing and dancing on a peg leg, although reticent about the role as written. Logan recounts this conversation with Huston:

> "He's an old scoundrel," Walter said.
>
> I began to knot up inside.
>
> "Oh, I like the nasty part, except that the character's pretty skimpy."
>
> "It can be longer," I said.
>
> "Not longer, just better. It's too one-note, too cool-headed. Couldn't this old bastard make love to that pretty young girl a bit? Not win her, just give her a squeeze or tickle her under the chin, and she could even consider him for a fraction of a second when she hears his song."
>
> "Song?" I said, not realizing I was making history by the question.
>
> "Sure—something nice I could sing to her. I like the other songs . . . but I mean something, you know, a moment for the old son of a bitch to be charming."[44]

According to Logan, this was the genesis of "September Song." Even an integrated musical by such highbrow writers as Weill and Anderson could be influenced by the clout of a badly needed performer as cocreator. Indeed, "September Song" was the most memorable moment in the piece.

Perhaps the salient example of a Weill musical in which text and production were at odds was the Group Theatre's production of the Weill–Paul Green *Johnny Johnson* (1936), inspired by *The Good Soldier Schweik* (1928). According to Wendy Smith, both the composer and librettist decided on their title because thirty thousand American "Johnsons" had served in

World War I, three thousand of whom were named "Johnny." Using diverse American idioms such as vaudeville, folklore, and satire, they aimed to adapt the Brecht-Weill musical form for Broadway.[45] The musical probably needed to be guided by an expert in epic theatre, such as Ervin Piscator, who had directed the original German production of *Schweik*. Instead, Lee Strasberg directed, and the results, as Smith notes, were disastrous: "In scenes with many characters, each actor was left to work out independently his or her character's motivations and actions, and the result was chaos and hard feelings. . . . There had always been a certain amount of collective criticism during Group rehearsals but the level of bitterness rose, a result of their terror over the lack of direction inside and outside the rehearsal hall."[46] According to Harold Clurman, the first two audience previews were "the most distressing experiences I have ever gone through in the theatre."[47] Indeed, *Johnny Johnson* caused such dissension among Clurman, Strasberg, and the cast in production that the Group almost disbanded.

Piscator's adaptation of the Jaroslav Haček comic novel concerned a Czech soldier drafted into the Austrian army in 1914. Although Schweik only wants to please, he unwittingly demonstrates the brutality and stupidity of his military superiors. According to Mordecai Gorelik in *New Theatres for Old,* Piscator's original intention was to have Schweik alone played by a live actor; all his military tormentors would be represented as (literally) painted caricatures, but Piscator modified this concept, as it was too limiting. In the Piscator production, Schweik wandered on a noisy conveyor belt as the comic world around him changed. More than three hundred satirical line drawings by George Grosz were projected onto a back screen. At the conclusion of the play, Schweik finally enters the battlefield only to be captured by his own side, whereupon he is hit by shell fire.

The Weill-Green musicalization severely altered the heavily ironic tone of the German original: "There was a lot to discuss, for *Johnny Johnson* had a special tone, elusive and tricky to capture. 'The first act is a comedy, the second a tragedy and the third a satire,' Paul Green told a reporter."[48] Green's "special tone" was mostly sweet rather than ironic. It was the Weill score that injected variety and bite; nevertheless, the antiwar message was appropriate for 1936, when another World War seemed inevitable. The libretto involved a pacifist stonecutter who enlists to fight in World War I despite his principles; he wants to be worthy to marry his sweetheart, Minny Belle. While overseas, he tries to institute a cease-fire and sprays the Allied High Command with laughing gas. Eventually he returns, finds that his sweetheart has married a draft dodger, and spends ten years in a mental hospital.

During the final scene he sells toys on the street as his fellow townspeople gather to celebrate the beginning of the next war. Johnny gains tragic stature by the final curtain, whereas in Piscator's *Schweik,* the protagonist was a victim of circumstance. Weill's score was eclectic, employing *Singspiel,* operatic ballads, French music hall songs, cowboy music, and a tune set first to an antiwar lyric, then later reset as a military anthem.

The social criticism of the piece borrows not only from epic theatre but also from German expressionism. Set during World War I, the musical traces the Christlike Johnny Johnson's failed journey toward self-education through metaphoric Stations of the Cross, outer manifestations of his inner anguish. Perhaps German expressionism and epic theatre were not compatible elements for a theatrical organization that did so much to advance American realism. In addition to Strasberg's contribution as director, the distinguished cast for *Johnny Johnson* included Robert Lewis, Elia Kazan, Sanford Meisner, Ruth Nelson, John Garfield, Phoebe Brand, and Morris Carnovsky, an illustrious group of method actors uncomfortably out of their element.

Whereas the often farcical Kaufman, Hart, and Ryskind libretti, for the most part, cannily entertained audiences of the time, the Weill musicals were misfits in terms of the Broadway fare of the day.[49] It was not until 1941 that Weill managed to find a commercially viable subject to match his eclectic musical style. Moss Hart's libretto for *Lady in the Dark* was a realistic play about psychoanalysis that framed four expressionistic dream sequences, which in effect were mini-operettas mounted on a series of revolving stages. The musical was a box-office triumph, in part because of the fascination at the time with psychoanalysis and in part because of the performances by Gertrude Lawrence and Danny Kaye.

Lady in the Dark opens, uniquely, without music. Liza Elliott, the editor of a fashion magazine, decides to undergo psychoanalysis to reconcile her feelings of failure as a woman with her career aspirations. The score surfaces only in the four dream sequences and in the childhood song, "My Ship," the words of which Liza struggles to remember throughout the play. Each dream is a fantasy that includes characters from her life whom we have encountered during the play's realistic scenes. Weill's music is as varied as it was in *Johnny Johnson;* fortunately, his collaborator for this work was Ira Gershwin, whose veneration for Gilbert and Sullivan turns each dream sequence into an extended operetta finale. Interspersed in these miniature operettas are also individual songs that range from jazzy show tunes such as "The Saga of Jenny" to patter songs such as "Tschaikowsky."

Moss Hart's libretto foregrounds realism to a degree unique in terms of the Broadway musical. This musical play is just that: nonmusical scenes that occur when Liza is at work at the magazine and when she is talking with her psychoanalyst. The musical sequences, however, are extended expressionistic fantasies that theatricalize Liza's inner neuroses and anxieties. Although there is no narrator in the realistic scenes, the dream sequences involve a master of ceremonies to narrate Liza's inner journey. In "The Circus Dream," the Ring Master is in control as he condemns Liza for not being able to make up her mind. This kind of bold experimentation was a forerunner to the Sondheim-Prince *Follies,* thirty years later, in which the angst of the four principals culminates in a dream sequence, "Loveland," which symbolically manifests the characters' neuroses. One can also argue that the contrast between the realistic book scenes and the musicalized dream sequences inspired Rob Marshall's 2003 film of *Chicago.* Although *Lady in the Dark* is regarded as a groundbreaking musical and has certainly been influential, it is a difficult piece to revive. Hart's take on psychoanalysis is simplistic in contemporary terms and should be rewritten; it is ludicrous that a patient could magically be cured after recounting a few Freudian dreams. Equally problematic has been the task of finding a suitable female star to inject charm, charisma, and glamour into a leading role that is often mannish and strident as written. Ann Sothern successfully negotiated a badly truncated television version in 1954. Rumors surfaced for years that Julie Andrews would make her Broadway comeback as Liza Elliott. It never happened.

While the Gershwins and Kurt Weill forged new directions for the serious musical, another thread in the development of the integrated musical appeared at the tail end of the decade. *Pal Joey* (1940), with a libretto by John O'Hara and a score by Rodgers and Hart, is the American musical's ode to naturalism. Introducing the antihero to the commercial musical, *Pal Joey*'s libretto applies Emile Zola's elimination of the "sympathetic character." Joey Evans, a down-on-his-luck hoofer and nightclub emcee, is simultaneously wooing Linda, a dim-witted secretary, and Vera, a wealthy, married society matron who eventually keeps Joey and sets him up in a chic nightclub. Mixed into the plot are Gladys Bumps, a blackmailing chorus girl who is the whore minus the heart of gold, and Ludlow Lowell, a thug masquerading as an agent. When the last two attempt to blackmail Vera, she dumps Joey. None of these characters is sympathetic; their dialogue is jagged, edgy, and full of underworld slang. Writing for the *New York Times,* Brooks Atkinson famously wondered, "Can you draw sweet water from a foul well?"[50]

Despite the grittiness of the dialogue, most of the songs are presentational performance numbers; they are sung and danced either as part of the floor show at the seedy Chicago nightclub that is the setting for much of the first act or at Chez Joey, the nightclub that Vera eventually bankrolls for Joey. Abandoning operetta conventions, the nightclub numbers are brassy, contemporary, tuneful, and full of double entendres. Joey extols his sexual prowess in the metaphoric "Happy Hunting Horn." "The Flower Garden of My Heart," a satiric recycling of a typical *Follies* production number, features a slightly off-key, Ziegfeldian tenor extolling the beauty of the chorus girls, who are the antithesis of the lilies, daisies, roses, and lilacs that they impersonate. "That Terrific Rainbow" satirizes burlesque numbers of the period in which the showgirls parade across stage playing with multicolored scarves. The lyric compares their passion to different colors of the rainbow, as the lights, in turn, change color, finally blending in a rainbow effect.

Here is a case of the musical as both transgressive and conservative. Audiences and critics were shocked by the amorality (and immorality) of *Pal Joey*'s characters and relationships. The casting, however, was geared to make the musical palatable to spectators used to the convention of the sympathetic character and was largely responsible for the musical's commercial success. Aware that an older married woman cheating on her husband with a conniving heel would be distasteful to musical theatre patrons, Rodgers and Hart cast the charming Vivienne Segal, a lilting soprano, against type. Listening to Segal on the 1951 studio recording that inspired the successful Broadway revival, one can hear the grace, class, and wit with which she transformed the hard-boiled comic lyrics of "What Is a Man?" and "Bewitched." Even more significant, Gene Kelly achieved the impossible by making Joey not only sexually attractive but also irresistibly lovable. In fact, the show folded soon after Kelly left to pursue a Hollywood contract. In choosing to cast charismatic performers as unpleasant characters in the original production, Rodgers and Hart anticipated John Raitt's sexy, virile Billy Bigelow as the wife-beating carnival barker in *Carousel* (1945), Robert Goulet's eight-by-ten-glossy interpretation of the priggish, arrogant Lancelot in *Camelot* (1960), Ethel Merman's hilariously raffish and outrageous portrayal of the monstrous Mama Rose in *Gypsy* (1959), Elaine Stritch's dry, droll approach to the acerbic Joanne in *Company* (1970), and Angela Lansbury's lovably comic accomplice to cannibalism and murder in *Sweeney Todd* (1979).

Pal Joey's subsequent production history goes a long way in demonstrating the close connection between performance and cultural zeitgeist. In its original incarnation, *Joey* was regarded as not only shocking but also groundbreaking in its integration of dialogue and song. By 1952, the year of its first Broadway revival, it was no longer quite so shocking; *Oklahoma!* had long overshadowed its attempts at integration. Producer Jule Styne shrewdly instituted some changes that downplayed the elements of integration and emphasized the musical comedy–burlesque elements of the piece, which wisely stressed escapism during the turmoil of McCarthyism. "Plant You Now, Dig You Later," originally a book song, now became a non-plot-related production number. The dialogue scene that involves the blackmail setup between Ludlow and Gladys was simplified, and Vera's character was softened at the end of the play. Originally, Vera left Joey destitute, forcing him to vacate his apartment to brave the winter without even an overcoat. In the revival, Vera just left Joey to his own devices, which seemed punishment enough without freezing to death in Chicago. Robert Alton, who had choreographed the original production, reworked his dances, emphasizing even more than originally the comedic aspects of the numbers. In "Flower Garden of My Heart," Helen Gallagher, as Gladys, appeared with a watering can. As she sang her chorus of the lyric, she proceeded to fertilize the crotches of the supine chorus boys downstage, each of whom promptly raised a stiff leg in response. Segal, twelve years older and consequently more vulnerable romantically than she had been in 1940, recreated Vera, while Harold Lang, a ballet dancer, gave Joey's numbers new choreographic dimension. The production was no longer a shocker but an enormously entertaining musical comedy that ran longer and was more profitable than the 1940 production.

Subsequent versions have been more troublesome. A 1957 film adaptation with Frank Sinatra, Rita Hayworth, and Kim Novak bore little resemblance to the Broadway text and score. Due to 1950s film censorship, much of the bite and spoofing of sex that had made the show so entertaining disappeared, and the film became a catalog of Rodgers and Hart favorites interpreted by Sinatra. In 1961 and 1963, two City Center revivals starred Bob Fosse, who scored a triumph as Joey, but featured Carol Bruce and Viveca Lindfors respectively as Vera. To accommodate Bruce and Lindfors, Vera's songs were transposed into a lower, brassier belt range. The toughness of the vocal delivery enervated the role, as it did when an overly mannered Patti Lupone played it in an Encores revival in the late 1990s. If Vera is too tough, she alienates the audience. It is not funny to see an unsympathetic, unfaithful wife joking about cuckolding her husband. Without wry self-deprecation, great charm, and a degree of vulnerability, a tough

Vera compromises the laughs in "Bewitched," which is fundamentally a sardonic comedy number. A disastrous 1976 Broadway revival found Edward Villela and Eleanor Parker jumping ship during rehearsals. Christopher Chadman, Villela's understudy, took over but was unable to carry the show. Perhaps the low point was *Pal Joey 1978*, produced for the Los Angeles Civic Light Opera as a vehicle for Lena Horne. The sexually liberated 1970s must have seemed an apt cultural moment for reviving the piece. Setting the show in the 1970s proved fatal, however. One of the traps in mounting the show is recreating the kinds of period burlesque-nightclub numbers that the show hilariously means to satirize. In a postfeminist world, it is far more politically correct to objectify the scantily clad man than the gum-chewing chorus girl. This phenomenon was reflected in a production number that featured Horne and a chorus of hard-hat construction workers. The orchestrations for *Pal Joey 1978* were updated to disco. The milieu remained sleazy, but the humor of the 1930s burlesque routines was gone. The production fell into the trap of so many *Joey* revivals. In trying to live up to its reputation as a groundbreaking, integrated musical, the production team destroyed the show's entertainment value as a musical comedy. The last revival I musical-directed was a 1981 benefit at Town Hall in New York, which starred Tammy Grimes, Michael Callan, Christine Ebersole, Laurie Beechman, and George S. Irving. Since it was a benefit, Grimes was unsure of the lyrics to the many choruses of "Bewitched" on opening night. She had cause for worry. Amusingly, a remarkable percentage of the men in the large audience knew the song backwards and forwards and were only too eager to correct any inaccuracies.

The Reemergence of Hammerstein During a Wartime Zeitgeist

With America's entry into World War II and a booming economy, the horizon of expectations for musical theatre audiences changed once again. The cultural zeitgeist during the early 1940s involved fostering community, promoting social responsibility, and defending democracy. Even before the United States entered the war, the best-selling book *How to Win Friends and Influence People* (1937) urged Americans to cooperate rather than to compete for success. In 1939 *The Wizard of Oz*'s Dorothy Gale charmed audiences while achieving her dream to return home by unselfishly helping her friends. In that same year, Hollywood also mythologized the old South in *Gone with the Wind*, a motion picture that preached about the need for community and healing. Americans were patriotic about a nation damaged by the Depression and now threatened by fascism abroad. For

Mark Fearnow, *Gone with the Wind* reconciled nostalgia for the past with anxiety about the future. Scarlett O'Hara journeys from barbecues and flirtations to a new and difficult world of Reconstruction in which she must mature to survive economically. At the end of the novel, unable to face her own anxieties, she romanticizes about the past and returns to Tara, at least temporarily, to find strength. Fearnow argues that "like Scarlett, America could return to its Tara, the body of myth and tradition symbolized by such projects as Rockefeller's [reconstruction of colonial] Williamsburg, and from this haven plan its campaign."[51] This nostalgia for the past, along with anxiety about rebuilding an uncertain future, helps explain Hammerstein's veneration of community in *Oklahoma!*

Like the old South of *Gone with the Wind,* the West in *Oklahoma!* is overly mythologized. The characters are hearty, boisterous, fun-loving, and reminiscent of a simpler time. The question that motivates the plot is, Who will take Laurey to the box social? This nostalgic look at America's past is marred by the violence that threatens the bucolic Oklahoma territory. Jud, the farmhand, is a psychopathic arsonist. He spends his time in a smokehouse gazing at dirty pictures and, presumably, masturbating. The cowboys, Curly and Will Parker, may seem sunny by comparison; however, it is likely that they spend their leisure time in equally antisocial pursuits: traveling to Kansas City to patronize whorehouses, drinking, carousing, and living a nomadic existence. By the end of the play, both Curly and Will have been socialized. They abandon their nomadic lifestyle and embrace marriage. In effect, the audience is instructed to believe what they already know—that community is all-important and requires hard work and self-sacrifice. By 1943 Rodgers and Hammerstein were preaching to the choir.[52]

The phenomenal success of *Oklahoma!* can be traced to audience reception of wartime nonmusical plays that basked in a nostalgic, romanticized glorification of American values. If one can see echoes of *Gone with the Wind* in the overly mythologized West of *Oklahoma!,* one can also see traces of an idyllic America in *Life with Father* (1939), a wartime play that ran for a record-breaking 3,224 performances. The Howard Lindsay–Russell Crouse script affectionately celebrates family life in nineteenth-century New York. Whereas *Oklahoma!*'s plot rather simplistically hinges on who will take Laurey to the box social, *Life with Father* revolves around mother's attempts to get father baptized. The play is a valentine to the past and a tribute to simpler values.

Perhaps more influential is Thornton Wilder's mythologizing of American life in *Our Town* (1937) and *The Skin of Our Teeth* (1942), the latter a

Pulitzer Prize winner produced a year before *Oklahoma!* Wilder, heavily influenced by the theatricalism of Pirandello, experimented with metatheatrical form. These experiments with form, however, cannot hide the rather simple parables at the heart of his plays, particularly *The Skin of Our Teeth,* which included an optimistic, if somewhat didactic, wartime message about the potential for American endurance in the face of all obstacles.

For Wilder the present and the future borrow from past accomplishments. Building on the past ensures the upward spiral of western civilization. In the final act of *Skin,* Mr. Antrobus functions as a kind of *raisonneur;* he clings to the speeches of Plato, Aristotle, Spinoza, and Moses to inspire him to survive the destruction of war. The speeches of these philosophers are not necessarily the most well known or obvious choices, but presumably they reinforce western values with which the audience is already familiar. The work of the philosophers is ensconced in the subconscious of what Gertrude Stein refers to in *The Geographical History of America* as "the human mind." Wilder is suggesting that wrapped up in the everyday life of Americans are the weaknesses that have threatened humankind, as well as the moral and religious values that have ensured its survival. The war between Antrobus and Henry becomes a struggle between the ego and the id, a somewhat pat explanation for Adolf Hitler and his brutal policies of racial extermination; nevertheless, patriotic audiences during World War II warmed to Wilder's idealization of the American spirit. In "Some Thoughts on Playwriting," Wilder claims the dramatist must deal with material that is "understandable by the larger number"; in other words, the author writes for the "popular mind."[53] In effect, Wilder, like Hammerstein, was preaching to the choir.

The Rodgers and Hammerstein solution to America at war—the glorification of family, community, and the nation—was not ensconced in the kinds of abstractions and intertextuality that permeated Wilder's work; nevertheless, in terms of content, Wilder and Hammerstein were soul mates. To cement a sense of community in *Oklahoma!* "the farmer and the cowman should be friends." Racism in *South Pacific* is not hereditary but "carefully taught." Faith enables Julie Jordan in *Carousel* to "never walk alone," whereas Maria von Trapp in *The Sound of Music* must "climb every mountain" to follow her dream.

Hammerstein's pat resolutions and liberal platitudinizing should zap him from any list of realistic writers. In mythologizing the American past in *Oklahoma!,* Hammerstein is definitely following a lyrical bent; however, even William Dean Howells was surprisingly generous about plays that merged romanticism and realism: "The fact is, the two kinds [realism and romanticism] do not mingle well, but for a while yet we must have the romantic and the realistic mixed in the theatre. That is quite inevitable, and it is strictly in accordance with the law of evolution. . . . Perhaps not till the next generation shall we have the very realist; which puzzles the groundlings, romantically expectant of miracles that shall clear away all trace of romanticism in an instant."[54] The year 1943 is part of the next generation that Howells foresees, but one must remember that Hammerstein was trained not only in the theatre of Ned Sheldon and Dorothy Donnelly but also in the presentational, vaudeville traditions so characteristic of 1920s musicals.

The distinction between the theatrical and the realistic is crucial to Hammerstein's structural contrast between the primary and secondary love triangles. Hammerstein fashions a subplot in which Hakim is typically played broadly and theatrically—for laughs—via the conventions of vaudeville. This harmless theatricality contrasts with the realism with which Jud is usually played and which renders him menacing. Jud's songs further character, whereas Hakim's "It's a Scandal, It's an Outrage" is more presentational and derives from earlier musical comedy traditions. Hammerstein had melded the two styles sixteen years earlier in *Show Boat,* in which the theatrical, show-within-a-show numbers sung by Frank and Ellie contrast with the more plot-driven numbers sung by Magnolia and Ravenal.

In *Oklahoma!* Hakim is not the only character who sings and performs in the vaudeville style. The secondary love triangle consisting of Hakim, Ado Annie, and Will Parker (the last character not in the original Riggs text), all sing quasi-presentational musical comedy numbers, while the numbers performed by the primary love triangle (Curly, Laurey, and Jud) tend to be more realistic and often involve journeys, by which I mean the song is constructed much like a scene, in which the character has an objective and, by the end of the song, an emotional change or decision occurs. For instance, in "People Will Say We're in Love," Curly wants Laurey to declare her love for him so she will cancel her plans to go to the box social with Jud. Laurey, in turn, is angry that Curly has brought the flighty Gertie Cummings to the farm and wants to tease Curly by playing hard to get. By the end of the duet, Curly seems to have won his objective: Laurey basically admits through song that she loves Curly. Terrified, however, that Jud will seek revenge, she unexpectedly refuses to break her date in the lines immediately following the duet, which prompts Curly's visit to the smokehouse to confront his rival. Laurey's inner turmoil is expressed through heightened emotion or song. Similarly Annie must make a decision between

Hakim and Will, although she does not care to, a feeling she laments in "I Cain't Say No." There is no inner journey here, rather a statement of character and purpose. The subplot, written around Ado Annie's vacillation between Will and Hakim, provides comic theatricality, in contrast to Laurey's more realistic, psychologized dilemma, which is to decide between Curly and Jud.

Certainly in his future work with Rodgers, Hammerstein manages to trim some of the musical comedy conventions of the 1920s. The subplots still exist, but the secondary romantic leads, the soubrette and her paramour, no longer have to be comic relief after *Oklahoma!* and *Carousel.* In *South Pacific,* Liat and Lieutenant Cable are a tragic pair; they reflect the racial conflict that haunts Emile and Nellie. The comic relief is provided by a kind of third "couple," Luther Billis and Bloody Mary. In *The King and I,* it is Anna and the King who provide the comedy, whereas the secondary lovers, Lun Tha and Tuptim, are tragic. Hammerstein often develops, in addition to the secondary lovers, the figure of the older woman, a motherly sort who provides a degree of wisdom and comfort in virtually all his libretti: Aunt Eller in *Oklahoma!,* Nettie in *Carousel,* the grandmother in *Allegro,* Bloody Mary in *South Pacific,* Lady Thiang in *The King and I,* the fairy godmother in *Cinderella,* Fauna in *Pipe Dream* (1955), Wang Ta's aunt in *Flower Drum Song* (1958), and the mother abbess in *The Sound of Music.* Hammerstein also regularly fashions a comic villain whose comedy or villainy varies from show to show: Jigger in *Carousel,* Billis in *South Pacific,* the Kralahome in *The King and I,* Hazel in *Pipe Dream,* and Max in *The Sound of Music.*

With *Oklahoma!* and *Carousel,* Hammerstein embarks on a collaboration with Rodgers that focuses on culture clashes and venerates postwar, middle-class American values. Cowhand Curly is domesticated by landowner Laurey and becomes a valuable member of the community. *Carousel's* Billy Bigelow manages to exonerate his sins by instilling faith in his daughter that she will no longer be a social outcast but can be accepted into her New England community. Joe Taylor, in *Allegro,* leaves his lucrative medical practice in a large city and his adulterous, socialite wife to return to a simpler life as a dedicated country doctor. In *South Pacific,* Nellie Forbush simultaneously sheds her southern bigotry while managing to Americanize her wealthy French planter, who wears GI fatigues by the final curtain. *The King and I* finds the British Anna Leonowens instilling middle-class, schoolmarmish western (read American middle-class) values in the King of Siam. When he resists, she somehow shames him into dying. Hammerstein's libretto for the first televised *Cinderella* (1956) finds the king praising the wine of his country: beer. Even he just wants to be middle class.

Hammerstein's veneration of middle-class, community values influenced many of his successors in the 1940s and 1950s. Although Frank Loesser's *Guys and Dolls* (1950) is usually considered a musical comedy in that its characters are uniquely New Yorkese and its songs contemporary and brassy, it owes much to Hammerstein's integrated musical play. Both Sky Masterson and Nathan Detroit, like Curly, agree to be domesticated and socialized through marriage to Sarah Brown and Miss Adelaide, respectively. One can argue much the same about the crooked Harold Hill in *The Music Man* (1957), who, far from corrupting the local librarian, finds himself settling down in the small-town Iowa community that he once ridiculed. Even *My Fair Lady*'s (1956) irascible Henry Higgins, despite wishing that women were more like men, confesses that he's grown accustomed to Eliza Doolittle's face. Conversely, the Jud–Billy Bigelow figure, who refuses to be socialized and consequently compromises his middle-class community, is evident in such characters as Harry Beaton in *Brigadoon* (1947), whose disregard for the well-being of his Scottish town spells his death.

After *Allegro,* Hammerstein focused on racism in both *South Pacific* and *The King and I.* The former, of course, is a wartime tale. One wonders how much Hammerstein was influenced by the spate of liberal plays about social injustice popular after World War II, including *Deep Are the Roots* (1945), *Strange Fruit* (1945), *Home of the Brave* (1945), and *All My Sons* (1947). Both *The King and I* and *South Pacific* (and later *Flower Drum Song*) condemn insularity and racial tyranny; the message was a common one in realistic plays at the end of the Second World War. Writing of *Deep Are the Roots,* a play about a black soldier who, upon returning home from the war, is falsely accused of stealing from an old southern planter, its director, Elia Kazan, questions its political liberalism:

> The effect of treating a social problem in this way is that there is never any doubt in the audience's mind as to what they're expected to feel. They have the assurance from the beginning that they are on the side of the angels—the falsely accused. They have never been challenged to doubt. This, of course, does not prepare them for life as it's lived. They are also often masochists—so it has seemed to me—enjoying the middle-class white man's guilt about the black man. They've been told where to stand and what to think, and guaranteed safe passage to the final curtain. We are in a kind of conformity tide. That is a word liberals say they hate, and they do—except

> when it's their own conformity. Such a play is not drama that informs life; it is liberal corn.[55]

Much the same criticism has been leveled at Hammerstein. If Nellie sheds her bigotry in *South Pacific,* she also manages to Americanize DeBecque and acquire an oceanside villa, whereas Lieutenant Cable, who stands to inherit only a shack in Bali Hai, dies for his intolerance. Bruce McConachie has attacked the implied imperialism in the Oriental musicals of Rodgers and Hammerstein. According to McConachie, Hammerstein's well-meaning liberalism planted the seeds of racism that led to America's involvement in the war in southeast Asia.[56] For Andrea Most, *South Pacific* is Rodgers and Hammerstein's attempt to reconcile their liberal politics with McCarthyism. By championing equal rights, Americans were attacking communism, which thrived on racial disaffection. According to Most, "American Jews—and in particular, assimilated New York Jewish artists like Rodgers and Hammerstein—had a personal stake in asserting this connection between anticommunism and civil rights."[57]

Most also maintains that the Nellie-DeBecque romance is passionless because the stage directions suggest that DeBecque not kiss Nellie after he sings "Some Enchanted Evening" during the opening scene. Ironically, after this opening scene, Ezio Pinza, the original DeBecque, found many onstage opportunities to kiss Mary Martin, the original Nellie Forbush. The kisses were so passionate that gossip had it that Pinza and Martin were having a torrid offstage affair, this despite Pinza's offstage marriage and Martin's own marriage to Richard Halliday (as well as her rumored relationship with Janet Gaynor):

> Pinza's long and enthusiastic onstage kisses had convinced their public that he and Mary Martin were madly in love. . . . Don Fellows said, "Pinza knew her entrances and he'd go to her dressing room door and take her by the hand and lead her onstage. I'd hear her in the wings saying, 'Ezio, when you kiss, kiss me nicely,' and he'd be saying, 'When I kees, I kees!' She'd be singing onstage and he'd be whispering, 'Mary, I love you!' into her ear. . . . He used to get love letters and he'd put them on the call board. Some of them were crazy, women offering to leave their husbands for him."[58]

Whatever did or did not happen between the two, kinescopes exist of Pinza and Martin singing "Some Enchanted Evening," both on *The Ed Sullivan Show* and on a General Foods tribute to Rodgers and Hammerstein. The look on Martin's face as Pinza sings in her ear is pure adoration, stage directions notwithstanding.

Performance also subverts text in *The King and I.* Hammerstein borrowed from nonmusical theatre in the persona of the male star as object of the sexual gaze. Yul Brynner's bare-chested king became a sex symbol, much as Stanley Kowalski, with his torn tee shirt, became the object of the gaze in *A Streetcar Named Desire* (1947). Brando's performance in the Williams play galvanized audiences not used to seeing the male on a sexual pedestal. His sensitivity, coupled with his intense sexuality, threatened to overturn the balance of the original production.[59] If audiences rooted for Brando's magnetic Stanley rather than Jessica Tandy's fragile Blanche, the legendary Gertrude Lawrence had her hands full trying to wrest audience empathy from the virile, shirtless Brynner. Lawrence was charismatic and held her own. Certainly the text confirms the Victorian victory of Mrs. Anna over the sexually instinctive king. After Lawrence's death, however, and throughout the many revivals of the show in which Brynner performed, it was he rather than Mrs. Anna for whom audiences cheered.

The Concept Musical

If musical comedy was typified by the star as cocreator and if the integrated musical, throughout the 1950s, increasingly repositioned the author as seemingly autonomous, the concept musical turned the integrated musical into a vehicle for the auteur-director. Jerome Robbins, Bob Fosse, Michael Bennett, and Harold Prince (the sole member of the group who was not also a choreographer) were often as bankable as their over-the-title performers. Fosse's vision in *Pippin* (1972) and *Chicago* (1975) arguably supersedes the text. In fact, Fosse banned composer-lyricist Stephen Schwartz from *Pippin* rehearsals. For *Big Deal* (1986), his last musical, he maintained control by writing his own libretto and using old tunes by dead composers. Similarly, Michael Bennett reportedly had such intense disdain for the score of *Ballroom* (1979) that he refused to choreograph when his dance arranger improvised melodies from the show. Instead, Bennett insisted on working to counts of eight without music. In both these examples, it was the director who was in charge rather than the authors.

The collaboration between director and designer is also crucial to the success of concept musicals. Prince's work with Boris Aronson is a case in point. *Cabaret* (1966) resembled an expressionist painting; *Fiddler on the Roof* (1964), a Marc Chagall canvas. *Company*'s commentary on the coldness of urban relationships was manifested in a constructivist set, with multiple platforms and chromium balconies and towers. Each show had a distinctive look.

Concept musicals also tend to have a circular structure. An opening number tells the audience what the show's idea will be, and this message is usually reiterated, with some variation, in the conclusion. The emcee welcomes the audience to a nightclub in *Cabaret*'s "Wilkommen"; at the show's conclusion, the number is reprised with ugly, discordant chords to underscore the effect the moral deterioration of Nazi Germany has had on the characters at the Kit Kat Klub. *Fiddler* begins with a song, "Tradition," that tells the audience what the show is about. Without tradition, sings Tevye, life is as fragile as a fiddler on the roof. The show closes with the image of the fiddler tucking the violin under his arm and following Tevye to America. *Sweeney Todd* begins and ends with a Brechtian chorus emotionally distancing the audience in the narrative "The Ballad of Sweeney Todd."

Jerome Robbins perhaps did the most to perfect this thematic opening-number convention. Historically, musical comedies and operettas began with a merry peasant number, establishing setting and mood. Hammerstein altered the tradition with *Oklahoma!,* but "Oh What a Beautiful Mornin'" still establishes mood and setting, although it is sung by a lone cowboy rather than a colorful chorus. It was Robbins who insisted that the opening tell the audience precisely what the show is about, most famously when he doctored the floundering out-of-town tryout of *A Funny Thing Happened on the Way to the Forum* (1962). Robbins insisted the original opener, "Love Is in the Air," misled audience expectations. He demanded a new number that would telegraph exactly what the show purported to accomplish. The result was "Comedy Tonight." Eventually he would inspire Jerry Bock and Sheldon Harnick to write "Tradition" to explicate *Fiddler*'s theme. Again, a genealogy of influence is in effect, since Robbins's apprentice work as choreographer in *On the Town* (1944) was with director George Abbott, a collaboration that lasted into the 1950s, while Prince, the producer of *Fiddler* and *Forum,* worked almost exclusively with Abbott earlier in his career. Abbott was famous for fixing an audience's horizon of expectations. William Goldman relates an anecdote about an Abbott failure, *The Education of H*Y*M*A*N K*A*P*L*A*N* (1968):

> A scene has just ended in a black-out, and as one set rolls off and another rolls on, there is almost a moment in which the audience doesn't know where it is. Almost, but not quite. Because an instant after the black-out, a spotlight picks up a pretty young girl crossing

> toward where the new set is going to be but isn't yet, and as she makes her cross, she says to another girl, who is standing on the far side of the stage, "And how are things in the teacher's room tonight?" This is a line that could happen only in a George Abbott musical. Because once the words are spoken, the audience relaxes; it knows that eventually all the rolling on of sets and flying in of drops are going to create a teacher's room.[60]

According to Goldman, Abbott avoided confusion by showing audiences exactly what to expect.

The concept musical, then, tends to be the work of an auteur-director, has a definite physical look or design, and, with its recurring "theme song," is often circular in structure. But what exactly is it? Perhaps the best definition is a musical that confronts the audience with ideas it usually goes to musicals to escape. The tired businessman and his harried homemaker wife of the 1940s and 1950s happily accepted Hammerstein's liberal platitudes about bigotry in *South Pacific* and *The King and I.* This same couple, by the 1960s and 1970s, was bombarded with crumbling American values in *Follies* (1971); the spiritual bankruptcy of Weimar Germany in the 1920s as a metaphor for American spiritual bankruptcy and racism in the 1960s in *Cabaret* (1966); western colonialism and its devastating effect on Japanese culture in *Pacific Overtures* (1976); the perils of emotional commitment in a cold, urban culture in *Company;* the dangers in creating poisonous popular-culture heroes in *Chicago* (1975) and *Evita* (1979); the tendency to prostitute one's integrity in a materialistic society in *Merrily We Roll Along* (1981); and the need for some Americans to cling to, in Andy Warhol's words, fifteen minutes of fame at any cost in *Assassins* (1991; 2004 revival). The appropriation of serious subject matter from nonmusical theatre was now intellectualized, not unlike Weill's experiments with theatricalism, epic theatre, and expressionism in the 1930s. Indeed, with *Follies,* Prince and Sondheim exploded Hammerstein's romantic idealization of postwar American values.

If the emergence of the concept musical follows several different threads, it is important to acknowledge two early precursors of the form: Rodgers and Hammerstein's *Allegro,* which bears a remarkable similarity to Thornton Wilder's *Our Town,* and Kurt Weill and Alan Jay Lerner's *Love Life* (1948), a history of a marriage told through the conventions of American vaudeville. Like *Show Boat, Allegro* is epic in scope; it covers the first thirty-five years in the life of Joe Taylor Jr., Hammerstein's vision of Everyman. Joe is an idealistic doctor who loses his way in a materialistic society. *Allegro* traces Joe's birth, his upbringing as the son of a country doctor, his years at college, his marriage to his childhood sweetheart, his migration to a big city, and his career as a successful physician in an urban hospital. By act 2, Joe has sold out. Instead of healing needy patients, he becomes a kind of rich quack, comforting wealthy neurotics and squandering his knowledge and talent. Jenny, his wife, is a materialist. Ultimately, she sleeps with the president of the board of directors of a major city medical center to help secure a position as chief of staff for her husband. Disgusted, Joe walks off into the sunset at the second-act curtain, accompanied by Charlie, his alcoholic best friend and colleague, and by Emily, the plain, sensible nurse who has loved him all along.

Hammerstein conceived *Allegro* as a kind of musical *Our Town.* Rather than a set to signify pictorial illusion, a bare stage was used. Projections on a huge cyclorama were sometimes representational (a huge spoon to show infant Joe learning to eat) and sometimes abstract (geometrical patterns and shapes to signify the hectic pace of modern urban life in act 2).[61] Hammerstein employed a third chorus in addition to the traditional (at the time) singing and dancing choruses—a Greek chorus, sometimes speaking and sometimes singing but, most important, commenting on the action and on the characters.

Hammerstein's Greek chorus deliberately interrupted the book scenes, underscoring the show's theme of compromise. Unlike the conventional chorus of a musical, this chorus carries scripts, introducing a theatricalism reminiscent of Wilder and Pirandello. At the beginning of the play, the chorus narrates Joe's birth. He is not visible onstage but is addressed as if he and the audience are one, which is partially true, since Joe is Hammerstein's Everyman. In act 2, the chorus expresses its antipathy to the frenzy of modern city life in a cocktail party chant that simultaneously entertains the audience and creates emotional detachment. The technique is reminiscent not only of Brechtian epic theatre (particularly with the use of slides projected on the rear cyclorama) but also of Wilder's comic theatricalism in *The Skin of Our Teeth,* notably Sabina's interjections about how much she hates the play in which she is forced to perform, the stage manager's explaining that various cast members have succumbed to ptomaine poisoning, and the antics of the dinosaur and the mammoth. Uncharacteristically borrowing a bit from expressionism as well, Hammerstein laces the tale of his Christlike central figure with archetypes: the Grandmother, the Mother, the Father, the Best Friend, the Wife, and the Loyal Secretary.

Agnes de Mille, who had found new and interesting ways to narrate plot and demonstrate character through dance in *Oklahoma!* and *Carousel*, contributed even more daring work in *Allegro*. *Oklahoma!*'s dream ballet, in which Laurey's sexual fears and neuroses are exposed somewhat expressionistically, was, according to Ethan Mordden, a miniature play, since it articulated emotions that the character herself could not express.[62] De Mille fearlessly staged *Allegro*'s final ballet to depict the brutality of modern urban society, with dancers crucified onstage—as close to an expressionistic statement of the Stations of the Cross as any musical is likely to achieve. Eventually, Rodgers and Hammerstein, eager to have a commercial hit, persuaded her to lose the crucifixions and focus instead on the speed and noise of city life.[63]

Perhaps de Mille's greatest contribution to the future of musical theatre, however, was the fluidity of her staging, since she directed as well as choreographed the musical, a harbinger of the superstar director-choreographers of the 1960s and 1970s. *Allegro* was close to ballet theatre, with virtually no wait between set changes. Since the stage was bare, characters would appear in spots or specials in a series of scenic dissolves. As one scene ended, the characters would exit offstage as new characters reappeared often in full view of the audience.[64] Designer Jo Mielziner's ramps and platforms helped differentiate space, whereas treadmills added to the constant sense of motion. Props and bits of furniture were used, but the production depended more on lighting and scenic projections. It was this cinematic fluidity that influenced Joshua Logan's staging of Rodgers and Hammerstein's next musical, *South Pacific*, and in effect the way musicals moved for the next fifty years. The series of dissolves in *Allegro* happened on a bare stage conceived in terms similar to the ancient Greek *orchestra;* two years later, *South Pacific* boasted more representational scenery by Mielziner. The audience saw characters exit and enter while complicated set changes were still in progress. The effect was perhaps even more startling than it had been with *Allegro*.

Allegro, which received mixed notices, was Hammerstein's first and last venture into expressionism. Stephen Sondheim, Hammerstein's gofer on the musical, suggested that his own career has consisted of attempts to rewrite *Allegro:* "In *Allegro*, Oscar used theatre convention frankly as theatre convention: the chorus that oversees the action, the abstract scenic design. These techniques have had a large influence on Hal's [Prince's] work and on mine."[65] Indeed, *Allegro* is pivotal to Sondheim's work with Harold Prince in the 1970s. The chorus of married couples who comment on the action in *Company* is a direct outgrowth of Rodgers and Hammerstein's Greek chorus. Hammerstein's libretto for *Allegro* bridges the world of the living and the dead, a concept that anticipates the use of ghosts in *Follies. Merrily We Roll Along* (1981) and *Sunday in the Park with George* (1984) involve roads either taken or abandoned. Both these latter Sondheim musicals also deal, in a somewhat postmodern fashion, with the plight of the artist in a commercial society, a predicament Hammerstein addressed metaphorically in *Allegro:* "It is a law of our civilization that as soon as a man proves he can contribute to the well being of the world, there be created an immediate conspiracy to destroy his usefulness, a conspiracy in which he is usually a willing collaborator. Sometimes he awakens to his danger and does something about it. This is the story of *Allegro.*"[66] Although credited as a revolutionary, Sondheim is firmly descended from the Hammerstein of *Allegro,* the most atypical of the Rodgers and Hammerstein collaborations.

Similar in its theatricalism to *Allegro, Love Life* (1948), with music by Kurt Weill and book and lyrics by Alan Jay Lerner, is another precursor to the Sondheim-Prince concept musicals of the 1970s. *Love Life* illustrates the effects of economics, particularly the growth of the industrial age, on one married couple from 1791 to the present. Rather than a linear plot, separate and connecting scenes span a period of 150 years. Like Weill's earlier work with Brecht, the songs comment on character and situation.

Love Life relied on the conventions of American vaudeville to dissect the interdependence of marriage and economics. Lerner details the presentational aspects of the show: "It began with a magician who sawed a lady, the leading lady, in half, raised the leading man three feet off the stage in the time-honored, elevated trick and then disappeared, leaving the couple to figure out how they had arrived in this awkward position, where the woman was half-homemaker, half-breadwinner, and part-time mother, and the man up in the air."[67] Other vaudeville turns included a trapeze artiste swinging over the proscenium arch and a Punch and Judy ballet. In effect, each scene ended with a vaudeville routine that traced the central marriage's economic disintegration. The techniques are similar to those Sondheim would use with Prince in *Company* and *Follies* more than twenty years later. Both Prince shows explore the difficulties of sustaining marriage within a wider social context: the pressures of urban life in *Company* and the collapse of the American dream in *Follies.* According to Cheryl Crawford, there was "no heart and no passion [in the original production of *Love Life*]. The audience couldn't get emotionally involved in the marital problems of the couple."[68] This, of course, was precisely the point, but emotional alienation is difficult to popularize in the American musical theatre. The most frequent criticism of the Sondheim-Prince shows has been that they are cold.

Also involved in the production was designer Boris Aronson, who later became part of Harold Prince's creative team, designing *Fiddler on the Roof, Cabaret,* and *Zorba* (1968), as well as the Prince-Sondheim *Company, Follies, A Little Night Music* (1972), and *Pacific Overtures* (1976). Both Aronson's contribution to *Love Life* and Sondheim's involvement with *Allegro* underscore the musical as a complex collaborative form that constantly recreates itself.

Perhaps *Love Life* is best remembered, however, as the show that created a schism between directors Elia Kazan and Robert Lewis. Originally Cheryl Crawford had approached Lewis about directing the musical, but Kazan had discouraged him from embarking on what he argued was a weak project. At Kazan's urging, Lewis declined the project. Months later, Lewis learned that Kazan had accepted the directing assignment himself. Irritated by this betrayal, Lewis resigned from the Actors Studio.[69]

Love Life's reliance on vaudeville conventions paved the way for Fosse's *Chicago* (1975), an indictment of America's media celebrities. Its original success probably had more to do with the razzle-dazzle of performance and Bob Fosse's staging than with authorial intent. Its cynicism was subordinated to audience adoration of its two divas, Gwen Verdon and Chita Rivera, both of whom played unsympathetic murderesses in ways that rendered them curiously and comically vulnerable. *Chicago* really came into its own with its 1996 revival during a cynical cultural moment that found Americans reeling not only from the O. J. Simpson murder trial but also from the Michael Jackson child molestation scandal and from President Clinton's affair with Monica Lewinsky.

Although precursors to concept musicals, *Love Life* and *Allegro* were by no means solitary threads in a direct lineage. The conventions Sondheim and Prince employed in the 1970s to underscore their intellectualized social and political messages date back to the 1930s, especially to the eclectic experiments of Kurt Weill with Brechtian alienation, expressionism, and theatricalism. *Sweeney Todd*'s Mrs. Lovett, for example, could well be the heroine of a Brechtian musical. She embarks on a life of crime, a comic attack on capitalistic enterprise. *Company*'s Bobby can be compared to *Johnny Johnson*'s pacifist protagonist; virtually ciphers, they both embark on a search for self-education and enlightenment through a kind of Stations of the Cross journey. Both musicals employ ironic choral commentary that distances the audience from emotional involvement and forces it to question social platitudes.

The Webber-Prince *Evita* asks questions similar to those of Weill's *Knickerbocker Holiday:* who are our popular culture heroes and why have we allowed them to manipulate us? According to Prince, *Evita* historicizes the American media's tendency to create false gods: "I wanted the audience to *examine* what they worship. Fifteen years ago I told editors at *Time* that they put villains and felons on their covers, powerful figures who weren't caught. What that show is about is as poisonous now as in Evita's lifetime: how dishonest the news is every night."[70] Here is a case in which the public response to a popular musical manages to ignore the negative message intended by its creators. Rather than distance themselves from Evita, audiences tended to root for her. Perhaps they read her as a victim of the system; perhaps she was a symbol of the independent woman in an era of the burgeoning feminist movement. Perhaps none of this seemed to matter, since the unwashed masses, whom she alternately reviles and reveres, are Argentinian rather than American.

Theorizing about cultural populism, John Fiske suggests that popular culture can be read by audiences in ways never intended by the writers and producers: "But audiences constantly engage in 'semiotic guerrilla warfare.' Whereas the industries seek to incorporate audiences as commodity consumers, the audience often excorporates the text to its own purposes."[71] For Fiske, Russian Jews who watch *Dallas* on television see it as a self-criticism of capitalism. Sylvester Stallone's portrayal of *Rambo* becomes relevant to Australian aborigines' political struggles. Fiske's theory can be applied to the reception for a musical such as *Evita,* in which the text itself condemns the media for canonizing the unworthy. Whereas Harold Prince tried to make the audience question the celebrities it worshiped, spectators seem to respond to the musicalized Evita as they would to Dolly or Mame, cheering her on for her grit, determination, and charisma.

Fiske's theory can similarly be applied to *Sweeney Todd* (1979), another Sondheim-Prince concept musical that revolves around the evils of industrialization. According to Prince, "I felt that by placing the action in its late nineteenth-century context, we could say that from the day the Industrial Revolution entered our lives, the conveyor belt pulled us further and further from harmony, from humanity, from nature."[72] The suffocating smoke that emanates from the onstage factory in Eugene Lee's set design for the original production suggested that the effect of industrialization on humanity was akin to the Holocaust; individuals were being sacrificed to a dehumanizing system that amounted to a huge gas chamber. Certainly Sweeney, in his quest for vengeance, has been sacrificed to this dehumanizing system. If Sweeney seeks revenge against a society that has destroyed his innocence, not to mention his family, he is nonetheless a serial killer. The victim of a corrupt society, he in turn has been corrupted and has lost his mind in the process. This is his tragedy. Like Evita, however, the character of Sweeney Todd seems to invite cheers from the audience. Spectators seem not only to root for him as victimized underdog but also to cheer his every brutal murder. Despite Prince's avowed intent, *Sweeney Todd* remains a Victorian melodrama rather than a parable of the horrors of industrialization. Like *Evita,* it is an example of a serious musical that succeeds despite (rather than because of) its serious message.

Concept musicals tend to express their intellectualizing through musical comedy conventions reshaped to comment ironically on character and situation. *Cabaret* is divided into both realistic dialogue scenes in the rooming house and performance numbers onstage at the Kit Kat Klub. The nightclub numbers comment on the action. Like Cliff, *Cabaret*'s *raisonneur,* the audience initially is lured by the show-business glitz of the Kit Kat Klub. As Cliff's disillusionment grows, however, so does that of the audience as it becomes increasingly disturbed by the performance numbers that reflect the moral corruption of a Germany under the sway of the Third Reich. The emcee, like a character in a Brecht-Weill musical play, steps downstage into an eerie spotlight to comment on the play, simultaneously entertaining and distancing the audience in routines like "Wilkommen," "The Money Song," and "Two Ladies."

Employing theatricalist techniques, Prince used a distortion mirror in the original production through which the audience, at times, was permitted to see its own reflection. After "If You Could See Her Through My Eyes," the number in which the emcee dances with a gorilla, the mirror stopped distorting and became reflective just as the emcee sang the punch line: if we could see the gorilla through his eyes, she would not resemble a Jew. I remember seeing the show during its Boston tryout, and the effect was chilling. The audience was able to witness its individual reactions to this racist joke. Some laughed, some were shocked, while others were simply hypnotized into watching their own reactions and those of their fellow spectators. Eventually, the Anti-Defamation League demanded that the joke be softened. During New York previews, the gorilla became a "meeskite," the Yiddish word for "ugly," rather than a Jew. The original punch line, however, appears in the published version of the script.[73]

In the original production, Prince tried to create the impression that the moral corruption of the Kit Kat Klub was seeping into the everyday lives of Cliff and the others in the rooming house. Kit Kat Klub girls lingered onstage and watched as the set changed to the rooming house. In the 1998 Broadway revival, director Sam Mendes takes the limbo world one step further. Borrowing from the ghosts of the Prince–Michael Bennett *Follies*, the Kit Kat Klub girls no longer just linger; they act as an otherworldly presence. The emcee and chorus girls infiltrate the rooming house as they eavesdrop on and whisper about the characters in the more realistic rooming-house scenes. For Mendes, the moral corruption is everywhere.

The revival also illustrates performance subverting the text. In 1966 Cliff was written as heterosexual. Although initially fascinated by the seedy glamour of the Kit Kat Klub, he gradually sees the horrors of Nazism permeating the club, as well as Berlin, and his fascination turns to disgust. Without this change of character, his final scene with Sally, in which he confronts her with the ugliness all around them and begs her to accompany him to America, makes little sense. In the 1998 version, Cliff is written as bisexual, as he was in the Fosse film version and in the Christopher Isherwood source material; nevertheless, the script indicates the same change of character as Cliff progressively becomes aware of the corruption around him. In Mendes's staging, it is clear from the opening that the Kit Kat Klub is not divine but sordid. The chorus girls have track marks on their arms. The "Two Ladies" number is performed in shadow behind a scrim with suggestions of fist-fucking. If the Kit Kat Klub is Berlin's answer to the infamous New York gay sex club the Mineshaft from the beginning of the show, there is no discovery, either for Cliff or for the audience. As a result, the final confrontation scene with Sally has little resonance. One wonders why he did not escape Berlin after the opening number. Mendes's second-act curtain, in which the emcee, along with the other denizens of the Kit Kat Klub, are killed in a gas chamber, is certainly a coup de théâtre but makes little sense in terms of the text. As written, the script does not suggest that a backlash against sexual hedonism caused Hitler's rise to power. This vision is interesting and possibly historically accurate, but it is not written. On the contrary, the text specifies that the emcee, the waiters, Frau Kost, the Kit Kat girls, and other Berliners are gradually seduced by Nazism. Mendes's production and directorial touches are nonetheless brilliantly theatrical and show how an auteur director can manipulate the text for his own purposes.

A product of its cultural moment, *Follies* was written as the tumultuous

1960s came to a close. Exploring America's crumbling values and shifting social arrangements, it attacked the postwar mythologization of America that was so endemic to the Rodgers and Hammerstein canon. In addition to songs that reveal character and emerge from dialogue, Sondheim uses pastiche and performance numbers to comment on the dichotomy between present and past, youth and maturity, reality and fantasy. The score, like those of *Johnny Johnson* and other Weill shows of the 1930s, is eclectic, a kind of time travel through varying musical theatre styles. One hears echoes of Romberg in "One More Kiss," Cole Porter in "Lucy and Jessie," DeSylva, Lou Brown, and Ray Henderson in "Broadway Baby," and Irving Berlin in "Beautiful Girls." Through these performance numbers, Sondheim enables the characters to express neuroses they would otherwise be unable to verbalize. Indeed, the "Loveland" sequence becomes a kind of Walpurgisnacht, in which the four principal characters expose their psychological demons to the audience and to themselves.

Here is a case in which text was overshadowed by a legendary production. Prince and codirector Michael Bennett staged the more realistic book scenes as well as the performance numbers with onstage ghosts. By juxtaposing young and old versions of the principals, Prince was also able to comment on their false dreams and illusions. During an emotional confrontation between Sally and Ben when both realized the foolishness of their illusions, one of the ghosts, a tall, statuesque showgirl, suddenly turned her back to the audience, whereupon the strand of pearls she was wearing made a loud, swooshing noise. The unexpected, haunting sound of the pearls reinforced Ben and Sally's shattered illusions about their relationship. The 1971 production was filled with moments of breathtaking theatricality: Dorothy Collins's exquisitely economical rendition of "Losing My Mind," the stunning dichotomy between past and present in Bennett's choreography for "Who's That Woman," the elderly Ethel Shutta's magical ability to shed seventy years as she belted "Broadway Baby," Alexis Smith's electrifying dance number to "Lucy and Jessie," not to mention the unforgettable image of a gorgeous, Amazonian showgirl ghost who posed while a thunderbolt crashed and the curtain rose. Besides being incredibly lavish and virtually impossible to recreate in terms of today's Broadway economic climate, this production was also the high point of the careers of Bennett, Prince, and Boris Aronson—a trio not easy to best. When performance supersedes text, as was the case with the original production of *Follies,* new interpretations inevitably struggle with a phantom memory, which is why I referred to the show in chapter 1 as the *Rebecca* of musicals.

Indeed, since the show's debut, critics have attacked the libretto. The script focuses on a reunion. Without the director and actors magnifying the stakes, it is difficult to become emotionally invested in the four somewhat unpleasant protagonists. Dorothy Collins filled in many of these gaps in the original production. When she first entered as Sally, she wore a dress more appropriate for a younger, cuter, less plump woman than herself. Here was someone desperately trying to recapture her past. More memorably, when she first bolted onstage she looked as though she had run all the way to New York from the Midwest. This was not just a reunion but a matter of life and death. If this Sally failed to win Ben, one feared that her life might well be over. In the final scene, Collins sat motionless. Without moving, she brokenheartedly kept muttering that she had left the dishes in the kitchen sink. Faced with the death of her illusions, she dreaded returning to a life with no hope. "Losing My Mind" aptly foreshadowed Sally's state at the final curtain. In the revivals on Broadway (2001) and at the Paper Mill Playhouse (2000), the Sallys were unable to recreate this sense of urgency and loss. If Sally perkily, or even resignedly, rises and refers to the unwashed dishes as if she is ready to return home, it is not only the dishes that remain in that kitchen sink but the emotional trajectory of the character.

Assassins, a newer Sondheim concept musical, asks its audiences to puzzle the significance of nine Americans obsessed with killing various presidents of the United States. Opening in 1991 during the midst of the Gulf War, the original production played a limited run at New York's Playwrights Horizons. Commercial producers shied away from a move to a Broadway theatre during that turbulent political crisis. The musical was slated for revival by the Roundabout Theatre Company in 2001 but was pulled from the schedule because of the aftermath of September 11, 2001. In 2004, timing seemed ripe for a musical about terrorists, even if the terrorists were American rather than radical Islamicist fundamentalists.

Critics hailed the revival. Finally New York had a politically relevant musical to challenge audiences. Pondering why the reception of the show had changed so drastically from that of the original, Frank Rich devoted a column to the musical's relevance in 2004: "Though the text has been slightly tweaked, a song added and the production overhauled, it's not the show that has changed so much as the world. The huge difference in response to 'Assassins' from one war in Iraq to the next is about as empirical an indicator of the larger drift of our post-9/11 culture as can be found."[74] As Rich points out, two of the assassins now hit considerably closer to home. In 1974 Samuel Byck attempted to hijack a commercial 747, thirteen months after weapon detectors had been installed at American airports. His goal was to fly into the White House and kill Nixon. Byck's saga resonates creepily with Condoleezza Rice's testimony that hijacking a plane as a suicide weapon was incomprehensible before September 11. Moreover, Charles Guitreau, a religious fanatic who shot James Garfield in 1881, regarded his suicide mission as God's will. As Rich wondered, "You find yourself wondering if he is expecting 72 black-eyed virgins as his posthumous reward."[75] Writing for the *New Yorker,* John Lahr disagreed:

> It [the revival] was meant to have its Broadway debut just after September 11, 2001. The delay of more than two years has not helped the show's karma or its message. The musical views terrorism as the random acts of individual madmen, not as the coordinated civil mayhem we now know. . . . The jihadists of September 11 imprinted their sense of death irrevocably on this nation. In one way or another, we are all now survivors. "Assassins"'s portrait of American invincibility has come to feel almost as Pollyannish as the traditional musicals against which Sondheim's work rebels. . . . In light of our new hell, the violence that "Assassins" addresses seems antique, quaint, almost sweet: Terrorism Lite.[76]

Certainly the musical raises many questions and provides few answers. Political assassinations are not uniquely an American phenomenon. What *is* peculiarly American about this assortment of murderers and would-be murderers? Are the assassins psychotics who reflect a common American lust for celebrity? Are they representative of the disappointment and rage that consume those whom the American dream passes by? Perhaps most important, are the assassins reflections of America's obsession with violence and power? It seems to me that this last question is the one that begs clarification in the aftermath of September 11 and the preemptive bombings of Afghanistan and Iraq. While the failure to rework and refocus the script seems to be a missed opportunity, *Assassins,* like most of Sondheim's work, succeeded in providing fodder for intellectual discourse and disagreement.

Sondheim credits Hammerstein's theatricalist techniques in *Allegro* as the inspiration for much of his own work. Both Prince and Sondheim, however, swear they are not influenced by Brecht. According to Sondheim, "Brecht and Weill worked in a tradition of *Lehrstück;* my background is Broadway and the two are very different. . . . I like *Threepenny Opera* but not really anything else. Basically, I hate Brecht."[77] Sondheim and Prince are commercial Broadway showmen, not Marxists, but in the ironic, often jeering choral commentary and use of musical comedy and vaudeville conventions to underscore intellectualized ideas, they incorporate elements of anticathartic epic theatre, as well as other forms of antirealism. The use of narration and the Christlike protagonist on the road to self-knowledge in a musical such as *Sweeney Todd* is reminiscent of expressionism, just as the ironic choral commentary and the emotional distancing of actors through song are characteristic of Brecht and epic theatre, despite Sondheim's denials.

Prince, on the other hand, likens himself to Meyerhold rather than to Brecht:

> Unlike Brecht, my purpose is not to eliminate emotional response—it isn't by design that a show of mine is cold. Brecht flooded his stage with white light; I like shadows. I was flattered when the widow of [Brecht's teacher] Erwin Piscator said *Evita* was close in spirit to her husband's work, but in fact Russian theatre has influenced me far more than Brecht's tradition; Joshua Logan told me my work resembled Meyerhold's. Furthermore, I've been bored to death by Brecht-inspired productions.[78]

Prince seems to ignore some important information here. Brecht did not totally eliminate emotional response. His characters are often sufficiently complex, most notably Mother Courage, that they inevitably elicit a degree of emotional response, including empathy. Secondly, Brecht was a disciple of Piscator, who borrowed many ideas from the expressionists and, before them, from Meyerhold. It was Meyerhold who first advocated a kind of theatricalism. What Meyerhold, Piscator, and Brecht have in common is the use of antirealistic theatrical conventions to frame their politicized ideas. This is also the tradition that Weill's American musicals followed in the 1930s; so did the American satirical musicals of the Gershwins, Kaufman, and Ryskind. We also see the tradition in *Allegro* and in *Love Life* in the 1940s. Once again, the development of the form is not a linear one but the history of a genealogy of influence with various interweaving strands that cross through decades.

Searching for a New Horizon of Expectations

At the same time that the concept musical was emerging, artists such as Tom O'Horgan and Tom Eyen tried to apply what was vital in the experimental New York theatre to the musical: O'Horgan with *Hair* (1968) and Eyen with *Caution: A Love Story* (1968), which combined the saga of the Duke and Duchess of Windsor with a band of gypsies performing excerpts from *The Kama Sutra.*[79] Both O'Horgan and Eyen worked at La MaMa and were part of a cultural zeitgeist that included the experiments of the Living Theatre, the Performance Garage, and an emerging eclectic postmodernism that began to chip away at the realism of the Broadway commercial theatre. As nonmusical theatre struggled to find new structural and performance conventions, the conventions of the serious musical began to change as well. Popular music was forever altered with the emergence of rock, which became the music of the hit parade, rather than the peculiar hybrid of Jewish–Eastern European–African American jazz that had influenced Tin Pan Alley and show music for most of the century.

Hair, the first successful rock musical, with book and lyrics by Gerry Ragni and James Rado and music by Galt MacDermot, emerged concurrently with the concept musical. If the concept musical was a product of its cultural moment, so was *Hair* but in a different way. Whereas one can trace influences from Hammerstein to Brecht and Weill in the Prince-Sondheim collaborations, *Hair* was part vaudeville, part rock concert, and part loosely structured political satire that involved the day-to-day concerns of young people in the turbulent 1960s: the war in Vietnam, the draft, sexual identity, and a postromantic concern with individuality threatened by the establishment. The musical broke many musical theatre conventions. The plot, thin as it was, unfolded in a revuelike format. As such, *Hair* was as much a happening as a musical. Presentational in style, the concept was metatheatrical, with performers using handheld microphones throughout the show. It was clear from the beginning of the performance that the musical was just that, a performance. The *Hair* tribe appeared before the show and wandered through the audience, much like the members of the Living Theatre troupe that had performed *Paradise Now* a year earlier. The tribe consisted of actors telling their counterculture story to a largely middle-class audience.

During the year it took to transfer Gerald Freedman's original production at the Public Theatre to Broadway, the text was progressively altered when O'Horgan joined the show as director to underscore the show's youthful spontaneity. The seriousness of the antiwar theme contrasted with the campy staging of O'Horgan and the casting of authors James Rado and Gerry Ragni, both of whom were approaching middle age, which seriously dislodged a sense of reality in their portrayal of draft-aged teenagers. O'Horgan's staging was far more concerned with drug fantasies and gender ambiguity than with the war in Vietnam. The book scenes, as well as the musical numbers, were characterized by gender role reversals, in which men played women and women played men. Jonathan Kramer played Margaret Mead in drag and sang "My Conviction," while another character, Woof, was avowedly bisexual. The musical also featured a now legendary nude scene, which was an outgrowth of the nudity prevalent at performances of controversial experimental works by the Living Theatre, the Performance Garage, and La MaMa. Moreover, the demands of singing rock eight times a week (not to mention the availability of drugs) took its toll on the company. Cast members often missed performances. Women sometimes replaced men and men, women. Certainly, the performance was open in that each actor was free to bring his or her personality (and gender) into this fluid structure.

Marvin Carlson observes that the location of the theatre, the neighborhood surrounding the place of performance, the lobby, and the auditorium itself are crucial elements in reception.[80] *Hair* played at the Biltmore in New York. The outside of the theatre was spray-painted to look like an East Village tenement. The inside of the Biltmore was deliberately defaced and decorated with old tires and refuse to resemble the kind of neighborhood its middle-class audience probably avoided. In its alteration of the theatre building, *Hair* anticipates *Rent* (1996). Both musicals enable a middle-aged, middle-class audience to "visit" a provocative bohemian milieu in a safe, protected environment.

Hair's disregard of standard musical theatre conventions was symptomatic of changes in Broadway audiences' horizons of expectations by the 1970s and 1980s. As both the rock musical and the concept musical thrived, the British poperetta, a sung-through musical with operatic aspirations, arrived in America with Tom O'Horgan's staging of Andrew Lloyd Webber's *Jesus Christ Superstar* (1972) and continued with *Evita* (1979), the revuelike *Cats* (1982), *Les Misérables* (1987), *Phantom of the Opera* (1988), and *Miss Saigon* (1991).

Like the rock musical and the concept musical, the poperetta renegotiates musical theatre conventions. Poperettas have little or no dialogue. The assumption is that everything that is sung is emotionally heightened, which often makes the faux opera recitatives, particularly since they are in English, sound banal. With the use of recitative comes another alteration in the musical's ongoing negotiation between the realistic and the presentational: amplification. Body mikes are easily detected on the current Broadway stage. A microphone sticking out of a performer's spit curls is a fourth-wall-shattering experience, at least for me. My own suspension of disbelief is not heightened when I hear an amplified voice but cannot tell where it is coming from.

One wonders about the extent to which amplification in the late 1960s encouraged the birth of the sung-through poperetta. One of the first fully amplified musicals was *Promises, Promises* (1968), which offered a rather conventional Neil Simon libretto of realistic dialogue scenes and a contemporary score by Burt Bacharach. Bacharach insisted on an amplified sound for the songs. He installed pit voices in the orchestra to replicate a recording-studio sound rather than that of the typical hard-sell Broadway show tune. What happens to realistic dialogue scenes, however, when all the songs are amplified? It is almost impossible to make a seamless transition between dialogue and song when orchestra and voice are amplified but dialogue is not. The realism of unamplified book scenes and the artificiality endemic to musical amplification make for an unbridgeable chasm. If one agrees to mike the dialogue, the lines no longer sound realistic. One solution, of course, is to eliminate the dialogue, which is exactly what poperettas do.

Phantom, a Webber poperetta directed by Prince, is a backstager set in the opera house that the phantom haunts. Whereas a poperetta–concept musical such as *Evita* is structured around a complex character with complex relationships, *Phantom* offers considerably less psychologizing.[81] Christine is a singing cipher. What are we to make of her feelings for the phantom? Is she sexually attracted to her abductor? Are they sleeping together? The script offers little help in decoding the relationship. The work is puzzling; nevertheless, it is one of the most commercially successful musicals in the history of the American theatre. Perhaps its popularity lies in its openness. It avoids defining the sexual relationship between the phantom and Christine while, as Foster Hirsch notes, simultaneously creating metaphors for it: the phantom's charisma, his musical genius, his Svengali-like control over Christine's throat and body, her fascination with his mask.[82] As Hirsch observes, Michael Crawford played the role not as the freak depicted in the Lon Chaney film but "with unexpected realism, as an obsessed lover craving acceptance."[83] Certainly, Crawford, an ex-dancer, is a very physical actor with enormous magnetism. Here is a case of performance fleshing out an open text.

It is impossible to predict the direction musicals will take in the future. As soon as a pattern occurs, a new hit show seems to break the trend. In the aftermath of September 11, audiences seemed to cling to escapist fare. *Hairspray,* an old-fashioned musical comedy that starred Harvey Fierstein in drag, became the hit of the season. By 2004, shocked by American soldiers' abuse of Iraqi prisoners of war, the nation grew increasingly skeptical about the Bush administration's handling of the war on terrorism. *Assassins,* Broadway's terrorist musical, won the Tony for best revival, but the public flocked to *Wicked,* an escapist fantasy. As American involvement in Iraq becomes increasingly reminiscent of the war in Vietnam, a new production of *Hair* is scheduled for a national tour, presumably gearing itself toward a Broadway revival. If musicals constantly switch direction, they also assimilate and reflect changes in society. In effect, the development of the form is an ongoing sociology of American culture.

4

◆ ◆ ◆ ◆ ◆ ◆ ◆

Popular Musicals as Utopia

If musicals reflect the material conditions in which they were originally produced and received, popular musicals, through their wide and broad range of appeal, become markers that document American attitudes toward identity during the past half-century. It seems logical that particularly successful musicals typically unite the world of the author with the concerns of the audience. Writing of Michel Saint-Denis' theory of style, Jane Baldwin summarizes the importance of filtering the text through the tensions and anxieties of the culture that receives it:

> Style is both internal and external: it is composed of language, behavior, fashion, prevailing aesthetic(s), social structure, and belief system(s). All these elements are filtered through the play's text. Style is not static; the playwright's word is fixed in time but not the audience's perception of it. Although Saint-Denis believed that universality was the test of a play's greatness, he realized that a given style's contemporaneity is related to the anxieties, fears, desires, and values of the audience."[1]

Along these lines, Richard Dyer suggests that popular entertainment reconciles and resolves perceived social tensions by suggesting alternatives to needs or desires in society that can make life better. Through binary oppositions, Dyer lists the social problems experienced by audiences and the textual solutions provided by popular entertainment.[2] For instance, scarcity (poverty) becomes abundance (elimination of poverty for self and others) in *My Fair Lady* (1956). Dreariness is transformed into intensity in *On the Town* (1944), which creates a fantasy world of New York City during wartime, and in *The Sound of Music* (1959), in which the von Trapp family escapes the Anschluss by singing and climbing over the Alps. Stereotypical notions of the performance of female gender, challenged by the wartime emergence of women in the work force, result in spontaneity (nontraditional male-female relationships) in *Annie Get Your Gun* (1946), which revolves around the romance between two competitive sharpshooters.

Dyer's theory that popular entertainment provides solutions to social problems experienced by audiences during specific cultural moments suggests a useful way of thinking about popular musicals. I have chosen to discuss four: *Oklahoma!* (1943), *Fiddler on the Roof* (1964), *A Chorus Line* (1975), and *Les Misérables* (1987). Each is a cultural marker that reflects a turning point or profound sociocultural change. In *Oklahoma!,* the endorsement of community over fragmentation helped to heal wartime tensions not only between isolationist and interventionist but also between conservative and New Dealer. The generational conflicts that threaten tradition in *Fiddler on the Roof* reflect the generational conflicts between Broadway audiences in the 1960s and an emerging youthful counterculture that threatened hegemonic, middle-class values. *A Chorus Line* traces the tensions between insider and outsider. Written amidst the rhetoric of the 1970s "me" generation, the musical tries to resolve the anxieties created by valuing one's individual autonomy while simultaneously capitulating to an increasingly corporate America. Finally, *Les Misérables,* although conceding the futility of social revolution, optimistically endorses the power of the individual to create change. These musicals provided hope that tensions in society, seemingly insoluble and bitter, could indeed be bridged. Their enormous popularity sprang, at least in part, from their affirmation that the system could be fixed.

Oklahoma! and the 1940s

Reconciliation of perceived social tensions helps explain *Oklahoma!*'s role in American political consciousness. The fragmentation of community in the Rodgers and Hammerstein musical, exemplified by the conflict between the farmer and the cowman, is hypothetically resolved when the territory becomes a state. In a larger sense, the focus on fragmentation versus community historicizes the isolationist-interventionist conflict that preceded and shadowed America's participation in World War II. Before entering the war, America was divided between interventionists, who wanted to join the Allies and fight fascism abroad, and isolationists, who believed that Americans had no business meddling in European affairs. Isolationists often accused the media and entertainment industry, which many perceived as predominantly Jewish, of trying to coerce the United States into joining a war that centered on the persecution of European Jews; this interventionist stance suggested a motive of self-interest for the Jewish American. Although Roosevelt's administration was officially neutral, New Deal liberals were linked with interventionists, whereas conservatives were aligned with isolationists. *Oklahoma!* offered a solution to these wartime tensions: if American values were to be safe from fascism abroad, America had to bond together to fight the enemy. For Rodgers and Hammerstein, both of whom were Jewish supporters of FDR, the solution to these political tensions involved the mixing of wartime conservative ideology that glorified a grassroots, 1890s populist vision of small-town America with New Deal notions of an assimilationist society. In *Oklahoma!,* the writers provided reconciliation and resolution by retaining a vision of rural America that appealed to conservatives and populists while inserting a New Deal message that even grassroots America could be a model of assimilation and tolerance.

The result, a mythologization of the American community, toured for sixteen years and ran almost four times as long on Broadway as any book musical that had preceded it. Just as Curly, the musical's hero, must settle down, become a farmer, marry, and nurture a new generation of Oklahomans, the Oklahoma territory itself must become a state that embraces the Union. Rodgers and Hammerstein fashion a middle-class utopia where liberals and conservatives can be friends. The writers present this vision of American life under an idyllic populist banner. Part of the conservative, grassroots rhetoric against the New Deal attacked Roosevelt's alliance with the labor unions and his support from urban constituencies, which were perceived as ethnic, Jewish, or communist, depending on the rabidity of FDR's detractors. In his libretto, Hammerstein redefines populism as all-inclusive by melding what Michael Kammen terms a soothing nostalgia for a bygone America with assimilationist, interventionist strategies.[3] *Oklahoma!* contributed to the healing of a nation divided by its role in World War II, an America where middle-class values could potentially be inclusive of ethnic outsiders, including Ali Hakim, as well as the "territory folk," native-born Americans who were not yet citizens of the United States. At the same time, Hammerstein warns against the politics of exclusion through Jud

Frye, whose insistence on his own individualized needs at the expense of those of the community alienates him from the social contract. Metaphorically the musical endorses New Deal ideology within a populist framework, minus the isolationist rhetoric of wartime conservatives. The feat here is one of complex topsy-turvydom; in effect, *Oklahoma!* demonstrates that fragmentation, in the guise of insularity, enervates the grassroots American values that wartime conservatives believed were menaced by the New Deal.

The original Broadway production of *Oklahoma!* opened fifteen months after the bombing of Pearl Harbor. By that time, America had banded together to join the war; however, the tension between isolationist and interventionist remained deep-seated, despite the efforts of the Office of War Information and the Bureau of Motion Pictures, which mobilized support for the war effort by disseminating propaganda through the entertainment industry and other media.

To understand the political ideology behind *Oklahoma!,* it is important to grasp the meaning of the conflict between isolationist and interventionist, conservative and New Dealer, as well as the origin of American anti-Semitic populist rhetoric that was key to the debate about whether to enter World War II. Much of this rhetoric involves what Steven Carr terms "the Hollywood question," or the extent to which immigrant Jews were perceived as controlling the American film industry in the 1930s and 1940s, which was symptomatic of a larger anti-Semitism at work in American culture at the time. According to Carr, stereotypes of Jews fed into two long-standing sources of American anxiety: "fear of the Other and fear of potentate."[4] Although Rodgers and Hammerstein endorsed a New Deal message of tolerance in *Oklahoma!,* the political ramifications of the piece are not overt. The authors were vulnerable to attack by conservatives and by anti-Semites; it was in their interest, both as Jews and as creators of what they hoped would be a broadly commercial, popular entertainment, to assuage America's anti-Semitic fear of the Jew as racialized Other by promoting a concept of community that would embrace strategies of tolerance and assimilation.

Rodgers and Hammerstein capitalize on the political similarities between 1890s insularity and conservative isolationist ideology prior to World War II by venerating the middle class while managing to overturn the anti-Semitic rhetoric common to both periods. Historically, grassroots populism emerged during the economic depression of the 1890s, just as isolationism and the reemergence of populist rhetoric in the 1930s were, in part, products of the Great Depression. Populists of the 1890s, many of whom operated small farms or small businesses at which the farmers traded, were convinced that big business and government were antigrassroots America and anti-middle class. For example, an editorial in the *Representative*, the official paper of the Populist Minnesota State Farmer's Alliance, described the sale of the *New York Times* in 1894 and compared Jewish control of the press to fin-de-siècle industrialism: "In these evil conditions, made by bad laws, the Jews alone thrive. . . . The reason is they deal only in money, they have no belief in farming, manufacturing, or any other industry; they are money-mongerers."[5] Populist rhetoric maintained that Jewish capitalists squeezed the lower and middle classes, Jewish journalists printed lies and distorted truths, and Jewish entertainment moguls polluted high culture.[6]

Both before and after the United States entered World War II, xenophobic populist sentiment once again demonized big business, labor unions, and ethnoracial urban centers as enemies of the ordinary, hard-working middle-class American. As Michael Kazan argues, populist rhetoric venerated a self-sufficient middle class: "Populist speakers typically expressed their highest esteem for citizens who inhabited what the novelist E. L. Doctorow calls 'the large middle world, neither destitute nor privileged . . . that of the ordinary working man': yeoman farmers, urban craftsmen, native-born factory workers, home owners struggling to pay their taxes."[7] "Native born" is a significant phrase here, since Jewish control of the media, the press, the theatre, and the film industry had long served as a mainstay of populist rhetoric.[8]

Wartime isolationists transformed populism into an idealized vision of small-town American life. For Carr, "The America that . . . most western progressive isolationists spoke for . . . was overwhelmingly rural and small town. It was an America consisting largely of farmers on the soil and of small businessmen buying and selling to those farmers in countless small towns scattered across the prairies and Great Plains."[9] This populist view of American small-town life not only excluded the ethnic outsider but also demonized the Jew as a threat to these nostalgic American values. By the late 1930s, isolationists such as John Rankin, Burton K. Wheeler, and Gerald P. Nye appropriated traditional populist ideology as well as anti-Semitic rhetoric. Moreover, editorials in publications such as *Social Justice*, the weekly newspaper of isolationist Father Charles Coughlin, opposed any U.S. sanctuary for Jewish refugees from Hitler's Germany.[10]

Clearly, one problem interventionists faced in fighting Hitler was American anti-Semitism. Just as the original populists of the 1890s were suspicious of Jewish control of the theatre, isolationists during the late 1930s were similarly suspicious of Jewish control of the media. As a Jewish interventionist,

Hammerstein was virulent against this anti-Semitic zeitgeist. By 1936 he had all but abandoned Broadway for Hollywood after a string of stage flops. While working with Jerome Kern on the film musical *High, Wide, and Handsome* (1936), he joined liberals in the motion picture community, including Dorothy Parker, Alan Campbell, Donald Ogden Stewart, Fredric March, and Florence Eldridge, to form the executive council of the Hollywood League Against Nazism. Hammerstein regularly hosted meetings at his home, organized radio broadcasts, wrote articles, and prepared short films that condemned Nazi anti-Semitism.[11] Eventually he chaired a special interracial commission designed to "combat racial intolerance and thus combat Nazism, which uses intolerance as a weapon to attain power."[12] Perhaps his most eloquent interventionist statement is expressed in the lyrics to "The Last Time I Saw Paris," written immediately after the Nazi occupation in 1940. The song won Hammerstein an Academy Award.

Hammerstein's political stance fed populist, isolationist fears that New Dealers had aligned themselves with interventionist policy. As a Jew working in Hollywood, Hammerstein was particularly vulnerable to attack.[13] The war in Europe involved the persecution and annihilation of Jews. Hollywood studios were perceived to be run by Jews; it was clearly in their best interest to distribute films proselytizing that America join the war effort. In 1936 Joseph Breen, speaking for the Production Code, warned Hollywood film producers against making anti-Nazi propaganda films: "There is a strong pro-German and anti-Semitic [*sic*] feeling in this country . . . and while those who are likely to approve of an anti-Hitler picture may think well of such an enterprise, they should keep in mind that millions of Americans might think otherwise."[14] Joseph Kennedy, then the U.S. ambassador to Great Britain, similarly warned American film producers against an interventionist stance in 1941. After one of Kennedy's banquet speeches, Douglas Fairbanks Jr. wrote to President Roosevelt that "the less than admirable [Kennedy] apparently threw the fear of God into many of our producers and executives. . . . The Jews were on the spot, and they should stop making anti-Nazi pictures or using the film medium to promote or show sympathy to the cause of the 'democracies' versus the 'dictators.'"[15] Since Jews had founded, to a large extent, the motion picture industry at the turn of the century and were responsible for many of the films distributed throughout America, they were indeed on the spot. If they did nothing, they were turning their backs on their fellow Jews in Europe. If they intervened, they would be attacked as warmongers coercing the nation to join the war on their behalf. Furthermore, Jewish film producers who recruited Jewish refugees from Europe to write and direct their films were accused of harboring communists.

A 1939 Gallup poll confirmed that 42 percent of Americans were concerned more about the promotion of war propaganda by Jews and European refugees than about the infiltration of Nazism, Fascism, or Communism in America.[16] According to polls sponsored by the American Jewish Committee and conducted by the Opinion Research Corporation, by 1940, a year before Pearl Harbor, more than 50 percent of Americans believed that Jews held too much power. Intuitively, one would assume that the Holocaust would help eradicate American anti-Semitism, particularly since the Office of War Information and the Bureau of Motion Pictures mandated popular culture, at least through the film industry. In fact, anti-Semitic attitudes toward Jewish control of the media had increased by the end of the war when, ironically, American distrust of Jewish power was at an all-time high: "By July 1945, the number of people who responded yes to the question 'Do you think the Jews have too much power and influence in this country?' had peaked to 67 percent."[17] Although the Bureau of Motion Pictures tried to resolve American anti-Semitism through censorship and propaganda, America's distrust of Jews lasted well beyond World War II.

To counter this anti-Semitism, Hammerstein would become active on the Writers War Board from its inception in the spring of 1942 to its expansion as a liaison with the Office of War Information. One of the primary goals of the board was to change American attitudes about Jews: "Distressed by the racism and anti-Semitism existing in America even while it fought the Nazis, the board not only tried to change attitudes, but pressured the government and other organizations to stop racist practices. Its efforts were instrumental in getting the Army to hire black medical personnel and the Red Cross to stop typing blood by racial group."[18] According to chairman Rex Stout, Hammerstein never missed any of the board's all-day Wednesday meetings, even after the success of *Oklahoma!*[19]

By the time America had entered the war, the nation remained deeply divided between New Deal ideology and conservative, populist values. Phillip Murray, John L. Lewis's successor as leader of the CIO, forged an alliance with FDR, but by 1943, the year that *Oklahoma!* opened, this union was perceived by conservatives as unholy. The alliance ignited the prejudices of middle America against Jewishness, radicalism, the new immigrant, and racial egalitarianism. According to Kazin, "The strains of right wing populism, intermittently strummed by the KKK in the 1920s and by [isolationist] Coughlin in the 1930s, were swelling again."[20] The thinnest of lines separated the myopic isolationist from the closet fascist, even after America had entered the war.

To underscore the political implications behind *Oklahoma!*'s enormous appeal, the CIO set up PAC, the Political Action Committee, in the summer of 1943. PAC mobilized union staffers to register voters, canvass workers, and seduce potential voters to believe that grassroots liberalism could curtail the momentum of the resurgent Right and provide a new era of reform in which every American would find a good job in a thriving economy: "'This Is Your America' was the title of the PAC's widely distributed introductory pamphlet. Superimposed over the photo of a small farm on a gently rolling hill with cows grazing behind a picket fence, those four words were meant as a declaration and a promise. The PAC's program would enable 'the Common Man of this earth' to realize his dreams."[21] The photo on the pamphlet looked surprisingly similar to the original sheet music design for *Oklahoma!,* which also pictured a small farm with a picket fence in a rural setting.[22] *Oklahoma!* had opened the previous March. Here was an instance in which the musical offered a utopian solution to the conflict between the New Deal and mid-American conservatives and populists.

Hammerstein counters conservative opposition to FDR and anti-Semitic rhetoric that the Jew posed a threat to American society through the character of Ali Hakim, the libidinous Persian peddler. Hakim represents the ethnoracial foreigner in this idyllic populist landscape, and it is clear from his profession, as Andrea Most stresses, that he is meant to be Jewish, although slightly disguised through a bit of geographical displacement.[23] His Semitic speech inflections, love of haggling, and humorous tendency to wallow in self-pity fed into stereotypical perceptions of the acquisitive Jewish merchant. Hakim is a clown, written in the tradition of the Jewish star comics of the 1920s and 1930s. If his one number, "It's a Scandal, It's an Outrage," is presentational, so are his vaudevillian "Persian Hello's" and "Persian Goodbye's." By turning the Jew into a comic, vaudevillian character, Hammerstein undercut American anti-Semitic rhetoric during World War II. Despite his Otherness, Hakim is accepted by the community and assimilated socially. The play ends with his comic declaration that he has been married in a shotgun wedding. The message is clear: it is possible to be assimilated in this grassroots idyll, as long as one buys into middle-class ideology and agrees (if at gunpoint) to be a fruitful member of the community.

Most attributes another motive to Hakim's function in the musical. She argues that *Oklahoma!* provided an assimilationist strategy for the Jew by promoting racialist ideology:

> Unlike race, ethnicity was presented as a set of transient qualities that was nonthreatening because it could easily be performed away. As long as the characters could learn to speak, dress, and sing, or dance in the American style, they were fully accepted into the stage or screen community. . . . The emphasis on ethnic inclusiveness did not preclude the perpetuation of racial stereotypes about blacks. Jews (and many other immigrant groups) found that a powerful strategy for becoming fully American was to adopt the prejudices of whites toward blacks.[24]

Most's argument is similar to Michael Rogin's assertion that Jews in show business used blackface to align themselves with the dominant, white culture. By appropriating stereotypical racialist traits associated with the African American, Jews, according to Rogin, achieved a degree of assimilation, although the price involved essentializing the African American.[25] For Most, a similar dynamic applies to *Oklahoma!* During "The Farmer and the Cowman Must Be Friends," Hammerstein cleverly includes the merchant along with the farmer and the cowman in his lyric; everyone, including the Jew, must bond if the community is to thrive. Jud, on the other hand, is also dark and, in a different sense, foreign. Most argues that Rodgers and Hammerstein assimilate the Jew, in the persona of the nonthreatening, theatricalist Hakim by demonizing Jud as a more realistically fashioned racialized Other or, metaphorically, as the African American.

To build on this argument, I suggest that Jud can be read as the embodiment of several kinds of Otherness, encompassing both race and class. Hammerstein's strategy for assimilating the Jew into the community involves turning Jud into the metaphorical racialized Other who cannot be "whitened." This Other includes not only the African American but also the Native American, particularly with *Oklahoma!*'s setting in Indian territory. The implied concept of manifest destiny endowed white settlers with providential powers to possess and "civilize" the West by appropriating Indian land. According to manifest destiny, genocide, slavery, and displacement of indigenous people were justifiable. It was the stereotype of the violent, sexual savage that threatened the taming of the wild frontier.

In *Celluloid Indians,* Jacquelyn Kilpatrick documents the shifting misrepresentations of the history and culture of Native Americans in Hollywood westerns. Dividing the stereotypes into three categories, mental, sexual, and spiritual, Kilpatrick explains how Hollywood has managed to do what thousands of years of social evolution could not accomplish. In effect, Hollywood turned the Native American into the homogenized celluloid Indian, a clearly definable racialized Other:

> One way to see how a group defines itself—to itself as well as to Others—is to look at those it makes its heroes. The self-definition at stake in most films with a Native American presence has been the Euro-American westering male. When we look at the writing of James Fenimore Cooper or the films of John Ford, we see this American self-definition repeatedly reinforced by its juxtaposition to the image of Native Americans. In that way, the challenge presented by the "savages" can be interpreted as a confirmation of the dominant value structure.[26]

The dominant value structure here is represented by *Oklahoma!*'s hero, Curly. In *Unthinking Eurocentrism,* Ella Shohat and Robert Stam further explore this ideological process of identification: "Native-Americans are usually portrayed as mean-spirited enemies of the moving train of progress."[27] The stereotype of the celluloid Indian, depicted as the bloodthirsty enemy of law-abiding Americans in 1940s westerns, historicized the Bureau of Motion Pictures' celluloid wartime depiction of the fascist or Nazi, whose murderous disregard for civility similarly threatened democracy.

The stereotyped Jew, on the other hand, is more complex, since, according to Carr, he channels his savagery within the socially acceptable:

> Racism directed toward blacks and Native Americans has traditionally located nonwhites outside the walls, displacing the actual brutality and violence meted out to these groups as an imagined, projected savagery of an uncivilized Other. American anti-Semitism, however, conjured a different kind of projection. Recalling the myth of the Trojan Horse, traditional anti-Semitism envisioned the Jew inside the walls, abusing the rules of assimilation to amass greater power and special privileges, much to the detriment of communal welfare.[28]

Oklahoma! turns this perception of the Jew upside down, in that Hakim is assimilated into the community almost against his will. He is nomadic and does not want to settle down but is forced into sociability through the end of an irate father's shotgun. Rather than connive to amass power, he connives to sell his goods and thus be free to continue his solitary life on the open road. Ultimately he succumbs to marriage and civilization. Hakim is willing, if not eager, to work within the walls of the community. Jud, like the myopic isolationist or closet fascist, works outside those walls.

In fact Jud shares many of the traits of the stereotypical celluloid Indian. He is primitive, violent, and intellectually inferior. Although mental acuity is not the strong suit of any of the characters in this musical, Jud is particularly dim-witted. He speaks in short ungrammatical phrases and grunts, not dissimilar to pidgin English or Tonto-talk. His preoccupation with sex (the pictures of nude women in the smokehouse) and his lust for Laurey cause her to fasten her door against "it," when she hears Jud prowling about at night. Laurey's allusion to Jud as "it" coincides with the stereotypical image of the Indian as sexual and bestial: "Sexuality has historically constituted an important dimension of Hollywood Indians, both male and female, producing a very scary character. We repeatedly see the lustful savage attacking the white woman, requiring that he be killed immediately."[29] This image of the Indian is consistent with James Fenimore Cooper's nineteenth-century novels as well as Robert Montgomery Bird's *Nick of the Woods* (1837), in which the title character, Nathan Slaughter, is virtually a one-man white genocide squad dedicated to exterminating the "savages." Literary scholar Curtis Dahl explains Bird's vision:

> Bird, perhaps from his travels through the frontier, had assimilated the feelings of the frontiersmen toward the savages. Thus in the novel they are "red niggers," dirty and drunken, with an unquenchable bloodlust. The frontiersmen who are nearly as savage (they, too, delight in taking scalps) slaughter them like rattlesnakes. Though Bird does not express approval of the extremes to which the whites go, he certainly makes the reader sympathize with Nathan's wish for bloody vengeance, and he pictures the Indians as a brutish race which must inevitably be destroyed by the advance of white civilization. He will stand for no romanticizing or sentimentalizing of the Indians.[30]

Dahl's analysis of perceived notions of the Indian bears much in common with Jud, who appears murderous and drunk at the shivaree. Jud's brutishness must be destroyed if the community is to survive, and much like Bird's vision of the Indian's ultimate fate, Jud's death or extinction is both desirable and inevitable. That Curly is forced to murder Jud in self-defense resonates with interventionist ideology that American heroes (GI's) should be willing to sacrifice their lives, if need be, to defend their country from the fascist menace abroad.

Just as there is a long-standing kinship between Jew and African American as racialized Others, musicals have employed perhaps an equally close kinship between the Jew and the Indian. Most points out this relationship in two musicals of an earlier era, *Whoopee!* (1928) and *Girl Crazy* (1930):

> They [Jews] had to confront an increasingly racialist culture which defined them as biologically (and hence immutably) alien. As one method of countering this prejudice, Jews strove to associate themselves with the founding mythos of America and hence to prove that they, like the Indians, were *already* American and that America was *already* Jewish. They supported historians and societies that argued that Columbus was a Jew, that the Puritans were actually a Hebraic sect, and that the Indians were the Ten Lost Tribes of Israel.[31]

One can argue within this context that Hakim is already "Native American," but *Native* here ironically resonates between outsider and insider, as opposed to the explicitly racialized Otherness of the stereotypical, savage Indian. Hakim is acculturated if not fully assimilated. If he is already part of the community, bringing him in fully through marriage means "whitening" him through the Anglo-American melting pot. Hakim is a liminal figure, who represents the space between the acceptable and the unacceptable. "Whitening" him through marriage to Gertie promotes his acceptability or assimilation.

Within this liminal space, Hakim acts as mediator between Jud, the outsider, and Curly, the insider. Whereas Jud wants to purchase the "little wonder," a gadget with a hidden switchblade, Hakim says he does not handle such dangerous items. Eventually Jud buys the knife from Will, who does not know that a switchblade is attached to the gadget. At the box social, Jud hands the "little wonder" to Curly, and Hakim, aware of Jud's murderous intent, seeks Aunt Eller's intervention to save Curly's life. The kinship between Hakim and Jud lies in their shared sense of outsider status, but Jud's violence promotes Hakim's acceptability. Hammerstein employed a similar strategy nineteen years earlier in *Rose-Marie*, in which the noble, half-Native-American heroine is victimized by the machinations of the evil Indian murderess Wanda. Rose-Marie ends up marrying her white lover, whereas Wanda is escorted to prison. It is Hard Boiled Herman, the Jewish comic in the show, who paves the way for Rose-Marie's happiness by exposing Wanda as a murderess. Herman is a mediator between the acceptable (Rose-Marie) and the antisocial (Wanda), just as Hakim is a mediator between the "white" hero (Curly) and the racialized Other (Jud).

In both *Oklahoma!* and its source play, *Green Grow the Lilacs* (1931), by Lynn Riggs, the conflict between Curly and Jud for possession of Laurey can be read as a metaphor for possession of the land or, within the World War II context of *Oklahoma!,* for possession of America. In having to make up her mind between Curly and Jud, Laurey is in the position to bestow land—the farm—on whomever she chooses: the fascistic bully who will manage the farm efficiently but whose steep price is usurpation or the white American hero who will cherish, nurture, and protect both Laurey and the farm but whose freewheeling lifestyle has made him more ambivalent about his responsibilities. In *Lilacs,* Curly says he is not worthy to marry Laurey because he has nothing:

> If I'd ever a-thought—! Oh, I'd orta been a farmer, and worked hard at it, and saved, and kep' buyin' more land and plowed and planted, like somebody—'stid of doin' the way I've done! Now the cattle business'll soon be over with. The ranches are breakin' up fast. They're puttin' in barbed w'ar, and ploin' up the sod fer wheat and corn. Purty soon they won't be no more grazin'—thousands of acres—no place for the cowboy to lay his head.[32]

Curly's speech predicts the historical evolution of Oklahoma. When statehood finally arrived, the farmer and the cowman did not become friends. As farms proliferated, ranchers were criticized for letting their cattle roam freely. In time, the cowboy all but became extinct.

In the musical, Hammerstein omits Curly's speech, with its wistful ambivalence about the extinction of the nomadic cowboy and his lifestyle. The point of *Oklahoma!* is not to create an accurate history but to mythologize community and the unification, acceptance, and tolerance of all who agree to abide by the social contract. Curly has the good sense to realize that he must settle down, accept his social responsibilities, and manage the farm as Laurey's husband and inheritor of the land. Similarly, Hakim, who does not particularly want to inherit the land, nevertheless agrees to accept society's rules. Unlike Jud, he functions within the walls of the community.

The difference between *Oklahoma!* and Riggs's source play involves questioning what constitutes an American. In *Lilacs* Curly is arrested, goes to jail on his wedding night, escapes, and returns to prison for sentencing at the end of the play after consummating his marriage. When the posse of townsmen try to take him away before he can spend a night with his bride, Aunt Eller reminds them that they are territory folk, not Americans, and that the U.S. marshall is a foreigner. They respond by affirming that they all have Indian blood:

Aunt Eller: Why, the way you're sidin' with the federal marshal, you'd think us people out here lived in the United States! Why, we're territory folks—we ort to hang together. I don't mean hang—I mean stick. Whut's the United States? It's jist a furrin country to me. And you supportin' it! Jist dirty ole furriners, ever last one of you!
Voices (outside, grumbling, protesting): Now, Aunt Eller, we hain't furriners.

My pappy and mammy was both borned in Indian Territory! Why, I'm jist plumb full of Indian blood myself.

Me, too! And I c'n prove it![33]

The townspeople's protestations of their "native" heritage set up a complicated moment. Here the supposedly "white" people are really outsiders, or native in a way that implies outsider status. Riggs, a Cherokee from Claremore, Oklahoma, was aware that before statehood, territory folk had intermarried and were of mixed blood. Everyone is an outsider unless they band together into a community of outsiders that will produce something new—not necessarily white but a melding and mixing of Indian, Jew, and white. This bonding is compatible with Israel Zangwill's original notion of "melting pot," in which off-white or racialized groups were not whitened by an Anglo melting pot but presumably would be acculturated and thus produce something dynamic and new in terms of American identity.[34]

Clinging to the notion of the Anglo melting pot, Hammerstein has Aunt Eller bend the law in *Oklahoma!* as well, but there is no mention of Indian blood, miscegenation, or the U.S. marshall being a foreigner. She merely coerces the judge into giving a verdict of not guilty on the spot so Curly and Laurey can proceed with their honeymoon and Curly can be exonerated of the crime. This change promotes the idea that territory folk do not regard the United States as foreign. Hammerstein's mythologizing of rural populism implies whitening, just as Hakim is whitened by his marriage to Gertie. Hammerstein refuses to acknowledge that these territory folk may have Indian blood; they are white Americans eager for Oklahoma to become a state, which is why they celebrate the land in song. It is Jud's insularity and refusal to become part of the community that label him as Other, and no one seems particularly disturbed by his death. If the farmer, the cowman, and the merchant can be united, the New Deal liberal, the populist-conservative, and the ethnic outsider can bond during World War II, as long as they share common, civilized goals. It is the man who rejects the communal bond during wartime America, the isolationist tacitly endorsing the threat of fascism, who becomes the outcast. Unlike the characters in *Lilacs,* it is only Hakim and Jud who are racialized Others in *Oklahoma!* Although the farmer and the cowman may not be happy about it, they accept Jud into the community. His inability to assimilate is the result of his own brutality and his insistence on his separateness from communal existence.

Jud is a sexual psychopath, but his sociopathology seems a product of class as well as race. Paul Filmer, Val Rimmer, and Dave Walsh argue that Jud is a threat to middle-class values: "The challenge to the integrity of this envisioned order comes in the form of the primordial instinctuality of Jud Frye. Jud is an outsider in every sense: neither farmer nor cowman, he is Aunt Eller's hired hand, a status that he uses to justify his low self-esteem, despite Aunt Eller's insistence that she and Laurey could not manage to run the farm themselves without his aid."[35] Jud is motivated by a sense of injustice. Aunt Eller acknowledges that she may not be better than anyone else, but she is certainly just as good; Jud, on the other hand, bitterly informs Laurey that she looks down on him because he is only a hired hand. In fact, Jud is disruptive and threatening because he is convinced that his position as a hired hand excludes him from acceptance by the rest of the community. His isolation is, to a large degree, self-made, which he acknowledges in "Lonely Room." No one stops Jud from taking Laurey to the box social. The community allows Jud to bid for her box lunch. Filmer, Rimmer, and Walsh imply that Jud is a product of the city and poses an urban, racial threat to small-town values. Actually, Jud is a hired hand whose employment history precludes the city. His last job was on another farm, where he developed a similar, psychotic sexual obsession with his female employer. His reaction to sexual rejection in that situation—setting fire to the farm—mirrors his reaction when he is rejected by Laurey. Jud is unwilling to be assimilated or whitened. His "primordial instinctuality" is characteristic of the bully who threatens civilization, the individual versus the social contract, the prioritization of fragmentation over community.

In 1943, as Meryle Secrest notes, Oklahoma had only been a state for thirty-six years: "When people thought of it, they thought of immigrants struggling to put down roots in a brand-new world, a struggle that, far from being in the distant past, was very much alive in people's memories."[36] With hindsight, one can see how wartime audiences would recognize it as a metaphor for melting-pot America. Here is *Oklahoma!*'s complexity. Hammerstein creates a nation of territory folk, but they are Americans, not foreigners, who struggle to bond together to become a civilized nation, where the ethnoracial foreigner (Hakim) can be assimilated through whitening and intermarriage. Jud is the villain, both in *Lilacs* and in Hammerstein's musical adaptation, but the distinction between Riggs's melodramatic villain and Hammerstein's usurping, antisocial bully is profound.[37] In *Oklahoma!,* Jud, who bristles at all social authority, threatens civilized values by taking what he wants with no regard for the social contract. Baiting civilized order and decency is the work of a bully or, within the context of World War II, of a fascist. Domestically, as Hammerstein demonstrates in a complex, dense context, it is also the work of the isolationist, who undercuts the necessity of banding together to fight the threat of fascism. Whereas Riggs fashions a melting pot of foreigners who unite to create something new, unpredictable, and dynamic in terms of American identity, Hammerstein creates an Anglo melting pot that endorses the assimilation and tolerance of ethnoracial Otherness. True to his Jewish roots, Hammerstein works within the walls of the community. Rather than creating a New Deal utopia, which would only be attacked by American conservatives and anti-Semites, he redefines American populist ideology to include what populism has traditionally railed against: the ethnoracial Other. It is not the liberal but the country's own insularity that threatens grassroots America.

Through performance, specifically through the casting of Hakim, *Oklahoma!* provided resolution to populist anti-Semitic rhetoric that the Jew posed a threat to small-town, rural values. Joseph Buloff, a veteran of the Yiddish theatre as well as the Broadway stage, played the peddler in the musical, whereas Lee Strasberg, also Jewish, played Hakim in the original production of *Lilacs.* Since Strasberg was immersed in the acting techniques of Stanislavsky and Vakhtangov, it is logical to assume that his performance was nonpresentational and, to an extent, rooted in realism. In contrast, Buloff was a Broadway musical theatre clown, in the tradition of Webber and Fields, Leon Errol, and Willie Howard. Celeste Holm, the original Ado Annie, recalled his antics in an interview with Max Wilk:

> The first day we did our scene he came on eating a banana. Well, the chorus girls thought that was the funniest thing they'd ever seen. The next day he came on with a cane, with which he began hitting me on the ass. He seemed to have no sense of the other actor's responsibilities or his needs. One day Joe stood on my foot; didn't even *know* he was standing on my foot! So I went to Mamoulian [the director] and I explained very quietly that I'd have to get this scene set, one way or the other. I said, "I'm his partner in this scene and I want to know what he's going to do!"[38]

At the same time, Buloff's outrageous stage business was rooted in believability. His persona was gentle and lovable; his ability to make fun of his own defeats and failures could be read as stereotypically Jewish in its ironic self-mockery. This ability to ingratiate himself with his audiences and remain empathetic played against Hakim's libidinous, sexual pursuit of Ado Annie and his aggressive haggling. The actor also spoke with a thick Russian accent, which further linked him with Eastern and Central European immigrants.[39] Buloff was probably the best-known performer in the original cast; it is his picture that accompanied the *New York Times* review of the opening.[40] That Hakim became a nonthreatening, racialized Other in the original production had much to do with Buloff's presentational performance style, his skill as a Jewish star comic, and his gentle, self-mockingly charismatic persona.

Ironically, by the time the film version of *Oklahoma!* was released in the mid-1950s, it was no longer necessary to make Ali Hakim explicitly Jewish. The role was performed by Eddie Albert, who exhibited no stereotypical, ethnoracial traits. By that time, Hammerstein had succeeded so well with his assimilationist strategy that the Jew no longer had to perform Jewishness to make the point that the farmer, the cowboy, and the merchant could all dwell in a productive community. Assimilation no longer demanded ethnic buffoonery. The merchant remained, but the performance of Jewishness vanished from Albert's performance in the film. Carr notes,

> Rather than defining ethnicity either for laughs or sympathy, the new image of America emphasized the American that the ethnic could become. One can thus view the disappearance of the Jew from the screen, not as acquiescence to the Hollywood Question, but as an ideologically charged assertion challenging an older set of assumptions.[41]

No longer a liminal figure hovering between the acceptable and nonacceptable, the Jew had been whitened. *Oklahoma!* had become an assimilationist fantasy. In mid-1950s America, Jewishness no longer had to be burlesqued to be rendered nonmenacing. By the time the film was released, Hakim was simply the merchant. Audiences could see him as Jewish, Persian, or an assimilable, ethnoracial Other.

In the 2002 Broadway revival, mounted just six months after the devastating events of September 11, 2001, Trevor Nunn cast Aasif Mandvi, an Arab, as Hakim. The casting of Mandvi functioned similarly to that of Buloff in the original production, although the Other has changed. At a time when racial profiling exists because of radical Islamicist terrorism, the

Arab American faces hostility and exclusion from a nation engaged in a different kind of war and embroiled in a different concept of Otherness. By rendering the stage Arab nonthreatening after September 11, Nunn endorsed an assimilationist strategy similar to that of Rodgers and Hammerstein, who had portrayed the Jew as harmless during a cultural moment of considerable American anti-Semitism.[42]

Fiddler on the Roof and the 1960s

Fiddler on the Roof offers utopian solutions to the generational clashes produced by an emerging 1960s counterculture. Tevye, a Jewish dairyman living in a Russian *stetl,* confronts challenges to the traditions of both his community and his faith. The play details the compromise necessary for him to accept the marital choices of his three daughters and still retain his own belief system. During the final scene, Tevye and the villagers of Anatevka are forced to leave their homes, many of them bound for America. The implication is that they will carry their traditions with them. At the same time, assimilation will logically result in even greater compromise.

Fiddler opened in September 1964. Although one tends to associate social change in the 1960s with its most turbulent year, 1968, there was much by 1964 to threaten the ideological postwar America of Rodgers and Hammerstein. The assassination of John F. Kennedy occurred ten months before *Fiddler* opened. Before Kennedy's death, Americans, glued to their television sets during the 1962 Cuban missile crisis, faced the real possibility of nuclear war. Martin Luther King delivered his "I Have a Dream" speech in 1963 amidst racial unrest in America's cities, which resulted in the landmark Civil Rights Act of 1964. In 1963 Timothy Leary was fired from Harvard University for conducting experiments with LSD on campus. Even more threatening was the potential for radical activism and campus unrest when students occupied a building at Berkeley in the fall of 1964.[43]

Equally disturbing were challenges to the nuclear family as alternative lifestyles became more visible in urban centers, particularly New York City. One of these alternate lifestyles was homosexuality. In 1963 Robert Doty wrote an article for the *New York Times* entitled "Growth of Overt Homosexuality in City Provokes Wide Concern," which stressed the increasing visibility of homosexuals in New York City and the perception by heterosexuals that public space was being threatened by this sexual subculture.[44] In 1964 a fourteen-page article appeared in *Life* magazine about gay male life in the United States. According to Michael Bronski, "This had the immediate effect of making it clear to mainstream culture that gay people existed and that they had claimed, by a conscious act, public space for themselves in the urban landscape. The gay ghetto, now exposed, could function more overtly as an erogenous zone."[45] With photographs of street hustlers, leather bars, and gay cruising spots in assorted urban areas, the *Life* article forced the heterosexual majority to recognize not only the existence but also the growing openness of gay life.

According to Martin Duberman, a growing awareness of homosexuality was only a signpost for the emergence of an increasingly visible New Left. In *Stonewall,* Duberman argues that the early 1960s telegraphed a significant shift in American consciousness:

> The new homosexuality was part and parcel of a much larger cultural upheaval. The conformity and dutiful deference to authority that had held sway during the fifties were giving way under the hammer blows of the black civil rights struggle, the escalating war in Vietnam, and the emerging ethos of a counterculture that mocked traditional pieties and valorized "doing your own thing." A rapid-fire succession of events from 1963–1965 marked a seismic shift in national consciousness. The number of civil rights demonstrations in 1963 alone reached 930; they were highlighted by "Bull" Connor turning his police dogs loose on demonstrators, the bombing of Birmingham's Sixteenth Street Baptist Church, which took the lives of four little black girls, and the massive civil rights march on Washington.[46]

In a similar vein, Sally Banes argues in *Greenwich Village 1963* that the seeds for cultural change—for postmodernism and the emerging counterculture—were in place by 1963 in Greenwich Village. For Banes, 1963 was a pivotal year:

> In the early Sixties, the arts became an important arena in which aesthetic, personal, and polemical energies were galvanized by people who were convinced, with evangelical fervor, that they had entered into a new covenant with history through the rediscovery of their chosen medium. . . . The early Sixties avant-garde artists did not aim passively to reflect the society they lived in; they tried to change it by producing a new culture.[47]

Banes believes that a radical egalitarianism was the motivating force of the avant-garde of this period and stresses that the ordinary became a crucial element of artistic content. Banes's argument supports 1963 as a time of change, at least in New York, but perhaps it is a bit hyperbolic. In reviewing her book, Robert Brustein commented, "The avant-garde of any period is ultimately significant less for its artistic postures than for its artistic achievements."[48] At the same time, there is something to Duberman and Banes's belief that the seeds of the sexual revolution, the counterculture, the peace movement, gay pride, and postmodernism were being sown by 1963.

Popular music also represented a mainstream change perceptible by the time *Fiddler* opened. With some notable exceptions, the hit parade no longer reflected the Broadway musical. Although songs like "Hello, Dolly" and "The Impossible Dream" could still be popular hits, and the soundtrack album of *West Side Story* was phenomenally successful, these were exceptions rather than the norm for the music industry, which by 1964 catered to a youth culture. Elvis Presley had become a national icon for young Americans by the mid-1950s. Motown, founded by Berry Gordy in 1960 with his recording of the Miracles singing "Way Over There," was entrenched in the national youth culture by 1964 with recording artists such as Martha and the Vandellas and the Supremes.[49] Equally significant, the Beatles' first American recording was released on December 26, 1963.[50] Within a year, the British rock group was immortalized on film with *A Hard Day's Night.*

I do not mean to overstate my case. If the birth of Motown and the rise of the Beatles did not revolutionize American musical tastes for all its citizens, it was difficult in 1964 to live in a vacuum, unaware of a rebellious youth movement, racial unrest, and the need for civil rights legislation. *Fiddler*'s focus on tradition encapsulated the potential threat of disempowerment to its audiences. Although 1964 predates systematic marketing statistics and thorough surveys of audience demographics, *Fiddler*'s success implies a middle-aged (or older) audience likely to identify with a musical about the generation gap. Broadway comedies, such as *Generation* (1965) and *The Impossible Years* (1965) similarly reflected the loss of parental authority. Both comedies were financially successful and became films.

Director-choreographer Jerome Robbins, a Jew, was apparently scrupulous in reworking *Fiddler*'s Sholem Aleichem source material so that it would have more universal appeal. Every effort was made to de-emphasize the Jewishness of the piece by eliminating any Yiddishisms that would limit its audience. In an interview with Stuart Little before the musical opened, Robbins tried to frame *Fiddler* in terms of the social conflict in America at that time: "The play is about tolerance. And about change. This community, because revolution was in the air, lived in a time of great change. And so do we today. When there is change, you gain many things. You also lose many things."[51] In addition to the emerging youth counterculture that threatened the establishment, Robbins referred to "the many parallels [that] exist between the life of the Jewish community in the play and the life of the negro in America today."[52] Although he had testified as a friendly witness before the House Un-American Activities Committee in 1953, an action that might seem to link him with many prominent conservatives, Robbins, in his work for the stage, had a history of investigating social problems, particularly those of discrimination. Civil rights foregrounds "The Small House of Uncle Thomas" in *The King and I* (1951) and the racial intolerance and bigotry of gang warfare in *West Side Story* (1957). During an early rehearsal for *Fiddler*, Robbins asked the actors to improvise a scene in which blacks would try to buy books in a white bookstore in the South.[53] Robbins was clearly trying to make parallels between the Jews in Anatevka and the cultural changes in America in 1964 by broadening the appeal beyond a strictly Jewish audience.

When a Yiddishism or Jewish word is used, as in the song "To Life," the audience is told—in no uncertain terms—exactly what the word means: "To life, to life, l'chaim." According to Robbins's biographer, Greg Lawrence, when Zero Mostel started ad-libbing and inserting Yiddishisms soon after the show opened, Robbins discouraged friends from seeing the show until the star had been replaced. He was well aware that without focusing on the larger issues of social change and the threat to tradition, the musical's chances for success were limited. Before Robbins's involvement in the project, librettist Joseph Stein maintained that most Broadway producers evinced little interest in the material.[54] Even after *Fiddler* opened to affirmative notices, David Merrick declared, "It's a Jewish show. . . . No one will go."[55] In downplaying the Jewishness of the show, Robbins, according to Walter Kerr, was too successful: "'Fiddler on the Roof' takes place in Anatevka, a village in Russia, and I think it might be an altogether charming musical if only the people of Anatevka did not pause every now and then to give their regards to Broadway, with remembrances to Herald Square."[56] Kerr, of course, was in the critical minority. *Fiddler* ran for eight years, managing to comfort a hegemonic Broadway audience for the remainder of the 1960s and through the early 1970s.

At the same time, Robbins's insistence that *Fiddler* transcend its Jewishness implied a change in this audience. Unlike films, which tended to appeal to as broad an audience as possible, Broadway musicals and plays had always catered to an ethnic, urban, sizably New York audience, many of whom were Jewish. Between 1961 and *Fiddler's* opening in 1964, a spate of Jewish musicals opened on Broadway: *Milk and Honey* (1961), *A Family Affair* (1962), *I*

Can Get It for You Wholesale (1962), *What Makes Sammy Run* (1964), and *Cafe Crown* (1964). These musicals all had Jewish themes. *Milk and Honey* focused on American Jews transplanted to an Israeli kibbutz, *A Family Affair* chronicled a Jewish wedding, *I Can Get It for You Wholesale* dealt with the Jewish garment trade, *What Makes Sammy Run* involved the machinations of an overly ambitious Jew in Hollywood, and *Cafe Crown* concerned the Yiddish theatre. All of these musicals lost money, including *Milk and Honey,* which even featured a Yiddish theatre icon, Molly Picon. Similarly, established Yiddish stars who worked in the nonmusical theatre were faring poorly with their vehicles. Menasha Skulnick failed in *The Forty-Ninth Cousin* (1960), while Gertrude Berg flopped in a comedy entitled *Dear Me, the Sky Is Falling In* (1963). Both had long been Broadway box-office draws.

In *The Season,* William Goldman argues that musicals in 1969 were patronized predominantly by Jewish audiences. He defends his position by describing the new musicals of the 1968 season: "Of the standard-brand musical comedies, three out of ten were about Jews: *Golden Rainbow, The Education of H*Y*M*A*N K*A*P*L*A*N,* and *I'm Solomon.*"[57] What he fails to mention is each of these musicals was a financial flop. He goes on to describe planned musicals about Jews: "a musical based on the Rothschilds, a musical based on *Our Crowd,* a musical based on the radio serial *The Goldbergs,* something based on *Everything but Money,* something else about anti-Semitism in the Soviet Union . . . plus a musical version of Bruce Jay Friedman's classic Jewish mother–type novel, *A Mother's Kisses.*"[58] The statistics seem impressive, except that only two of these musicals ever made it to Broadway. *The Rothschilds* (1970) and *Molly* (1973) both lost money. *A Mother's Kisses* closed during its disastrous out-of-town tryout, and, to my knowledge, the other projects never found backing. Goldman does not mention Richard Rodgers's then projected *Two by Two* (1970), a musical based on the Biblical story of Noah, derived from Clifford Odets's *The Flowering Peach* (1954), which had originally starred the previously mentioned Skulnick. *Two by Two,* like *Fiddler,* featured a high-voltage star performance. Danny Kaye injected the Rodgers show with much of the Jewish humor that Robbins found repugnant in Mostel's performance in *Fiddler.* The result was a failure. Maybe David Merrick knew what he was talking about when he refused to produce *Fiddler* because it was a Jewish show.

The failures of these musicals imply several possibilities. Either the New York Jewish audience was not as substantial as it had been in the past or was not sufficient in number to fully support Broadway musicals, whose capitalizations were soaring with inflation. Perhaps changing demographics—

the move to suburbia, to Florida, or to other parts unknown—were responsible for the abdication of an aging Jewish audience. Another possibility is that Jews were more thoroughly assimilated into American culture by the 1960s and were no longer interested in musicals that pandered to their Otherness. Whichever was true, Robbins's focus on tradition and insistence on de-Judaizing the musical was canny and commercial. Audiences were given what Dyer would call a utopian solution to the changes in American society. Compromise between the cultural hegemony and an emerging youthful counterculture was inevitable, but tradition, in the guise of the fiddler following Tevye and his family to America, would remain. Robbins was promising that America was capable not only of incorporating change but also of surviving.

A more radical production of *Fiddler* was staged in 1968 for a nonelitist audience at the Harry A. Eiseman Junior High School 275 in Brownsville, Brooklyn, during the original long-running engagement of *Fiddler* on Broadway. Richard Piro, the drama teacher at the high school, who happened to be of Italian ancestry, decided to mount *Fiddler* to ease tensions between African Americans, who constituted the majority of the student body at Eiseman, and the Jewish community, who comprised the bulk of faculty and administration. Rather than soothing an elitist Broadway cultural hegemony, Piro's production was aimed at an African American audience in an urban ghetto during a moment of great racial unrest between African Americans and Jews. At first, Piro encountered anti-Semitism from his students, who ridiculed the Jewish characters and music. He finally was able to make the students identify their own heritage with that of the denizens of Anatevka. He was not, however, successful in convincing the faculty, most of whom were Jewish, that a black *Fiddler* would not ridicule their traditions and heritage. They feared that the production would add fuel to the racial fire that was already consuming Brownsville and other urban ghettos. In fact, one of the Jewish teachers tried to stop the production by contacting Music Theatre International, who controlled the rights.

Piro nonetheless managed to convince the Brownsville community and school board of the importance of a "black" *Fiddler*. One African American parent welcomed the idea of black Jewface: "Ever since before I was hatched, the white man was playing Negro. They blacked their faces. They wore our clothes and were entertaining people by imitating us and making fun of the way we spoke, we walked, and we sang. And who was there to object? Nobody."[59] Another woman answered objections to the production raised by a Jewish faculty member:

> Many of the boys and girls in this school only know you because you are the teacher who comes to them. They do not know Jews as neighbors. I do. I know you as a neighbor because I grew up in the atmosphere of your people. Therefore, I see you differently. I get the impression that you're worried the children may see you differently. Neighborhoods are changing with people running from one another. . . . The average human being seldom knows other human beings. The situation here can bring awareness.[60]

The final production, although successful as entertainment and as a lesson in cultures for those who participated, provided little resolution to the racial and class struggles in Brownsville. Although the black *Fiddler* received much publicity and apparently was beautifully performed, militant African Americans resented that a ghetto school could demonstrate excellence and tried to stop performances through violent demonstration. The production's success undercut their argument that poor urban African Americans were receiving an inferior education. Jewish teachers were still uncomfortable that their heritage was being embodied by African American students onstage. Piro's *Fiddler* briefly and heroically bandaged the racial turmoil of the community. Although the production received national press coverage and was televised, within a year Piro admitted defeat and resigned from his job.

Piro's experiment was at once inspiring and heartbreaking. Attempting radical social change through musical theatre is an admirable goal and one to be encouraged; on the other hand, it was beyond the parameters of theatre to solve the racial tensions in Brownsville in the 1960s. Although such experiments are enviably altruistic, they often lead to disappointment and disillusionment. For instance, the Living Theatre, in the 1960s, hardly put an end to American capitalism; the company eventually was jailed for tax evasion. Even Brecht, certainly a champion of radical social change, acknowledged the value of offering audiences choices and alternatives to the status quo. Serious musicals mounted on Broadway tend to offer far more conservative solutions to social problems. They paper over unsolvable tensions by proposing utopian solutions to problems that capitalism itself can presumably fix. These solutions satisfy commercial audiences hungry for peaceful change but averse to revolution.

A Chorus Line and the "Me" Generation

If *Fiddler on the Roof* focused on the conflict between an older generation threatened by changes in the fabric of American life, *A Chorus Line* tried to reconcile the 1970s "me" generation with the need for conformity. This alliance would not be easy to achieve. By 1975 the desire for individual autonomy and alternate lifestyles was challenged by an increasingly corporate society that celebrated mediocrity. *A Chorus Line* glorifies the cog in the American wheel. Its conflict is that of insider (the corporate hegemony) versus outsider (the individual).

Not since *Oklahoma!* has a musical so reflected the profound changes in middle-class ideology, because that ideology no longer involved Rodgers and Hammerstein's post–World War II idealization of community or *Fiddler's* tacit acknowledgment of middle-class values. *A Chorus Line* deals with the need to compromise individual autonomy with the corporate establishment. This is a far cry from the Rodgers and Hammerstein canon, where Mr. Snow can become a tycoon, Maria can marry a captain, Anna can domesticate the king of Siam, and Nellie can earn an oceanside villa by marrying a rich Frenchman. The reward for the aspirants of *A Chorus Line* is Andy Warhol's fifteen minutes of fame. In fact, the gypsies (dancers who move from show to show) recognize the brevity of their careers in "What I Did for Love."

During the showstopping finale, "One," they sing of the unseen female star of the musical-within-a-musical. What they are telling us is that the charisma of the female star exists in the audience's perception, and that perception is created not by her but by how the chorus frames her. Their goal is not to share her success but to assure it through their hard work and talent. If her reward is stardom, their glory lies only in their anonymity and loss of identity; they are all the same. The message here is not an egalitarian ideal but a demand for mediocrity. The finale is rousing if dark: metaphorically, the Horatio Alger myth is dead. Individuality, will, and desire no longer guarantee the success that Rodgers and Hammerstein had nostalgically helped to mythologize. The tension in *A Chorus Line* is between the autonomy of the individual and the need to be a team player or, put differently, between outsider and insider. Assimilation of varying lifestyles, gender preferences, races, and ethnicities is still possible but at what cost?

Whereas *Fiddler*'s characters struggle to maintain their identities in a world where their traditions were being challenged, the characters in *A Chorus Line* fight for assimilation into insider status by ultimately losing their identities. Cassie's number, "The Music and the Mirror," represents the striving of the most talented of these aspirants. She is too good to be in the chorus and must fight her talent and genius to acquire a job that necessitates mediocrity. *Fiddler* espouses compromise but suggests, through the final image of the fiddler following Tevye to America, that compromise can be achieved without loss of integrity. *A Chorus Line* seduces its characters into total compromise by promising them the opportunity to do what they love—to dance. In other words, they accept compromise to achieve insider status. The price, however, is painfully steep.

According to Michael Bennett, the director and choreographer, the goal was to make the audience learn and care about each of the characters vying for a job. The reward for each of the aspirants, by the finale, is anonymity and negation of self:

> You're going to get to know all these dancers as individuals and care about each one. Then, at the very end of the play, they're all going to come out in tuxedos and top hats, and you're not going to be able to tell one from another. They're going to blend. They're going to do everything you've ever seen anyone in a chorus line do. It's going to be the most horrifying moment you will ever experience in a theatre. I have a vision of them forming a VF and marching with frozen smiles, like in *Metropolis*. If I do this right, you will never see another chorus line in a theatre. Everybody will reevaluate what it is they're watching.[61]

As the finale of *A Chorus Line* ends, the lights fade on a chorus that looks like high-kicking Rockette übermarionettes. Just as Robbins de-emphasized the Jewishness of *Fiddler,* Bennett related his show business story to the audience's struggles with individual autonomy and corporate acceptance by employing mirrors throughout the production, so that spectators would identify with the plight of the auditioners.

Bennett, however, was too shrewd and commercial a showman to emphasize the more chilling aspects of the loss of individuality and its implications for the audience. The finale, "One," is the quintessential Broadway production number, full of glitz and glamour. Audiences watch it and tend to see this jubilant production number as a reward for the successful gypsies rather than as a cruel debasement. According to John Fiske, "It [entertainment] sees popular culture as a site of struggle, but, while accepting the power of the forces of dominance, it focuses rather upon the popular tactics by which these forces are coped with, are evaded, or resisted."[62] Here, as in *Evita,* the audience subverts the text for its own purposes, but Bennett and the creators of *A Chorus Line* encourage the audience to cheer along with the joyous finale rather than see the dark message behind a stage full of frozen smiles.

Also subverting the text for his own purposes, John Clum attacks *A Chorus Line* for perpetuating false American values: "The musical offers an uncritical presentation of the American notion that personality and private life, not talent or mastery of one's craft, get one a place on America's figurative chorus line."[63] Clum seems to miss the point that Bennett and his collaborators were making. *A Chorus Line* obliterates the Horatio Alger fable of success through hard work and talent. The world of *A Chorus Line* is not the postwar world of Arthur Miller's *Death of a Salesman* (1949); it is indeed personality and lifestyle *in addition to* mastery of one's craft that ensure success. We are meant to see each aspirant for a job as an individual who is willing to sacrifice his own autonomy for a place on the team. Bennett's underlying message is not the glitz of a high-kicking chorus line or a tribute to the Rockettes but a cruel vision of the loss of individuality. These dancers are not Willy Lomans who have the wrong dream; they have no other recourse to make their dream come true than to become team players in the corporate game. What is heartbreaking about the show is how much they want and need to become insiders and how little they anticipate the sacrifice that a position on the "line" will entail.

A Chorus Line mirrored real social problems in 1975. One year earlier, Richard Nixon resigned in disgrace over the Watergate cover-up. Cynicism among the young, however, predated Watergate. In 1968, Americans saw not only the assassinations of Bobby Kennedy and Martin Luther King but also the Columbia University student riots, which ended with students occupying campus buildings, police committing acts of brutality, a dean being shot, and Mark Rudd and the Students for a Democratic Society ordering Grayson Kirk, the president of Columbia, "up against the wall, motherfucker." Following within a year or so were Woodstock, the Stonewall riots, and violent demonstrations at the Chicago Democratic Convention.

By 1970, the best-selling book in America was Richard Bach's *Jonathan Livingston Seagull*. Bach instinctively knew that the search for authenticity and individual autonomy was no longer a function of radical 1960s counterculture politics but of self-actualization: "It [the book] described a corrupt, unworkable society that needlessly constrained its true soarers and seekers. . . . National politics, a sense of national identity and community, strove to bottle up the centrifugal forces that tore at American society, to hold together its diverse, competing elements."[64] After Watergate, the dichotomy between individuality and a corrupt establishment became even more strained and begged some healing solution. By the early 1970s, a vociferous counterculture rejected the establishment and valued individual identity:

> In 1970–1971, one-third of America's college-age population felt that marriage had become obsolete and that having children was not very important. The number identifying religion, patriotism, and "living a clean moral life" as "important values" plummeted. Fifty percent held no living American in high regard, and nearly half felt that America was a "sick society." In this setting, many young Americans no longer saw any reason to heed established conventions about sex, drugs, authority, clothing, living arrangements, food—the fundamental ways of living their lives.[65]

After Watergate the cynicism was, if anything, greater. How does one reconcile one's identity with an establishment that devalues it? On the other hand, if one wishes to succeed, how can one totally reject society and its criteria for success? How much compromise is necessary?

In *A Chorus Line,* the solution is not as utopic as it appears. Bennett apparently had something darker in mind, with his reference to the finale being like *Metropolis,* but he opted for a more optimistic conclusion to please his audiences. In 1971 he had codirected *Follies,* which deals with middle-age disillusionment and the death of the American dream. He apparently fought with codirector Harold Prince during the show's out-of-town tryout to lighten the book and offer audiences hope. According to Ken Mandelbaum, Bennett wanted Neil Simon and George Furth to add some humor to the dark script, whereas Prince insisted on the integrity of the show's original vision. Mandelbaum describes Bennett's frustration:

> One night, Hal grabbed Michael and said, "Michael, trust me. We are in Boston. This is not New York, and the audience is not as sophisticated. The reaction will be very different in New York." . . . At a late [New York] preview, Hal took him out to the lobby and said, "We just got our first review. It's incredible. We're a smash. Of course, she didn't like the book, but we always knew that was a problem." Michael said Hal went on talking but he never heard another word.[66]

The pessimistic *Follies* failed at the box office.

Bennett was not about to make the same mistake twice. By the time he created *A Chorus Line,* he reinvented the very process of developing a Broadway musical. Rather than opening cold on Broadway (or risking a by-then prohibitively expensive out-of-town tryout), Bennett enlisted Joe Papp's help in bankrolling a series of workshops at the Public Theatre to prepare for a commercial Broadway transfer by the Shuberts. In this way, Bennett retained autonomy and control of the project. Besides the finale, Bennett made another concession to guarantee popular success. During previews at the Public, Zach rejected Cassie. Bennett felt that she would never be hired; she was too much of a threat to Zach. Actress Marsha Mason finally persuaded him to change the ending, winning Cassie her place on the line. She argued that audiences would be disappointed; everyone hopes for a second chance.[67]

This same aesthetic can be applied to *Cats* (1982), the longest-running musical in Broadway history, which borrows heavily from *A Chorus Line.* The Lloyd Webber musical focuses not on a diverse group of dancers but on a diverse group of cats, who audition for a second chance or second life on the Heaviside layer. Grisabella, the least likely candidate, wins. *Cats* offers a much more naive solution to the loss of individuality than *A Chorus Line* does. Even though Cassie wins her position on the line, she loses her identity once she becomes a member of the chorus. Grisabella, scruffy and socially outcast, manages to be reborn without having to compromise. Her individuality is rewarded by the establishment in a solution that is commercially inspirational if unlikely.

Les Misérables and the Depoliticization of the 1980s

Les Misérables (1987) marks a turning point in shifting social arrangements but is difficult to isolate in terms of changing American attitudes toward class for a variety of reasons. Audience demographics had changed by the time of the 1980 marketing study conducted by the League of New York Theatres, just as ticket prices had escalated.[68] New audiences, mostly younger and more elitist than ever before, were drawn to Broadway musicals and were willing to pay increasingly astronomic prices.[69] By 1987 marketing strategies had also changed. Nationwide ticket services such as Ticketmaster, the availability of half-priced seats at TKTS on the day of the performance, massive television advertising, and the promotion of megaspectacles for foreign tourists all worked in favor of British imports like *Cats, Les Misérables,* and *Phantom of the Opera* (1988) and contributed to their long runs.[70] In addition to changing audience demographics, *Les Misérables* was an international hit rather than a homegrown American product. It was created in Paris, then produced in London by the Royal Shakespeare Company. After a commercial move to the West End, Cameron MacIntosh remounted the show for Broadway. Certainly the shape of the musical changed drastically from its initial unenthusiastic reception in Paris to its successful New York production. The show premiered in March 1987, during the height of

Reaganism. *Les Misérables* managed to survive that year's stock-market crash, but then so did Broadway megamusicals of the period in general.

Based on the Victor Hugo novel set in Paris during 1832, *Les Misérables* chronicles the life of Jean Valjean, arrested for stealing a loaf of bread. Valjean constantly reinvents himself over the years to conform to society and even becomes the mayor of his town, but despite his saintliness and good deeds, he is hounded by Javert, a policeman determined to send him back to prison. During the course of the play, Valjean befriends the dying prostitute Fantine; rescues Fantine's young daughter, Cosette, from servitude and raises her; risks his life to help Marius, Cosette's lover, during the futile and tragic student revolution by carrying the wounded young man through the sewers of Paris; and finally dies a martyr's death after the suicide of Javert. Authors Boublil and Schönberg address issues of class as well as the conflict between the disenfranchised "poor ones" and the status quo.

The musical is very much a part of its cultural moment, when 1960s radicals such as Jerry Rubin had long since given up the notion of revolution and had embraced Wall Street networking parties. By 1987 the yippies had become yuppies. If the government was corrupt and materialistic, it was nevertheless here to stay; revolt by that time seemed futile. Lawrence Grossberg quotes politician Lee Atwater: "If you want to look at a solid trend for the last fifteen or twenty years, it is that the American people are cynical and turned off about all the institutions and politics is one."[71] Certainly cynicism about the government was nothing new in 1987, but the yuppie's aesthetic of complacent acquisition and the decentralization of government during the Reagan years had led to a resigned, apathetic, depoliticized America: "The proliferation of statements suggesting, not only that the various movements of the 1960s and 1970s are dead but that their struggles were largely ineffective, is part of a larger rhetoric of helplessness which entails that control has always to be surrendered to someone else, whether corporate technology or the new conservatism."[72] The government may not be good, but revolution is futile. The counterculture of the 1960s and 1970s realized that rebelliousness had changed nothing; if anything, it had led to a greater conservatism.

Similarly, in *Les Misérables,* the student revolt does nothing to change the government. The students are slaughtered behind the barricades. Marius sings "Empty Chairs and Empty Tables" to his dead comrades, who have sacrificed their lives in vain. Even poor Eponine, who leads Valjean to Marius, is killed, as is the child Gavroche. Each time Valjean reinvents himself as a respected member of the community, he is exposed as an ex-convict and must create a new life for himself. What the musical does preach is the potential for individual good despite social evil, a kind of utopian solution for the politically cynical. Altruism becomes a goal that can be better accomplished by the individual, particularly a saint like Valjean, rather than through the government or through society. Even the relentless policeman Javert finally realizes that the value system he has believed in all his life is a lie and commits suicide.

Les Misérables revels in the misery of its characters, with little promise of any real solution. The outcasts and social renegades are doomed. When MacIntosh first acquired the rights to the French musical, he approached Alan Jay Lerner to adapt the lyrics and the book. Lerner was loathe to tackle the project; he wrote about people's dreams, not about their misery. In fact, the enormous appeal of the musical reminds me of Robert Brustein's assessment of *Miss Saigon* (1991), which he labels an example of the theatre of guilt:

> But it is a real question whether this glitzorama is an appropriate vehicle for stimulating charitable impulses—and whether people seeking a night on the town are going to respond to such exhortations with anything more practical than passing nods and sentimental sighs. I seem to remember audiences at *Nicholas Nickleby,* after the curtain came down on an impoverished waif in the hero's arms, gingerly wending their way past the homeless lying on the streets of New York.[73]

If there is a solution to social problems in *Les Misérables,* it lies in preaching liberal homilies to the already converted, which is perhaps the root of Dyer's pessimism about musicals and class: musicals tend to reject solutions to social problems that capitalism cannot potentially supply.

In a similar vein, Brustein questions, as does Peter Brook, the real power of theatre to create social change. He stresses Chekhov's position that it is the job of the playwright to present his case to the jury (the audience), not to provide solutions. Serious musicals, like *Les Misérables,* are at best well-meaning but fairly ineffectual in any real sense of healing social problems: "Theatre people have always had a soft spot for causes—rarely the cause of theatre. Smarting over recurrent charges that their work lacks social dimension, many American playwrights have begun to compensate through displays of conscience, preaching liberal sermons to already converted parishioners."[74] Here Brustein reiterates a very old argument. St. Augustine questioned the potential for change in theatrical works that pandered to audiences who delighted in wallowing in their own guilt and in the sufferings of others: "Why is it that men enjoy feeling sad at the sight of tragedy and suffering on the stage, although they would be most unhappy if they had to endure the same fate themselves? Yet they watch the plays because they hope to be made to feel sad, and the feeling of sorrow is what they enjoy. What miserable delirium this is!"[75] Rather than incite audiences to relieve the misery of the unfortunate, theatre, for Augustine, dangerously encouraged audiences to enjoy the misfortune of others.

Despite Brechtian distancing techniques employed by Trevor Nunn and John Caird, *Les Misérables* seems to confirm Augustine's theory. D. A. Miller agrees. He argues that the sung-through musical destroys the structural opposition between narrative and number, which is also consistent with Richard Dyer's theory that songs often provide utopian solutions to social problems raised by the libretti of musicals. The finale of *A Chorus Line* is an appropriate example. Michael Bennett ultimately chose the glamour and glitz of show business rather than the horror of *Metropolis,* which the book scenes confirm. Bennett's finale opts for the utopian solution to the problem of individual autonomy versus the corporate establishment: escapism.

The sung-through musical, on the other hand, destroys "those continual feats of negation that made the Broadway musical uniquely, preciously utopian."[76] For Dyer, musical numbers were an attempt to deny the misery or unhappiness that preceded and sometimes survived them in the dialogue. Miller's conclusion is that the sung-through musical destroys the concept of entertainment as utopia: "The unbroken lugubriousness of the score of *Les Mis* (a show in which the few characters who don't die remain permanently guilt-tripped by those who do) conduced to so numb an acquiescence in the status quo that it was doubtful whether the same theatregoer who had just finished weeping for 'the miserable ones' even recognized them when they reappeared outside the theatre asking for spare change."[77] *Les Misérables* is depoliticized in that it seems to offer no practical solutions to social problems; it asks nothing of its audiences except empathy for the downtrodden. Indeed, its utopian solution is Valjean's martyrdom, which predates Bush's thousand points of light. Martyrdom is an attractive idea but hardly a compelling, practical solution to individual suffering.

The tension between the original cultural moment and the world of subsequent audiences remains a challenge for each of the musicals discussed in this chapter. Even the most popular of musicals is universal and timeless *only* in its willingness to adapt to the values, anxieties, and tensions of new audiences in new cultural moments. *Oklahoma!* has recently been revived unsuccessfully on Broadway. Rumor has it that a new production of

A Chorus Line is in the works. Whether the revival will be a recreation of the Michael Bennett original or a reenvisioning is unclear. *Les Misérables* has only recently ended its marathon long run.

In this context, perhaps it is worth looking at the 2002 Broadway revival of *Oklahoma!,* since it illustrates the discrepancy between the world of the author and the world of contemporary American audiences. Certainly the Broadway transfer of Trevor Nunn's acclaimed London restaging was eagerly anticipated by New York audiences after September 11. The Nunn revival opened on Broadway in March 2002 to surprisingly lukewarm reviews. Margo Jefferson, in the *New York Times,* observed that this *Oklahoma!* was "lovely to look at and delightful to hear, but once it's over, there isn't much to feel or remember."[78] It is ironic that this archetypal slice of Americana was greeted with faint praise at a cultural moment that seemed perfect for its restoration. The publicity generated by the 1998 production in London suggested a reenvisioning—a more sexually raw, gritty interpretation. For Clive Barnes in the *New York Post,* "Nunn gives us 'Oklahoma!' raw—complete with a near-rape of its heroine and tensions between the farmhands and cowboys—and some will miss the sugarcoating."[79] Just as *Oklahoma!* mythologized an idyllic, rural America, the musical itself seems to have been mythologized and to have taken on a life independent of its own production history, another example of the inadvertent epic. For instance, Barnes's comments and those of the other reviewers in praise of Schuyler Hensley's revisionist Jud are strange, since his portrayal was very much in line with that of Rod Steiger in the film version, in which Jud tries to rape Laurey on the way to the box social. Certainly, Hensley's performance was no more nuanced than Steiger's or Martin Vidnovic's in the 1979 Broadway revival, or from all accounts, Howard Da Silva's in the original production.

Perhaps Nunn's Broadway *Oklahoma!* was disappointing because it was not dark enough. Americans raised during the 1960s amidst the war in Vietnam are more cynical than the generation that greeted the original production. During World War II, America could easily identify its enemies within clear geographical and national boundaries. The war against terrorism is not analogous. Terrorist cells are not limited to Afghanistan, Iraq, and North Korea but exist in countries allied to America, including Saudi Arabia, Germany, and, ironically, the United States itself. The enemy, unfortunately, remains faceless; its future plan of attack, mysterious. As Americans progressively realized this new situation after *Oklahoma!*'s March 2002 Broadway premiere, the show's weekly grosses continued to decline. The revival closed after less than a year's run at a substantial financial loss.

Moreover, American attitudes toward class and race have shifted dramatically since the 1940s; the issue of community versus separatism has not disappeared but only become more complicated as old Anglo-American notions of the white melting pot have turned to a multiracial salad bowl. This notion of a salad bowl is closer to Lynn Riggs's vision of an Indian territory filled with multiracial foreigners who nevertheless band together to coexist in a community than it is to Hammerstein's midcentury belief in an Anglo melting pot, in which the Jew or ethnoracial outsider achieves assimilation by being whitened. For years, *Oklahoma!* has represented an archetypal slice of Americana; however, Hammerstein's canny wartime ability to reconcile rural populism with urban notions of New Deal assimilation and tolerance seems a bit naive in the disturbingly complex political and sociological climate of 2005. It will be interesting to see how future productions of the Rodgers and Hammerstein musical, along with *Fiddler, A Chorus Line,* and *Les Mis,* adapt themselves to the tensions and anxieties of new audiences in new sociocultural moments.

5

◆ ◆ ◆ ◆ ◆ ◆ ◆

Enigmatic Characters and the Post-Stonewall Musical

In discussing nonintegrated musical comedy in chapter 2, I noted that star comics played with notions of ethnicity, race, and gender in fashioning fluid star personae. As writers of the integrated musical gradually try to shift authority from the performer as cocreator to the text, often the text itself features at least one leading character who is written in an especially enigmatic manner, by which I mean open or incomplete. In a form noted for stereotyped lines of business (the comic soubrette, male dancing lead, romantic hero), it is ironic that many of the most memorable characters and relationships in the integrated musical are conceived as unfinished. Just as the star comics of musical comedy commented provocatively on the messiness of American identity, enigmatic characters in the integrated musical similarly draw attention to provocative issues about gender and sexuality. Sometimes the incompleteness is filled in by performance; sometimes it is left unfinished, a nagging reminder that happy endings in musicals are akin to the Euripidean deus ex machina. They are attempts to paper over the disturbing issues that the plays raise.

This chapter deals with enigmatic characters in three musicals produced during the season that followed the Stonewall riots: *Company* (1970), *Coco* (1969), and *Applause* (1970). The musicals are open and incomplete in that the principal characters are sexually ambiguous, either through text, performance, or both. These musicals, products of a definite cultural marker, bridge the closeted attitude of mainstream musical theatre with a sexual revolution increasingly difficult for audiences of the time to ignore. Before discussing how each of these musicals deals with homosexuality, however, I will make my case for the power of the unfinished, scripted character.

Writing of dramatic characterization, Eric Bentley observes that often the greatest characters are "open," by which he means incomplete. Often, performance is an attempt to fill in what is written as unfinished:

> The great characters—Hamlet, Phaedra, Faust, Don Juan—have something enigmatic about them. . . . A mysterious character is one with an open definition—not completely open, or there will be no character at all, and the mystery will dwindle to a muddle, but open as, say, a circle is open when most of the circumference has been drawn. Hamlet might be called an accepted instance of such a character, for, if not, what have all those critics been doing, with their perpetual redefining of him? They have been closing the circle which Shakespeare left open.[1]

The openness or mystery often stems from several causes: the audience has incomplete information about a character, the character behaves in ways that are inconsistent and puzzling, the motivations behind a character's actions are either incomplete or omitted. Inconsistency and incompleteness open the character.[2] Sometimes the circle is closed in production choices; sometimes it is left open. For example, the reasons for Iago's extreme villainy are puzzling. Is he inherently evil? Is he in love with Desdemona and jealous of Othello? Is he in love with Othello and jealous of Desdemona? The last was Sir Laurence Olivier's motivation when he played Iago opposite Ralph Richardson's Othello. Shakespeare never tells us. Is Gertrude a loving mother or a monster? Is she oversexed and rather foolish? Was she unfaithful to Hamlet's father while the former king was still alive? Is she aware that Claudius has murdered her husband? Does she know the poison is meant for Hamlet when she drinks it? Again, through omission, Shakespeare enriches the character.

Often the most memorable characters in integrated musicals are similarly mysterious. Julie, in *Show Boat*, appears in a mere three scenes and sings only two songs; yet, she is unforgettable because Hammerstein shrouds her in mystery. During the first act, Julie is presented as a mulatta married to Steve, a white man, who is her protector and with whom she is very much in love. Midway through the act, she is banished from the show boat because she has tried to pass as "white." The next time she appears is halfway through the second act. At this point she has become alcoholic, is working in a Chicago nightclub, and is without a mate. In the first act, she sings "Can't Help Lovin' That Man," a tune that presumably refers to her husband. In the second act, she croons "Bill," a number she rehearses at the nightclub and which again presumably refers to Steve. Hammerstein, however, omits the history of her marriage. Did Steve walk out on her? Did she leave him? Did he die? Why did she become an alcoholic? Is there a hint that she is promiscuous now that she is alone? What happens to her after she leaves the club to give Magnolia her break? Julie is as fluid a character as any of the female stars or male star comics that played with identity in the non-integrated musical. Racially, she is neither black nor white and plays with both of these identities in "Can't Help Lovin' That Man." The first chorus is sung as the white Julie advising Magnolia to be careful about love. The second chorus is a defiant proclamation that she is not ashamed of her black heritage. Julie is memorable for her complexity, but that complexity stems from the character's openness.

Laurey is similarly enigmatic in *Oklahoma!* She is obviously attracted to Curly. Is she sexually attracted to Jud, against her better judgment? Does Jud's preoccupation with sex disgust her, titillate her, or both? Is she attracted to Jud *because* he disgusts her? How does her lack of a father leave her prey to Jud? How does the ballet reveal her sexual fantasies? What are these fantasies? Is she dreaming dirty dreams of being one of Jud's postcard girls so that she can be forced to submit to him against her will? Does Curly's cockiness attract her, repel her, or both? Do her reservations about Curly involve his inability to provide her with the fancy lace tablecloths and other expensive items the peddler brings back from Kansas City? Hammerstein's refusal to provide answers to these questions makes Laurey the most interesting character in the text. The production (or performance) will either close the open circle of her character or leave it for audiences to decode. The same can be said of Julie Jordan in *Carousel.* Is this a musical about the victim of a wife beater? Why does Julie remain with a husband who refuses to find work and abuses her? The libretto tells the audience about Julie's strength but, at the same time, implies her masochism. If there are answers to these questions, they appear in production, not in the text itself.

Alan Jay Lerner, a much-married, presumably heterosexual lyricist and librettist, specialized in sexually ambiguous yet provocative love triangles in his texts written during the 1940s, 1950s, and 1960s. In *Brigadoon* (1947),

Tommy and Jeff, best friends, wander through the Scottish highlands and discover a town that awakes for one day every hundred years. Tommy falls in love with Fiona but leaves her to return to New York with Jeff, knowing she will disappear, along with Brigadoon, for another hundred years. At the final curtain, however, he is drawn back to the Scottish highlands, where magically he is reunited with Fiona. How significant is the homosocial bonding between Tommy and Jeff? Is Jeff the obstacle that keeps Tommy from staying with Fiona? Lerner's script obliquely fails to spell out any answers, and this failure is, paradoxically, its strength, as alert performers and playgoers will sense. In *My Fair Lady* (1956), Eliza Doolittle shares a house with Professor Higgins and Colonel Pickering, two self-confirmed old bachelors who not only declare they are likely to remain so but also wonder why a woman can't be more like a man. How will Eliza accommodate herself to their relationship after the final curtain? Lerner tacks on a romantic closing scene, in which Eliza returns to Higgins with the strains of "I Could Have Danced All Night" playing in the background, but the audience is left wondering whether she will enjoy fetching and carrying for Higgins and Pickering when the music stops playing. The musical is more interesting for the provocative, unanswered questions it raises than for its "happy ending."

In *Camelot* (1960), Arthur and Lancelot love Guenevere, as well as each other. In T. H. White's *Once and Future King,* Lerner's source material, Lancelot is physically ugly. In the original Broadway production, Lancelot was played by Robert Goulet, the archetypal eight-by-ten glossy of his day. Lerner's glamorization of Lancelot turns the love triangle into a classic, closeted homosexual fantasy: one man symbolically sleeping with his powerful male friend by seducing the friend's wife. Perhaps the most startling version of this gender-fluid fantasy occurs in the film version of *Paint Your Wagon,* which portrays a ménage à trois that involves two gold prospectors, played by Clint Eastwood and Lee Marvin, and the woman to whom they are both married, played by Jean Seberg. Since the musical is set in the West during the gold rush, where the abundance of men and scarcity of women preclude traditional middle-class family values, Lerner is raising provocative questions about sexual behavior and its relationship to societal conditioning.[3] Each of these Lerner texts is open and enigmatic; each involves relationships that raise more questions than they answer. If Lerner is deliberately vague about the sex lives of his characters, that is what makes them so intriguing, particularly for their time. Perhaps the characters are no more aware of their sexual proclivities and yearnings than the members of the audience or, indeed, than their creator. Lerner's most successful musicals were written in an era of postwar family values and few alternative lifestyles besides the nuclear family. At the same time, the ambiguity of these relationships plays into American anxiety about gender and identity, much as the star performers of the 1920s, 1930s, and 1940s played with gender, class, race, and ethnicity. The texts are open to interpretation, as are the characters. It would be interesting to remount these productions and explore the homosocial or bisexual implications of these relationships in a twenty-first-century cultural climate. Eliza can still end up with Higgins, Tommy can still return to Fiona, and Guenevere can still enter the convent, but there is a rich, ambiguous subtext to be mined en route to the final curtain.

The Rise of the Double Entendre

Before discussing *Company, Coco,* and *Applause* and how they deal with homosexuality, gender, and identity, it will be helpful to examine both the attitude toward and treatment of homosexuals in both musical theatre and nonmusical theatre prior to Stonewall and then frame these musical within their cultural context. Much has been written about the relationship between musical theatre and a gay sensibility, including John Clum's *Something for the Boys.*[4] Gay men arguably have had a strong affinity for musicals, at least from the 1930s through the 1960s. Although Clum links this affinity to a gay sensibility, Gore Vidal dismisses the notion, arguing that there are no homosexual or heterosexual persons, only acts.[5] The notion of a gay sensibility essentializes the homosexual.

Edmund White is equally skeptical about the notion of a gay sensibility. In *States of Desire,* he frames the term in the context of historical relativism: "What we can discuss is the gay taste of a given period. A taste cultivated (even by some heterosexuals). What we can detect is a resemblance among many gay works of art made at a particular moment—a resemblance partially intended and partially drawn without design from a shared experience of anger or alienation or secret, molten camaraderie."[6] If one is to use White's definition that gay sensibility is the taste of a given period, what did the theatre, and more particularly, the musical theatre, offer from the 1930s through the 1960s that gays embraced so enthusiastically? Certainly as I mentioned in chapter 2, musical theatre stars of this era, through their playful and antic appropriation of a multiplicity of identities in their performances, helped allay gay anxiety about America's attitude toward gender and role playing. Central to this playfulness about gender was the use of the double entendre, which was particularly noticeable in the musicals of Cole Porter, Lorenz Hart, and Noel Coward and the performances of Beatrice Lillie and Mae West. Lillie attracted a particularly large homosexual following for her outrageous double entendres, most famously for her deadpan rendition of "There Are Fairies at the Bottom of Our Garden." West, whose repartee relied heavily on the sexual double entendre, lifted her comic persona from Bert Savoy, a female impersonator of the 1920s.

The double entendre was a product of an era repressive of homosexuals, which was characterized by antigay legislation and regulations. Homophobic laws, by their very existence, imply that gays were not always closeted. As George Chauncey points out, "If homosexuality had always been so invisible and homosexuals had always been confined to the closet, why were such rules even enacted?"[7] Obviously this was not the case. Chauncey describes the active homosexual presence on the streets and clubs of New York City between 1910 and 1930. One Broadway theatre was named after Julian Eltinge, a female impersonator and major star of his day. Although Greenwich Village and Harlem were centers of New York gay life, during the 1920s and early 1930s, gay entertainers and mixed clubs thrived in the Times Square area until the repeal of Prohibition.

Many of the Prohibition nightclubs were owned by racketeers and featured "pansy acts," a craze during the early 1930s. *Pansies,* a slang term for flamboyantly effeminate men, came into popular use during 1920–1933, roughly the Prohibition years. Many of these stereotypically effeminate performers began their careers in Greenwich Village or in Harlem. During Prohibition, they brought their acts to midtown venues. The pansy craze, according to Chauncey, was actually a function of the cultural upheaval caused by Prohibition:

> By criminalizing much of New York City's nightlife, Prohibition gave control of that nightlife to men and women from the "lower classes" who introduced middle-class audiences to "coarse" forms of entertainment previously restricted to working-class neighborhoods. Fairies were a part of the culture of those neighborhoods, and they moved with the gangsters to Times Square and other centers of middle-class nightlife.[8]

Racketeers fought over control of these midtown speakeasies. On January 25, 1931, gunfire erupted at the Club Abbey, a notorious "pansy" venue where Jean Malin was host and entertainer. The club's owner, Dutch Schultz, went into hiding, but the shootout marked the beginning of a war between rival gangs to control the midtown liquor trade.[9] With repeal, the gay men and women, so visible during the Prohibition era, were suddenly perceived as dangerous rather than amusing, as a backlash gained momentum to exclude them from public life and visibility. Curfews were enforced, and clubs that catered to a mixed clientele were instructed that homosexuals were not to be served. By the time LaGuardia was elected mayor in 1933, he outlawed the appearance of drag queens from Fourteenth Street to Seventy-second Street in Manhattan. By 1933 state regulations also prohibited gay men and women from gathering in licensed public establishments. Gay and lesbian bars still existed, but they were generally Mafia-owned, catered to a working-class clientele, and were subject to police harassment and payoffs. Gay men and women who were more well-to-do often frequented straight nightspots, where they were tolerated as long as they were discreet.

Just as the 1920s were characterized by a visible homosexual presence in the streets of New York, musical revues during the decade often featured homosexual innuendo, most notably in Frank Fay's monologues and routines in *Artists and Models* (1923 and 1924) and in *The Ritz Revue* (1924), which reportedly had so many references to homosexuality that critic Percy Hammond joked that Krafft-Ebing could have been one of the lyricists.[10] One sketch was entitled "The Four Horse-Women," a reference to lesbianism, and another involved "fairy tales" that Hammond thought needed decoding for many innocents in the audience. Gay themes were embraced by nonmusical theatre as well. Mae West's *Sex* (1926), *The Virgin Man* (1927), and most notorious, *The Captive* (1926), a play about a married woman drawn to a lesbian lover, were all raided by the police and forced to close. West's production of *The Drag* (1927), which culminated in an onstage drag ball, was raided in Bayonne, New Jersey, during its tryout engagement and never opened on Broadway. The explicit sexuality of these theatrical productions produced the Wales Padlock Act, which allowed the New York district attorney to padlock for a year any theatre that presented salacious material, namely gay characters or gay issues.[11]

The padlock laws did not eliminate homosexual themes, but producers and theatre owners were careful to make them considerably more oblique than they had appeared in the 1920s. In fact, the Shuberts capitalized on the Padlock Act immediately after the 1927 raids by presenting Texas Guinan in *Padlocks of 1927*, a revue whose title was obviously meant to titillate audiences. In 1933 both Mordaunt Hall's *The Green Bay Tree* and Noel Coward's *Design for Living* dealt with male homosexuality, but the productions were "tasteful," and the homosexuality was never explicitly mentioned. In 1934 Lillian Hellman's *The Children's Hour* dealt with a child's lies about an "unnatural relationship" between two women. Critics, concerned with censorship, tended to ignore or downplay the homosexual themes of these plays in their reviews, although this stance sometimes met with opposition. After the opening of *The Green Bay Tree,* one critic allegedly remarked, "My brothers of the First Night Garden, remembering the bad luck of 'The Captive,' are prone to pretend that Mr. Shairp's play . . . has nothing to do with the way of a man with a man. Well, if it has nothing to do with that, it has nothing to do with anything."[12] Reviewing *The Children's Hour,* Burns Mantle sidestepped the issue of lesbianism by arguing, "The true theme is the curse of scandalmongering . . . the kind of vicious lying that may easily wreck the lives of innocent persons."[13] Theatre still dealt with homosexuality, but gingerly.

By the early 1930s, as Chauncey observes, a concerted effort was in effect to make gays disappear in New York. Any licensed bar that served a homosexual male or female was subject to closure; any theatre that explicitly presented gay characters faced padlocking; and with the Hays code in Hollywood and the rise of the Catholic Legion of Decency, any film dealing with gay issues forfeited distribution.[14] By the mid-1930s, the pansy craze had turned into homophobia. It was common in burlesque shows for straight comics to ape the pansy acts that were so popular in Manhattan a few years earlier. Straight men donned drag and stereotypical swishy mannerisms; homosexual situations—men kissing and goosing each other—were exploited for laughter. Audiences roared at these antics, which amounted to the gay equivalent of blackface.

Even more disturbing, during the late 1930s gay men, like the Jews of the Middle Ages, were linked by the press to a series of crimes that involved the ritual murder of young boys. Homosexuals were no longer a spectacle of fun but a dangerous social threat.[15] The demonization of homosexuals continued through World War II and McCarthyism. It is ironic that America was fighting its own anti-Semitism and homophobia at the same time GIs were sent abroad to fight fascism and the persecution of these same two minorities. In the fall of 1959, *Coronet* magazine enumerated the homosexual menace: "Once a man assumes the role of homosexual, he often throws off all moral restraints. Some male sex deviants do not stop with infecting their often innocent partners; they descend through perversions to other forms of depravity, such as drug addiction, burglary, sadism, and even murder."[16] Under the circumstances, it made sense for homosexuals to keep a low profile, which often included double lives and marriage, as well as incidents of police entrapment and blackmail.

The closeting of homosexuals that began during the early 1930s led to coding and the use of the double entendre. The antigay laws and regulations turned the double entendre into a strategy to help gay men pass in straight culture.[17] Gay men appropriated standard terms and words and twisted them into gay meanings. The word *gay* itself referred to female prostitutes before it referred to homosexual men, just as *trick* and *trade* denoted the customers of prostitutes. *Cruising* alluded to a streetwalker's search for clients, while *coming out* was associated with debutantes.[18]

Gay men could frequent straight bars; they just had to be discreet. During World War II, the Astor Bar in Times Square was a notorious gay pickup spot. The huge bar was oval. One side was straight, whereas the other was gay. Often a stranger would sit unknowingly on the wrong side of the bar, so conversation had to be discreet and coded. "She" invariably referred to a man, possibly a boyfriend, even if "she" bought her suits at Brooks Brothers. According to Chauncey, coded conversations could be quite amusing: "'I adore seafood. Gorge myself, whenever the fleet's in. But I can't abide fish,' [a gay man] might say, and any gay man would instantly know that the speaker was turned on by sailors and turned off by women, while the puzzled Mr. and Mrs. Reader's Digest, listening in, would assume this was a discussion about food preferences."[19] Coding then became a humorous strategy in which gay men could communicate their sexual preferences in public spaces.

Since so many musicals were written, directed, choreographed, designed, and performed by gays, it was not surprising that the musical often offered both a plethora of double entendres during this period of gay repression as well as a soothing balm to gay anxieties about identity. Perhaps the most blatant coded references to homosexuality occur in *Jubilee* (1935), a musical with a Cole Porter score and a Moss Hart book, in which a royal family determines to spend a day as commoners. Although the queen, originally played by the deadpan, middle-aged comedienne Mary Boland, instructs her new friends to call her "Butch," she develops a letch for a narcissistic movie actor–bodybuilder modeled on Johnny Weismuller. Another character is suspiciously reminiscent of an effete Noel Coward. During a masquerade ball, a character modeled after the lesbian society hostess Elsa Maxwell tries to determine the identity of her blindfolded guests: "Are you a king?/ Are you a queen? / Well, you certainly can swing your swing."[20] The lyrics presumably refer to the sexual proclivities of most of the characters at the party.

If the double entendres became too noticeable and verged on the indiscreet, critics occasionally became uncomfortable. Lorenz Hart provoked *New York Post* critic Richard Watts with the book and lyrics to *By Jupiter*

(1942), a musical about a tribe of Amazons who rule their country while their milksop husbands skulk in the background. Watts complained, "What seems to me infinitely wearying [and] infinitely annoying is the attempted humor that is supposed to spring from homosexuality and kindred forms of degeneracy."[21] Several critics were similarly offended by Cole Porter's *Out of This World* (1950), a musicalization of Jean Giradoux's *Amphitryon 38.* Instead of scantily clad chorus girls, the show was marked by nearly nude, muscular chorus boys, perhaps an inspiration for Jack Cole's droll gym scene in the film version of *Gentlemen Prefer Blondes* in the early 1950s, where Jane Russell sings "Is There Anyone Here for Love?" to a chorus of uninterested bodybuilders.

During this period of gay closeting, homosexual men responded not only to the double entendres of the Cole Porter, Noel Coward, and Rodgers and Hart musicals but also to the strong female stars who crossed lines of gender and ethnicity and invariably succeeded in snatching the man of their choice through will and desire. Many of these musicals were nonintegrated and open in that they relied on the performer as cocreator of the text.

Later, integrated musicals became open or incomplete in different ways. For instance, *West Side Story* (1957) was created by a reportedly all–gay-bisexual-lesbian production team: Leonard Bernstein (music), Stephen Sondheim (lyrics), Arthur Laurents (book), Jerome Robbins (direction and choreography), Oliver Smith (sets), Irene Sharaff (costumes), and Jean Rosenthal (lighting). According to Ethan Mordden, the gay overtones of *West Side Story* are unmistakable. He claims that Riff and Tony are obviously lovers, just as Romeo and Mercutio are obviously lovers in *Romeo and Juliet.*[22] Although I would disagree on both counts, *West Side Story* has exerted an enormous appeal to gay men and lesbians:

> To many gay adults coming of age in the sixties, the romance, violence, danger, and mystery so audible on the original cast album, all felt like integral parts of the gay life they had embraced. The lyrics of "Somewhere," in particular, seemed to speak directly to the gay experience before the age of liberation. In 1996, it was one of the songs chosen for the first mass gay wedding of two hundred couples in San Francisco, presided over by the city's mayor, Willie Brown.[23]

Here is a case where authorial intent is irrelevant; the text is wide open. It is logical that various groups will choose to read a performance of a work of popular culture as containing a secret message for them. For Tony and Maria to be really together, everything in their past must die, including those they love (Bernardo and Riff). That is the fantasy of the "Somewhere" ballet. Whether one chooses to read *West Side Story* as a musical about bigotry between Polish Americans and Puerto Ricans, or whites and African Americans, or straights and gays, "Somewhere" is a new place, where the prejudices of the American past magically disappear. This meaning is certainly relevant to the era of the closeted gay, but the text, incomplete, is subject to coding by other groups as well; it is open to a plurality of readings.

Gay Characters and Gay Issues in 1960s American Theatre

Before discussing how the texts of three post-Stonewall musicals that dealt with homosexuality can be regarded as open, it is important to frame these musicals in terms of the cultural moment that led to Stonewall and gay activism. It is also important to frame the three musicals in terms of the American theatre of the 1960s, both mainstream and experimental, and how that theatre dealt with gay characters and issues.

As both Sally Banes and Martin Duberman argue, the 1960s set the stage for what finally erupted into the Stonewall riots.[24] Tired of antigay attitudes, laws, and regulations, a growing artistic community in Greenwich Village advocated sexual dissidence. As Alan Sinfield observes, "By 1966, *Time* was complaining that homosexual ethics and esthetics are staging a vengeful counterattack on what deviates call the 'straight' world."[25] Many who eventually turned the Stonewall riots into a revolution and founded the Gay Liberation Front had their roots in other activist causes during the 1960s, including the civil rights movement:

> From the black civil rights movement came an awareness of the inequities of American life; from the women's movement, consciousness of sexism and the profoundly important idea that the personal is the political, that one's experience *mattered;* from the antiwar struggle, the revelation that the government operated as a bulwark of conformity and privilege; from the countercultural revolution, the injunction to reject all received authority, to "do it now, to be what you want to be."[26]

Militant gays, unlike the earlier Mattachine Society, were no longer willing to concede that homosexuality was an illness or psychological disease. The strategies they were prepared to use to gain equality were the strategies they had learned from their participation in the civil rights movement, the defense of the Black Panthers, and the antiwar movement.

In a 1967 article, *Time* argued that homosexuals wanted to subvert straight society: "Even in ordinary conversation, most homosexuals will sooner or later attack the things that normal men take seriously."[27] Rather than feeling ashamed of their sexual feelings and sexual habits, gay men were beginning to wonder what exactly caused such antipathy among straight culture. For Michel Foucault, it was the gay lifestyle, not the gay sex act that threatened institutionalized straight society: "It is the prospect that gays will create as yet unforeseen kinds of relationships that many people cannot tolerate . . . and it is possible that changes in established routines will occur on a much broader scale as gays learn to express their feelings for one another in more various ways and develop new life-styles not resembling those that have been institutionalized."[28] Echoing Foucault, Arthur Laurents denigrates the attempt of gay men to ape heterosexual lifestyles: "Nothing could be more stupid. I mean that one is sort of the husband and the other is sort of the wife and they have to have fidelity and all this kind of nonsense—instead of seeing how lucky you are if you're two men and have this freedom."[29] Rejecting the need for double entendres and coding, gay activists, both politically and artistically, were positing that homosexuality was an alternative lifestyle, no better or worse than straight culture.

This reevaluation of the politics of the closet was mirrored theatrically in the Caffé Cino, the primary source of new gay plays in Greenwich Village between 1964 and 1967. Proprietor Joe Cino produced new plays by Doric Wilson, William Hoffman, Tom Eyen, Jean-Claude Van Italie, Paul Foster, and H. M. Koutoukas; sponsored directors, including Marshall Mason, Tom O'Horgan, Neil Flanagan, and Ron Link; and promoted actors such as Bernadette Peters, who originated Ruby in the campy *Dames at Sea* (1966) at the Cino before its off-Broadway transfer in 1968. To Arthur Bell, a *Village Voice* columnist and gay activist, the Cino "exemplified the freedom that was to come. . . . The Cino group made me want to assert my own gayness to the world."[30] Cino was a remarkable man; he was also haunted by his own demons. After his lover, an electrician, was killed, he committed suicide. Friends tried to sustain the theatre on Cornelia Street, but the doors closed in 1967. Before then, a remarkable body of work emerged that did much to change the image of the homosexual as he was represented in the New York theatre of the 1960s.

The Haunted Host (1964), a play by Robert Patrick produced at the Cino, chronicled the relationship between Jay, a gay writer, and his roommate, Frank, a straight man who has studied psychiatry only to learn that "people and homosexuals should try to understand one another."[31] The play is significant in that it is a comic representation of a gay character that is not patronizing. It is the straight man, the so-called intellectual, who is the object of ridicule. In Robert Heide's *Moon* (1967), three couples land on the moon. The two straight couples are edgy, violent, and distressed. Only Christopher, a gay man who paints and bakes bread with his lover, is calm and productive. Lanford Wilson's *Madness of Lady Bright* (1965) focuses on a forty-year-old screaming queen. He may lack pride and be stereotypical of a 1950s queen, but he is astute enough to recognize himself as the creature of a passing era.

Perhaps the most explicit portrayal of homosexuality of the period was Mart Crowley's *The Boys in the Band* (1968), which opened off-Broadway and was a significant commercial success that was later filmed. Although time has not been kind to Crowley's play, it was something of a milestone in the pre-Stonewall era in that the characters are not villains and reject suicide as a solution to their homosexuality. What they do long for is freedom from the self-hatred that society has foisted on them. The play focuses on a group of gay men gathered together in host Michael's apartment to celebrate the birthday party of Harold, an unattractive, bitchy, but wise queen. During the course of the evening, the partygoers play truth games, in which they reveal attitudes and feelings about homosexuality that have haunted them. As Harold leaves the party, he turns on Michael in a particularly acerbic speech:

> You're a sad and pathetic man. You're a homosexual and you don't want to be. But there is nothing you can do to change it—not all your prayers to your God, not all the analysis you can buy in all the years you've got left to live. You may very well one day be able to know a heterosexual life if you want it desperately enough—if you pursue it with the fervor with which you annihilate—but you will always be homosexual as well. Always, Michael. Always. Until the day you die.[32]

Harold suggests that Michael, a devout Catholic, will not find solace for his sexual orientation in either religion or psychiatry, two institutions that homosexuals of the time turned to in their struggle for self-acceptance and that failed them miserably. Although gay men thirty years later watch the film of Crowley's play and bemoan the self-hatred and misery of the characters, the message was positive at the time. Harold's speech maintains that gayness is incontrovertible and demands acceptance. The problem, according to Crowley, is learning to accept one's sexual orientation in a hostile society. The play is a benchmark for how far gay liberation has traveled in thirty years.

While *The Boys in the Band* broke new ground off-Broadway, gay writers, directors, and actors, many of whom had also worked at the Cino, formed an artistic community at Ellen Stewart's La MaMa. A fashion designer by trade, Stewart wanted to find a venue that would celebrate the work of the playwright. In effect, La MaMa was a community of theatre practitioners who set out to ridicule, among other things, the restraints of mainstream theatre and institutionalized culture.

Tom Eyen's *Caution: A Love Story,* which opened La MaMa's East Fourth Street theatre in 1969 and for which I composed the score, simultaneously retold the courtship of a sexually ambivalent Duke and Duchess of Windsor, while nude onstage gypsies extolled the techniques of the Kama Sutra and acted as a Greek chorus. Deliberately incorporating mainstream show business and musical theatre clichés, Eyen used intertextuality and pastiche to comment on the sexual and political trends of the day, which was typical of many of the writers involved with La MaMa and, earlier, the Cino. Lines such as "Years from now, when you remember this, be kind," "Conductor, Belle Reve," and "Very smart, Anita, very smart" were tossed in nonsensically but were immediately identifiable to gay or theatre savvy audiences of the period who were familiar with *Tea and Sympathy* (1953), *A Streetcar Named Desire* (1947), and *West Side Story* (1957). Eyen's intertextuality also extended to off-Broadway and experimental productions of the time. The gypsies were intent on finding an "author," whom they mispronounced as "Arthur," and whom they tried to summon throughout the performance—an allusion to Pirandello's *Six Characters in Search of an Author* as well as a comment on the auteur directorial projects currently in vogue with the Living Theatre and the Performance Group.[33]

In *Caution,* a black drag queen played the ultrasquare singer Kate Smith in a number called "When the Moon Comes Over Fire Island," a parody of Smith's signature tune, "When the Moon Comes Over the Mountain," that was staged on a ladder rather than on a large staircase but was choreographed and musically arranged to look and sound like Pearl Bailey's then current Broadway version of *Hello, Dolly.* One of the gypsies portrayed the Archbishop of Canterbury, who flung his clerical robes about as he defiantly announced, "I Feel Gay Today," à la Maria's "I Feel Pretty" in *West Side Story.* Another gypsy, dirndled like Maria in *The Sound of Music* and surrounded by other gypsies dressed like little children, sang about the decimation of a Vietnamese village in "P-E-A-C-E," an antiwar "Do-Re-Mi." The Living Theatre's *Paradise Now* and Tom O'Horgan's *Hair* were spoofed in a nude scene, in which the disrobed gypsies wandered through the audience intoning, "I am not allowed to smoke marijuana," "I cannot travel without a passport," and "I am not allowed to listen to original Broadway cast recordings." That "Author" or "Arthur" ultimately dies in a rowboat was more than a comical allusion to Dreiser's *American Tragedy* and the film *A Place in the Sun*. Writing in a way that gay men could easily decode, Eyen was also mourning the inability of the mainstream Broadway author to express himself honestly.[34]

Eyen and others in the off-off-Broadway movement had much to overcome. From approximately 1963 onward, publications such as the *New York Times* and *Time*, mainstream critics such as Robert Brustein, and authors such as Philip Roth outed closeted gay writers on Broadway, who, in their opinion, were not qualified to write about heterosexual relationships or marriage. In 1963, Howard Taubman, then the chief drama critic for the *New York Times*, wrote a primer on "helpful hints on how to scan the intimations and symbols of homosexuality in our theatre."[35] The Taubman article ostensibly focused on William Inge's *Natural Affection* (1963), an unsuccessful play about a sensitive young man saddled with a slatternly mother and an Oedipus complex. If Taubman seemed to be beating a dead horse, his real target was more clearly Edward Albee's *Who's Afraid of Virginia Woolf?* (1962), a success that galled him: "If only we could believe that people on the stage are what they are supposed to be."[36] According to Taubman, Albee was writing about four gay men, not two heterosexual married couples who couldn't possibly behave with the self-loathing and acerbity with which Albee depicted them. In fact Albee has refused to allow the play to be performed by an all-male cast. Similarly, Richard Schechner attacked Albee in a homophobic piece in the *Tulane Drama Review:* "I'm tired of morbidity and sexual perversity which are there only to titillate an impotent and homosexual theatre and audience. I'm tired of Albee."[37]

Vitriolic attacks continued throughout the 1960s. Most outed Albee, Inge, Tennessee Williams, and James Baldwin for writing closeted homosexual plays masquerading as mainstream drama. Addressing Albee's *Tiny Alice* (1964) in a particularly nasty piece in the *New York Review of Books* entitled "The Play That Dare Not Speak Its Name," Roth dismissed the play as a homosexual fantasy. His conclusion seemed to attack not only Albee but Williams and Baldwin as well: "How long before a play is produced on Broadway in which the homosexual hero is presented as a homosexual, and not disguised as an angst-ridden priest, or an angry Negro, or an aging actress; or worst of all, Everyman?"[38] Reviewing Albee's *Malcolm* (1965), Robert Brustein sarcastically labeled the play Albee's most homosexual work. Echoing his previous attack on Inge, Brustein challenged the ability of a gay playwright to understand heterosexual relationships: "As Albee gets closer and closer to his true subjects—the malevolence of women, the psychological impact of Mom, the evolution of the invert—he tends to get more abstract and incoherent until he is finally reduced, as here, to a nervous plucking at broken strings."[39] This is antithetical to the stand he would take thirty years later in his debate with August Wilson when he passionately defended the ability of white directors to understand African American plays.

In 1966 Stanley Kauffman, Taubman's successor as chief drama critic of the *New York Times,* wrote a notorious piece attacking closeted homosexual writers and their dissident agenda against a culture that victimizes them: "The marital quarrels are usually homosexual quarrels with one of the pair in costume [presumably, the female character is a man in drag] and the incontrovertibly female figures are drawn less in truth than in envy or fear."[40] Kauffman seems to be arguing that gay playwrights deliberately distort marriage and femininity as a vindictive gesture toward a homophobic culture that discriminates against them. In essence, Kaufman's criticism implied that only a heterosexual man having sex with a woman could possibly create a realistic female character. As Charles Kaiser points out, Kauffman's argument is naive and framed by a heterosexual denigration of women: "This argument grew out of a quintessentially fifties attitude: the idea that a woman's only value to a man was as a sex object, or as the mother of his children."[41] Certainly Kauffman ignores the female characters of Tennessee Williams, probably among the most complex and convincing ever written by an American dramatist.

Perhaps most vitriolic of these 1960s attacks against closeted homosexual playwrights on Broadway was William Goldman's chapter entitled "Homosexuals" in *The Season.* Reviewing Williams's *The Seven Descents of Myrtle* (1968), Goldman urges his readers not to place much stock in what the playwright has to say about sex or heterosexual relationships: "As far as Broadway is concerned, the three leading experts on heterosexual married life during the past twenty years have been Williams, Albee, and Inge, all of them—at least to my knowledge—bachelors, and I wonder if their knowledge of and attitude toward the subject might not be a little limited."[42] Goldman argues that society has forced these closeted playwrights to address material not crucial to their psyches, which in turn forces them to create vicious, distorted images of heterosexuality: "The married couples hate each other; the woman, with whom the homosexual tends to identify, is either a gentle dreamer destroyed by an insensitive man, or a destroyer herself. And the man is either a stupid stud, hot for a quick roll in the hay, or a weak, contemptible failure."[43]

Like Kauffman, Goldman trivializes not only the great women's roles created by Tennessee Williams but the great romantic films written or directed by homosexuals in Hollywood. George Cukor, noted as a woman's director, was responsible for many of Hollywood's greatest love stories. Indeed, he coached Vivian Leigh throughout the shooting of *Gone with the Wind.* In the 1970s, Arthur Laurents, who wrote the screenplay for *The Way We Were,* one of the most successful romantic films of the decade, was stunned by a comment from director Sydney Pollack, who casually mentioned that Laurents was a topic of wonder in Hollywood circles, since he had written the best love story in years and was a homosexual. Laurents was allegedly at a loss for words: "What do you say to a man like that? Do you attack him? Do you attempt to educate him? Or do you just say to yourself: What an asshole!"[44]

In essence, the mainstream Broadway playwright of the 1960s was in a no-win situation. Since the 1930s, homosexuals were supposed to be invisible not only onstage but on the streets and in the bars of New York. McCarthyism only exacerbated the situation. Blackmail was not uncommon. Unless they named names while testifying for the House Un-American Activities Committee during the 1950s, gay artists such as Jerome Robbins allegedly were threatened with being outed either by the government or by columnists like Ed Sullivan or Walter Winchell.[45] By the 1960s, with homosexuality more visible, gay playwrights who wrote mainstream works about heterosexual relationships were attacked for dishonesty; later, when they either were outed or had outed themselves, their works were trivialized, since the writers' homosexuality somehow diminished the importance and "authenticity" of their characters and themes.

From the 1960s to his death, Williams was accused of fashioning his aging female characters as gay self-portraits—a reductive critical analysis of a character such as Blanche DuBois. When a gay playwright did tackle a homosexual subject, he was often attacked by the gay community if not the mainstream press. Inge wrote a character in *Where's Daddy* (1966) named "Pinky" Pinkerton, who encourages Tom, a street hustler whom he has raised and bedded, to return to the woman he has recently married and left. Since heterosexuality is the prized way of life, Pinkerton becomes the spokesman for heterosexual family values. The closeted Inge sadly seemed to be arguing that homosexuality was, in effect, a case of arrested development. Even Mart Crowley's *Boys in the Band,* as we have seen, was brutally attacked by gay activists as self-pitying in its depiction of gay self-hatred.

Stonewall, Homosexuality, and the Broadway Musical

If gay characters and themes were closeted in the nonmusical Broadway play, how were they handled in the Broadway musical? Certainly, since the days of Madame Lucy in *Irene* and Russell Paxton, the Danny Kaye character in *Lady in the Dark,* musicals offered the occasional screaming queen. Gay audiences, however, were used to the coding and double entendres in Broadway musicals from the 1930s through the 1950s. Coding gender anxiety was intrinsic to the form before the cultural changes brought on by the sexual revolution and Stonewall in 1969. As mentioned earlier, the off-Broadway and off-off-Broadway theatre at the close of the 1960s contributed to the zeitgeist of social and sexual rebellion. Less than a week before Stonewall, *Oh, Calcutta!* opened at the Eden off-Broadway and began a 1,314-performance run before transferring to Broadway's Belasco Theatre. In 1968 *Hair,* which originated off-Broadway at Joe Papp's Public Theatre and later moved uptown to the Biltmore for an impressive 1,742 performances, featured a gay character and celebrated bisexuality. Despite these exceptions, mainstream Broadway musicals were still relatively closeted.

On June 22, 1969, a group of gay men rebelled against police harassment at a bar called the Stonewall on Christopher Street in Greenwich Village, and the gay liberation movement was born. According to Martin Duberman, harassment and police entrapment were still commonplace in the Mafia-owned gay bars of the 1960s. No one is quite sure precisely why the police met vigilant resistance on what should have been a routine raid; however, years of harassment, entrapment, forced invisibility, and exploitation struck a note not only in those in the bar during the raid but in gay men all over the city.

Duberman mentions the connection between Judy Garland's funeral and the Stonewall riots. Garland, probably the ultimate gay icon, had died the previous week in London. Her body was on view at Campbell's Funeral Home on Madison Avenue and Eighty-first Street for forty-eight hours prior to the Stonewall raid. Twenty thousand mourners paid tribute, including many gay men, both young and old, who brought portable record players and tapes while waiting to view the body. I remember, because I was one of those in line. The following night, I happened to be in the Village on my way to the Sheridan Square subway station when I stumbled upon the riot outside the Stonewall. Many of those who were most dissident and resistant were drag queens. The police had obviously picked the wrong night to harass them.[46] Throughout the 1960s, gay consciousness had been progressively raised; the Stonewall riots received national publicity and marked the beginning of a new American awareness of, if not respect for, the homosexual.[47]

Of the fifteen musicals mounted on Broadway between October 1969 and May 1970, the theatrical season that followed the Stonewall riots, only three were financially successful: *Company, Coco,* and *Applause.*[48] Surprisingly, all three dealt, at least indirectly, with gay, bisexual, or sexually ambiguous leading characters. All three also featured explicitly gay, if minor, male characters, whose relationship with the central character helps illuminate his or her enigmatic sexuality. Although their original cultural moment has passed, these musicals still raise provocative questions about gender. New readings inevitably will be equally revealing about shifting notions of American identity.

Company

Company, a concept musical with a score by Stephen Sondheim and a book by George Furth, has a cast of fourteen: Bobby, the leading man, five married couples who are his best friends, and his three girlfriends. Bobby is a thirty-five-year-old New York City bachelor, equally terrified of emotional commitment and of bachelorhood and its attendant loneliness. Plotless, the musical is a series of scenes that reveal the tensions and difficulties in the marriages of the five couples through Bobby's eyes, as well as the difficulties he has cementing an emotional commitment to each of his three girlfriends. The first couple, Sarah and Harry are neurotics. Sarah is constantly dieting; Harry has a drinking problem. Bobby witnesses their hostility when they start to quarrel and Sarah practices her newly learned karate techniques on her husband. Couple two, Peter and Susan, are getting a divorce so they can once more live amicably together. Jenny and David, the third couple, are worried about approaching middle age and try to sustain their youth by smoking marijuana. Couple four, Amy and Paul, have lived together for years and are about to marry, much to Amy's terror. The final couple, Joanne and Larry, are perhaps the most cynical and frightening. Joanne is rich and dominates her husband. She also propositions Bobby, who turns her down.

The wild card here is Bobby, who is a watcher rather than a participant. Even in his relationships with his three girlfriends, he is emotionally noncommittal. Bobby is forced to make a choice about his future based on his observations of his friends' relationships. Will he choose to remain free and a bachelor or commit to some sort of relationship, difficult and trying as it may be? During the out-of-town tryout, according to Foster Hirsch, three different solutions were offered. The first, voiced in a song called "Marry Me a Little," expressed Bobby's decision to embark on a safe marriage, one in which both partners would retain their independence. Unsatisfied with this compromise, producer-director Harold Prince asked Sondheim for a second solution. Replacing "Marry Me a Little" with "Happily Ever After," Bobby's choice seemed to be "the manifesto of a misanthrope."[49] The song confirmed Bobby's decision to escape marriage and remain single. According to Prince, the song was terrifying: "It was the most unhappy song ever written, and we didn't know how devastating it would be until we saw it in front of an audience. . . . If I heard that song I wouldn't get married for anything in the whole world."[50] Ultimately, "Happily Ever After" was replaced by "Being Alive," which argued that the only possibility for any sort of happiness is love and emotional commitment, even if that love is claustrophobic and frightening. This decision to commit emotionally is quite a leap, particularly after the previous, horrific examples of the five battling couples and Joanne's growlingly acerbic "Ladies Who Lunch," which immediately precedes it.

Apparently Sondheim was never pleased with the resolution, and Prince did not feel it was honest either; however, audiences expected a happy ending and happy endings involve marriage and commitment (although there is no one visible onstage to whom Robert can commit).[51] In the final scene, which follows "Being Alive," Bobby fails to show up for his annual birthday. The play ends with Bobby alone and smiling. Will he choose marriage? Is he rejecting the heterosexual world of his married friends? Is he embracing commitment to a gay relationship or lifestyle? After seeing the show, George Abbott allegedly asked Prince if the musical was promarriage or antimarriage. Prince's reply was noncommittal. The text is open; the character of Bobby, enigmatic.

From the outset, critics have argued whether Bobby is bisexual or a coded gay character. During the late 1960s and early 1970s, "coming out," as John Clum asserts, "meant cutting ties with one's straight friends," which would explain Bobby's refusal to attend his party.[52] Although Bobby has three girlfriends with whom he has sexual relations, they refer to him as a tease—an emotional vacuum—and imply that his lack of interest or commitment is perhaps a sign of his homosexuality in their trio, "You Could Drive a Person Crazy." Moreover, Furth's original script had a conversation between Peter, the newly divorced husband, and Bobby that made the latter's bisexuality explicit:

Peter: Robert, did you ever have a homosexual experience?

Robert: I beg your pardon?
Peter: Oh, I don't mean as a kid. I mean, since you've been an adult. Have you ever?
Robert: Well, yes, actually, yes, I have.[53]

Peter then propositions Bobby. What is unusual here is that both Peter and Bobby contradict the stereotype of the sissy or screaming queen associated with gay men in musicals up to that point. Both perform conventional, perceived notions of masculinity. According to the stage directions, Bobby takes a long time to respond. Is he seriously considering Peter's proposition? Is he reluctant to reject his friend or afraid to accept an attractive offer? Is he afraid of an emotional as well as sexual connection with a friend, or is he weaseling out of an uncomfortable confrontation? The text is open, since Bobby ultimately treats the proposition as a good-natured joke. Unfortunately this exchange was cut before *Company* opened in New York. It was reinstated by Furth for the London revival (1996) directed by Sam Mendes. By that time, it was difficult not to at least acknowledge the possibility of Bobby's bisexuality. In 1970 this possibility, even after Stonewall, would still have been threatening to the majority of Broadway audiences.

Nonetheless William Goldman, a fan of the original production, maintained that *Company* was about a homosexual and that the authors did not have the courage to deal with the subject: "I remember seeing *Company* five times and I loved it, and I had a huge fucking problem, which is that the main character is gay, but they don't talk about it."[54] Goldman is reiterating his own criticism of closeted Broadway playwriting, as well as the criticisms of Taubman, Kauffman, Brustein, and Roth throughout the 1960s. Sondheim and Furth's predicament was similar to that of Williams, Albee, and Inge. If the hero of *Company* were homosexual, how much appeal could the musical generate for a mainstream Broadway audience? A certain amount of gay coding had been standard since the 1930s in musicals, but if the authors acknowledged a gay hero, their musical would have limited popular appeal. If, on the other hand, Bobby was left sexually ambiguous, Sondheim and Furth were subject to attack because they dodged the issue of homosexuality, the same criticism that had plagued Williams, Inge, and Albee throughout the decade. The issue of authorial intent complicates matters even more. What *did* Furth and Sondheim intend? There is no conclusive answer.

In the thirty years since the musical opened, gay critics tend to see Bobby as a closeted homosexual. D. A. Miller, for one, is annoyed at the sexual openness of the character:

> This Bobby bubi is a Bobby bubba nonetheless. It is not just the characters in *Company* who all think so; in interview after interview, the show's creators continue to put their authority behind the same presumption, repudiating the possibility of gay representation with an emphasis that couldn't be firmer if they were organizing a St. Patrick's Day Parade. We, then, end up falling into the same furious incomprehension as Bobby's other girlfriends: we could understand a person if a person was a fag, but if he was not, he must be as crazy as he makes us.[55]

On the other hand, straight critics passionately defend Bobby's heterosexuality. According to Joanne Gordon, "Critics who dwell on Robert's possible homosexuality are clearly uncomfortable with the show's anti-romantic, unsentimental depiction of marriage."[56] The mixed reaction about Bobby is, after all, not significantly different from the mixed reactions to the plays of Tennessee Williams, William Inge, and Edward Albee during this same period. Both Furth and Sondheim were homosexual; Prince, heterosexual. Sondheim wanted to retain "Happily Ever After," the song that would resolve Bobby's dilemma by keeping him a bachelor. According to biographer Meryle Secrest, this preference very much mirrored Sondheim's own feelings of sexual ambivalence in his younger days.[57] However one chooses to read Bobby, the original production was a financial and critical success, although perhaps for the wrong reasons. It raised a complex issue after Stonewall about gay identity and coming out for the Broadway establishment that turned it into something of a cult show. Indeed, *Variety's* pre-Broadway review predicted its audience appeal: "It's evident that . . . George Furth hates femmes [women] and makes them all out to be conniving, cunning, cantankerous. . . . As it stands now [*Company* is] for ladies' matinees, homos, and misogynists."[58]

If the text is open, efforts were made to attempt to close it through casting in the original production. Anthony Perkins was originally slated to star in *Company* but left to direct the off-Broadway production of Bruce Jay Friedman's *Scuba Duba.* It is conceivable that Perkins's appeal as a film star and his ingratiating charm would have made the character less of a cipher and more subject to a heterosexual reading. He was replaced by Dean Jones, a Disney film star, who reportedly was terrified of the homosexual implications of the character and its long-range effect on his film career as a star of family comedies. Reviewing Jones's performance, Martin Gottfried commented, Dean Jones "can seem sexless and must watch it or the show's theme (and honesty) will be confused by hints of homosexuality."[59] Jones, a straight actor, walked away from his contract after five weeks and was replaced by Larry Kert, who played the role through the remainder of the Broadway engagement and in London. Although Kert was gay, his performance had a great deal of sex appeal and could easily be read as interpreting Bobby as straight. Ironically, Perkins and Kert, both gay men, were perceived as deemphasizing Bobby's homosexuality, whereas Jones, a straight actor with a wholesome Disney image, was perceived as lending more of a gay subtext to the character. The irony of this underscores the implicit playfulness and fluidity of identity that has characterized the American musical since the double doubling of minstrelsy in the nineteenth century.

Whether Bobby is straight or gay is (or is not) answered in performance. The original production, with Perkins deserting the ship, Dean Jones terrified of playing a "sexless" gay man, and Larry Kert somehow bridging the gap, was certainly not definitive—it begged the question. *Company* may have opened after Stonewall, but it was not ready to confront homosexuality openly in 1969. The text was altered, both literally and in performance, in Sam Mendes's London revival (1996), in which Bobby was played by the charismatic black actor Adrian Lester. The script was still open, but Lester was apparently able to fill in the gaps of the cipherlike hero and create a character who held some sexual fascination for the audience. Lester's race also added another dimension to the character. According to Alan Sinfield, homosexuality on the mainstream Broadway stage was usually divorced from race and ethnicity until the 1960s, mainly because nonwhite actors had limited opportunities to perform and because both blacks and whites found interracial sex too hot to handle.[60] After the 1980s, however, Sinfield argues that playwrights have increasingly explored the sexually dissident of various ethnicities and races. Sinfield speculates that this change may be an inheritance from gays who became militant after the Stonewall riots and who had learned their political strategies while fighting for racial civil rights and other nongay issues of the New Left. At any rate, it seems that a contemporary production of *Company*, thirty years after the original staging, needs to confront Bobby's sexual ambiguity rather than push it under the table. The character can still remain enigmatic, even sexually confused, but it is not enough in 2005 to leave him a cipher.

Coco

Like Bobby, the central character in Coco, with book and lyrics by Alan Jay Lerner and music by André Previn, is sexually mysterious. *Coco* chronicles the 1953 comeback of French couturier Coco Chanel, who walked away from her salon in 1939 during the height of her success. As the curtain rises, Chanel, convinced that her designs are timeless, wants to return to work. Her attorney, afraid her fashions are hopelessly outmoded, hires Sebastian Baye, a gay designer whose lover is the leading fashion critic in Paris, to supervise the new collection. Chanel rejects his designs, prepares the collection herself, and is devastated when the showing is calamitous. Four buyers from New York, however, offer to mass-market her designs for Ohrbach's, Bloomingdale's, Best, and Saks, and she is once more at the top of the fashion heap.

Lerner's script and lyrics seem like a reaction against the militant males of Stonewall and a valentine to the burgeoning women's movement and to feminism, years before feminism was embraced by mainstream American society. Fashioned as a vehicle for the iconoclastic Katharine Hepburn, the musical celebrates the sexual, material, and cultural autonomy of women. The heart of the show deals with Chanel's ambivalence about the conflict between her fierce need for independence and her need for a fulfilling personal relationship. She develops an attachment to Noelle, one of her young models with whom she has much in common. Both were orphaned before they were ten years old, both came to Paris, and both immediately found male lovers who refused to marry them. Noelle is currently living with Georges, a reporter, who wants her to abandon her modeling career to become his mistress. Coco advises Noelle to forge a career and life independent from Georges. She argues that a woman needs independence from a man, not equality. Equality, she affirms, is, in most cases, a step down.

Heeding Chanel's advice, Noelle informs Georges she intends to continue modeling. He puts her out, and she appears on Chanel's doorstep, suitcase in hand. The older woman takes her in but is afraid to become too emotionally involved with her protégée. Noelle insinuates herself into Chanel's life, soothes her when it looks as if her new collection has been disastrous, and encourages her to persevere. As the relationship between the two women grows, Noelle asks Coco why she never married. Coco explains that her father, whom she adored, abandoned her. She resolved never to depend on anyone again. Chanel, in turn, recognizes in Noelle a young woman like herself, who must eventually decide between independence and the normalcy that predicates that a woman have a husband and children. Deciding to mold Noelle in her own image, Chanel buys a new home that she intends to share with the young model, but Noelle returns to Georges. Finally realizing that she will remain, as ever, "Always Mademoiselle," Coco arranges to design a dress for Noelle's wedding as the curtain falls.

The real-life Chanel was bisexual. Although the character of Coco in the musical is shrouded in sexual ambivalence, the plot implies a love triangle between the aging Coco, her young model Noelle, and Noelle's lover, Georges. Almost immediately after meeting her, Coco urges Noelle to leave Georges and move in with her. Chanel predicts that Georges will conquer his aversion to marriage as soon as he recognizes Noelle's independence, but she nevertheless encourages Noelle to end the relationship and cherish her freedom. This prophecy eventually comes to pass:

> *Noelle*: It all happened just as you said, didn't it Coco? I became independent and he came around.
> *Coco*: It's a shame we're all so predictable. But everything about love is a shame, isn't it? Men and women deserve something better than each other.[61]

Perhaps Chanel is being more than epigrammatic here; if men and women deserve something better than each other, Chanel seems to be espousing a homosexual, rather than heterosexual, relationship. Early in act 2, Chanel is despondent that her collection has been ridiculed by the Parisian fashion press. Noelle, who has grown to love the older woman, berates Coco for her fierce independence, claiming her own rights in their relationship:

> *Noelle*: Coco, may I have dinner with you tonight?
> *Coco*: Noelle, if you don't mind . . .
> *Noelle*: Yes, I do mind. I refuse to go on being locked out like this without any explanation.
> *Coco*: Locked out? What on earth are you talking about?
> *Noelle*: I know you don't believe in leaning on anyone, Coco, but I care too much. You have no right to be unhappy without me.[62]

These are strong words for a girl who is being kept by an older woman, particularly one based on a real-life bisexual. Toward the end of the act, Noelle informs Chanel she is returning to Georges, rejecting not only the new home Coco has bought for her but the older woman's dreams for her future:

> *Coco*: What do you want me to say, Noelle? I understand . . . ? Well, I can't. And I do understand. It's you who understands nothing. *You need love and so you think you need him.* And why not? *It's the only love you've ever known.* Standing on your small hill of years, it is the only life you can see. But look out from Mt. Everest and I can see a future for you that you couldn't dream of with opium.

> *Noelle*: I know you can, Coco. But I want my own future. *I don't want to be made into someone no man can satisfy.*
> *Coco*: If my dreams are too big for you to carry, pick some up at the Flea market. Get out of here.[63]

Even without the italics, which are mine rather than Lerner's, the dialogue is filled with homosexual undertones. Noelle has had other lovers before George, so what does Coco mean when she declares that Georges is the only love Noelle has ever known? Is she proposing a lesbian relationship? Noelle rejects not only Coco's offer of love but Coco's belief in the value of independence and personal autonomy when she denigrates Chanel by refusing to be a woman that "no man can satisfy." Noelle goes from Coco's protection back to Georges'.

The ending, like most "happy" endings in musicals, is too neat, given the provocative issues the musical raises. Happily ever after, in terms of the musical, suggests an end to discourse. As Rick Altman observes, "The comic equivalent of apocalypse, marriage represents a timeless, formless state in American mythology, precisely so that it will not be open to question."[64] Here the romantic joining together of Noelle and Georges validates the heterosexual community and the sexual status quo. Noelle marries Georges, basically settling for a life as a housewife, while Coco, whom the audience has admired all evening, is left alone, seemingly punished for her insistence on personal autonomy. No doubt this is the happy ending that seemed inevitable to please a 1969 audience. At the same time, there is something triumphant about the androgynous Katharine Hepburn as Chanel once again ruling the world of fashion. Who could find an appropriate consort for such an overpowering personality?

Apart from the ending, Lerner underscores his admiration for Chanel's feminism and independence by creating two villains, both male. Georges is a male chauvinist, attractive but selfish. He denies Noelle the possibility of a career of her own. The other villain is Sebastian Baye, the gay designer who is at odds with Coco about her new fashion collection. Baye is stereotypically, cartoonishly homosexual. Observing Baye's behavior in the salon, one model inquires of another, "Is he homosexual?" The second replies, "It's gone beyond that."[65] This type of screaming queen was not new to the Broadway musical. As Walter Kerr noted in his *New York Times* review, the humor springs from stereotyping of gender, not from character: "Much of the comedy is bad fag comedy hung about the neck of a homosexual designer, the villain of the piece; at one point René Auberjonois squeals and snatches his hand away because he has inadvertently let it rest on the breast of a tailor's dummy."[66] Kerr's criticism points to the silliness and artificiality of the humorous gesture. A fitter or designer would certainly have to be used to touching female bodies. This is the same kind of criticism leveled against the stock "sissy" character and stereotyped gender jokes that Richard Watts attacked in *By Jupiter* and that the critics jumped on as early as 1924 with *The Ritz Revue.* The difference here is that the homosexual is not just an over-the-top figure of fun but a bona fide villain, out to destroy the heroine.

Many of Lerner's jokes center on Baye's effeminacy. Coco calls him a "wretched little UFO,"[67] whereas Baye himself insists that "there's no bitch like a man."[68] Lyricist Lerner gives Baye the comic showstopper of the evening, a song entitled "Fiasco," in which Baye, having been fired by Chanel, celebrates the failure of her comeback collection. By the end of the number, Baye is skipping and mincing across the stage as he gloats over Chanel's downfall. In the original production, Auberjonois emphasized the character's bitchiness and effeminacy. The number won him a Tony award as best supporting actor in a musical. It is ironic that Auberjonois was honored by the Broadway community for a performance that essentialized the post-Stonewall homosexual male. It is also disturbing that journalists such as William Goldman and Mark Steyn, who imply that the Broadway musical theatre community is something of a gay coven, ignore Auberjonois' acclaim for this particular role at this particular moment in time.

Both Steyn and Goldman write of a Broadway that seems vaguely mystical if not mythical in its gayness. In a chapter entitled "The Fags," Steyn constructs his version of the demographics of who mounts Broadway musicals: "There are no statistics for these things, but, on the basis of my own unscientific research, I would say that, of the longest-running shows of the 1940s, some two-thirds had a homosexual contribution in the writing/staging/producing department. By the 1960s, the proportion of long-runners with a major homosexual contribution was up to about 90 percent."[69] If Steyn admits that there are no reliable statistics to support his claims, where did he get these figures? Thirty years ago, Goldman wrote the following:

> Most of the major musicals of the sixties have been directed by homosexuals, the songs from most of the hits of the sixties have been written by homosexuals, the dances created by homosexuals, the clothing designed by homosexuals. In musicals, particularly, the homosexual contribution is tremendous: of the ten longest-running musicals of

> the decade, two, at the most, were accomplished without homosexual contributions in the writer-producer-director echelons.[70]

Goldman's statistics are questionable, particularly since the 1960s were the decade of such writers as Bock and Harnick (*Fiddler on the Roof*), Jule Styne and Bob Merrill (*Funny Girl*), Mitch Leigh (*Man of La Mancha*), and Galt MacDermot (*Hair*), not to mention such producers as David Merrick and Harold Prince, and choreographers such as Bob Fosse. Does one gay collaborator make a musical "gay?"

The sexual orientation of the much married Lerner also contradicts Goldman's statistics. Lerner's creation of the Sebastian Baye character is counterintuitive to a post-Stonewall cultural moment and demands some examination. It is actually not surprising that Lerner would create an explicitly gay male character in a post-Stonewall musical about the fashion industry. Lerner reverts to an older stereotype with Baye but updates and exacerbates it. Before *Coco,* characters of varying degrees of effeminacy were common in musicals, but they were usually not explicitly identified as homosexual. In fact, they often were married or about to be wed by the final curtain. Madame Lucy in *Irene* (1919), a dress designer with effeminate mannerisms, brags that the girls go simply wild over him; at the conclusion of the show, he marries Irene's mother. Reno Sweeney, in *Anything Goes* (1934), is prepared to marry the foppish Sir Evelyn Oakley. The effeminate stereotype appears frequently in film musicals as well, particularly with such character actors as Edward Everett Horton, and Erik Rhodes in the Astaire-Rogers films. The comic, stereotypical gayness of these characters, however, is inevitably papered over by a romantic entanglement with a woman or by marriage.

The salient exception is Russell Paxton, the dress designer in *Lady in the Dark,* which, like *Coco,* was a musical about high fashion. Playwright Moss Hart described Paxton as flighty and biting, "mildly effeminate in a rather charming fashion."[71] Hart insisted on casting Danny Kaye in the original production, and by all accounts, Kaye's performance was over the top and stereotypically, mincingly gay.[72] Paxton was the creation of Moss Hart, whose biographer, Steven Bach, acknowledges Hart's conflicted sexuality. According to Bach, Hart spent years with psychiatrist Lawrence Kubie trying to cure his homosexual urges.[73] Perhaps Hart's fondness for Kaye resulted in giving the comedian license to perform outrageously. Perhaps Hart's own conflicted sexuality and dogged attempts to live a respectable, married life led him to make the Paxton character a ridiculous cartoon.

According to Ethan Mordden, *Lady in the Dark* was a coded show, in which Hart's psychiatrist at the time, Gregory Zilboorg, encouraged him to write Liza Elliott as a metaphor for Hart and his own problems in emerging from the closet. Apparently, Hart went through analysis with Zilboorg before he ultimately switched his allegiance to Lawrence Kubie. The two psychiatrists differed in their philosophies and treatment. Whereas Kubie tried to "cure" Hart of his homosexuality, Mordden claims that Zilboorg encouraged Hart to confront it. For Mordden, *Lady in the Dark* is a gay coming-out parable: "The 'lady executive' is clearly a likeness of a gay man, capable and creative but alternate, not like most of us. . . . The Hollywood beauty [the male movie star in the play] as icon, the unnervingly masculine challenger who is at the same time an erotic figure . . . this is more gay imagery. And note that Hart intended his play for Katherine Cornell, a real-life lesbian wedded to a gay man, Guthrie McClintic."[74]

Unfortunately Mordden's speculations, like so much that has been written about musical theatre, are just that—speculations, not verifiable history. The same is true for Lerner, whose personal or psychological reasons for creating an explicitly gay figure of ridicule and villainy in response to Stonewall are equally up for grabs. According to Judy Insell, who assisted Lerner throughout the preproduction, rehearsal period, and Broadway run of *Coco,* Lerner was oblivious to Stonewall. Insell claims that Michael Bennett, in trying to make a musical comedy villain funny, did much to encourage Auberjonois' over-the-top characterization, including, of course, creating the outrageous tango for the "Fiasco" number. If the responsibility for Baye being portrayed as a camp villain lies at Bennett's door, it raises questions about the choreographer's attitudes toward his own bisexuality and possible self-hatred, even a year after Stonewall. This theory is plausible, since Bennett later married Donna McKechnie despite being homosexually promiscuous. All personal motivations of these men, unfortunately, remain speculation. I do find it hard to believe, however, that Lerner, who later was to write a musical about race relations and the presidency (*1600 Pennsylvania Avenue*) and nuclear devastation (*Dance a Little Closer*), was so apolitical that he was oblivious to or even uninterested in the Stonewall riots. Many of the New York drama critics were not oblivious, for several, including the aforementioned Kerr, lamented the cheap, derogatory laughs at the homosexual's expense.

What does seem likely is that the aftermath of Stonewall enabled Lerner to make the effeminate stereotype more explicitly gay than had been possible before, but unfortunately the explicitness, particularly through a twenty-first-century lens, was reductive and essentialist. Actually there is a certain logic to Lerner's reaction against gay male liberation, if that is indeed what it was. Throughout the 1960s, the New York press challenged closeted gay playwrights for being incapable of writing believable heterosexual relationships. As I mentioned earlier, the implication of much of this criticism seemed to be that gay men, resentful of their marginalization by the heterosexual hegemony, ridiculed and demonized women through their female characters. Lerner, a much married straight man, does the opposite. He demonizes, ridicules, and essentializes the gay male. If there is a point to this homophobic, gay cartoon, Lerner makes it through Chanel's comment about Baye's designs: "Do you know why fashion is so atrocious these days? Because men are making fun of women, that's why. And that's what he's doing."[75] If a straight man can appreciate a woman's beauty, Coco seems to imply, a gay man will jealously undercut her and make her look foolish. Lerner has Coco verbalize the criticisms leveled by Taubman, Kauffman, Roth, and Goldman throughout the 1960s about the female characters created by closeted, allegedly misogynist homosexual playwrights such as Albee, Inge, and Williams. If gay men are making fun of women, as Coco suggests, Lerner is making fun of the gay man. What is ironic is Lerner's glorification of feminism and, to an extent, Coco's bisexuality or lesbianism, which is implied by the text. In that sense, *Coco* does reflect a post-Stonewall sensibility, at least in terms of the Chanel character. Lerner can react in contradistinction to what he dislikes about Stonewall while venerating what he respects about the women's movement. Ultimately he leaves the character of Coco open by essentializing her comic, homosexual opponent.

Unfortunately the original production closed the text. Directed by Michael Benthal with musical numbers and fashion sequences staged by Michael Bennett, the production catered to Katharine Hepburn's huge following and safely sidestepped the potential sexual attraction between the two women.[76] Hepburn's star turn, however, involved her own nonmaternal star baggage. She brought the androgynous quality long associated with her from early films like *Sylvia Scarlett* in the 1930s, as well as her own reputation as a loner, an iconoclast, and a feminist. Her portrayal of Chanel seemed more a cartoon of Hepburn than a characterization of the bisexual couturier.[77] On the one hand, she failed to convey any great sense of maternal feeling toward Noelle. Conversely, the potential sexual attraction between the two women was ignored. As a result, little was at stake when Noelle leaves Coco at the end of the play to return to Georges. Part of this lack of emotional involvement conceivably involves Hepburn's own sexuality. Both Robert Parrish and William Mann have written forthcoming books that purportedly reveal Hepburn's bisexuality. Darwin Porter has recently published a fairly scurrilous book about Hepburn that recounts countless affairs with both men and women.[78] Judy Insell, who knew Hepburn well and worked with her on *Coco,* maintains that she was not a lesbian. In either case, the truth is difficult to verify, since most of the principals presumably involved are dead. Certainly, Hepburn's mania for privacy was legendary. If indeed she was bisexual, it would be logical that she would protect herself by refusing to explore the sexual ambivalence of the character and of the real-life Chanel. After Hepburn left the cast, she was replaced by Danielle Darrieux, who injected a glamour and warmth that did much to promote the mother-daughter aspect of the relationship with Noelle. Without the legendary Hepburn, however, the box office died. The show begs revival today, thirty years after the feminist movement. It raises issues of female autonomy that are embedded in parts of contemporary culture but that were far more dissident and transgressive in 1969.

Applause

Perhaps *Applause,* with a score by Charles Strouse and Lee Adams and the book by Betty Comden and Adolph Green, is the musical most directly influenced by the Stonewall riots. Its text is less enigmatic than that of *Company* and *Coco* and manages to literalize identity in a form that traditionally venerates the coded and sexually ambiguous. The musical is based on the 1950 film *All about Eve,* which in turn is based on a short story by Mary Orr, supposedly about a real-life incident in which either Elizabeth Berger or Tallulah Bankhead, depending on which version one believes, was sabotaged by an understudy. The Bankhead version is interesting in this context. While starring in *The Little Foxes* (1939) on Broadway, supposedly Bankhead was victimized by her understudy, Lizabeth Scott, who later became a film star and something of a lesbian icon. Bankhead's sexuality, as a matter of fact, was notoriously eclectic; she proclaimed herself a dedicated try-sexual.

In the musicalization, Eve Harrington, starstruck as well as seemingly mousy and self-effacing, manages to insinuate herself through fawning adulation into the life of her idol, an aging musical theatre icon named Margo Channing. She soon moves in with Margo and becomes her indispensable gal Friday. Eventually she also becomes Margo's understudy. Increasingly suspicious of Eve's motives, Margo begins to turn on her protegée, but friends and colleagues dismiss her misgivings as the paranoia of an insecure, middle-aged star. Margo's suspicions are ultimately confirmed. Eve betrays Margo by conspiring to cause her to miss a performance, goes on in her place after alerting the press that she will be performing in Margo's stead, and wins rave reviews. Eve manages to seduce both Margo's producer and favorite playwright. She also unsuccessfully tries to seduce Bill Sampson, Margo's director and lover. Eventually Eve talks her way into replacing Margo as the lead in a new musical, while the star, convinced that there must be something greater than the backbiting world of show business, marries Bill and settles for a life of relative normalcy outside the theatre.

In translating the film to the musical stage, Comden and Green make several significant alterations. In both film and musical, Eve uses men sexually to claw her way to the top of her profession. According to Vito Russo, however, two scenes in the film suggest that her real attraction is toward women:

> According to Ken Geist in his biography of Joe Mankiewicz [who wrote and directed *All About Eve*], the character of Eve Harrington, as played by Anne Baxter, was conceived as a lesbian, a predilection only subtly suggested in a scene with Eve's boardinghouse roommate and again at the end of the film when she impulsively invites an adoring young fan to spend the night with her. She is, of course, being taken in by a creature very much like herself.[79]

Russo observes that Eve's vulnerability to Phoebe, the conniving high-school girl in the film's final scene, is the product of Eve's lesbianism: "Eve does not have the kind of generosity that led Margo Channing to take a waif like her under her wing. To ask Phoebe to spend the night rather than take the subway home to Brooklyn could have only one motive, and it spells the beginning of the end for Eve Harrington."[80] Although both the boardinghouse scene and the final scene with Phoebe are relatively subtle, necessarily so for a film produced in 1950, Eve is arguably lesbian or, at the very least, bisexual. She doesn't care with whom she sleeps as long as she reaches her goal. The boardinghouse scene and the final scene do, however, show a rare vulnerability and honesty in the character. Eve is clearly more at ease with her roommate and with Phoebe than with the men she ruthlessly seduces.

In musicalizing the property, Comden and Green cut both scenes involving the roommate and Phoebe, thus eliminating any ambiguity about Eve's sexuality. This is in direct contrast to Joseph Mankiewicz's vision of Eve in the film:

> Whether in the theatre, or at *Harper's Bazaar, Vogue,* or I.B.M., Eve is essentially the girl unceasingly, relentlessly on the make. Not necessarily for men; as a matter of fact, only rarely. A particular man, perhaps, or series of men—or women—may be the means to an important end, but almost never the ultimate goal. The goal—toward which Eve is fanatically and forever at full charge—is no less than all of whatever there is to be had.[81]

Since Eve is the villainess of the piece, it is not surprising that Comden and Green skirt the issue of Eve's bisexuality in a musical that opened almost a year after the Stonewall riots. In 1950 Eve's lesbianism would have been consistent in the eyes of the general public with her ruthlessness and amorality. In line with pieces from *Time* and *Coronet* that I cited earlier in this chapter, homosexuality (whether male or female) was regarded not merely as a question of sexual preference but as a mental disorder that could easily lead to psychosis. The pre-Stonewall press depicted the homosexual as attempting to subvert all that straight society held dear, which led Foucault to theorize that it was the homosexual lifestyle and its implications rather than the homosexual act itself that rocked the status quo.

By 1970, with the increasing visibility of homosexuals after Stonewall and the rise of gay activism, it was necessary to take a different approach. This change is apparent in the liner notes to the original cast album, in which Comden and Green summarize the plot: "It is a tale of treachery, the humble underling, subtly boring from within to unseat and usurp the figure of power on the throne, told in terms of the witty, glamorous theatre star and the mousy, adoring girl from the sticks who ingratiates herself into the star's private world, and then systematically attempts to take over her career, her lover, and her life."[82] Comden and Green's description sounds potentially like the articles in *Time* and *Coronet* that accused the homosexual of deliberately undermining mainstream society.[83] With Stonewall fresh in the public consciousness, not to mention some critical brickbats aimed at the over-the-top homosexual stereotyping of the villainous Sebastian Baye, who was, after all, a minor character, it would be reactionary and counterproductive to create a lesbian villainess. Baye was a stereotypical joke of effeminacy, who fails in his attempted villainy; he was not nearly as threatening to Coco as the handsome, heterosexual Georges, who eventually wins Noelle away from her. Eve, on the other hand, was a predatory monster. Linking her villainy to her sexuality would feed into the almost pathological stereotypes that gay activists, particularly since Stonewall, had done so much to discredit. In the final analysis, the show highlighted a comforting message to straight audiences in 1970. By the final curtain, despite her glamorous lifestyle and exposure to a world of gay bars, amusing companions, and fast living, Margo Channing, in the guise of Lauren Bacall, chooses to take the commuter train home to a husband and white picket fence rather than remain in the amoral world of show business. She bequeaths that legacy to the likes of Eve Harrington, as played by Penny Fuller. Ironically the gay gypsies want no part of Eve; her success will depend on her ruthless, sexual manipulation of the straight men of the musical theatre.

Stonewall not only had established homosexuality as a presence that would not disappear from major urban centers such as New York City but also had endowed its increasing visibility with glamour. Comden and Green cleverly capitalized on this publicity by including explicitly homosexual minor characters and a scene that takes place in a gay bar. Audiences were titillated during the title number, in which three male dancers, satirizing *Oh, Calcutta!,* exposed their bare backsides to the audience. Gay bars were in the news but were certainly beyond the realm of experience of straight musical theatre audiences. *Hair,* a year earlier, had enabled Broadway theatregoers to taste the dissidence and controversy of the counterculture within a safe setting, the Biltmore Theatre, filled with graffiti and deliberately made to look run-down and seedy in keeping with the show's East Village setting. By featuring male nudity within a flashy production number in a gay bar, *Applause* similarly allowed audiences to be voyeurs of an alternate gay lifestyle from the safety of their seats at the Palace Theatre.

In musicalizing *All about Eve,* Comden and Green close Eve's sexuality but open the Margo Channing character. The musical is all about Lauren Bacall as Margo, not all about Eve. Basically a suspicious, bitchy character, Margo is made lovable through her sympathetic relationship with Duane, her gay hairdresser. Her relationship with Bill Sampson is not only volatile but also often lugubrious. She is never as happy with her lover, her straight producer, or her straight writer and his wife as she is with Duane and with the adoring gay men who worship her when she accompanies Duane to a gay bar. If Margo's heterosexuality is secured by the script, she becomes an icon for gay men in production. Director-choreographer Ron Field described the importance of making the audience cheer for Bacall and for her character:

> In the case of Lauren Bacall in the disco scene, I had wanted the audience to fall in love with Lauren Bacall at the beginning of the

> show because from then on her character had to be bitchy and suspicious. I knew I only had about fifteen minutes for the audience to fall in love with who she was. I thought, How can I get that to happen? In the script her hairdresser, who was gay, takes her to a Village disco and I had fifteen boys throw Bacall around. She looked wonderful.[84]

Margo's best friend is gay. Unlike Sebastian Baye in *Coco,* he is not out to destroy the heroine but to support her. Margo's acceptance of Duane's homosexuality, her embracing of the alternate lifestyle of the gypsies in her cast and in the world of the New York theatre are endearing characteristics, a bit shocking for 1970 but nonetheless endearing. Given the post-Stonewall cultural moment of the original production, villainous Eve is distrusted, perhaps hated by Duane and the other gypsies, many of them gay, while Margo, the heroine, is supported and supportive of her gay following. Comden and Green create audience empathy for Margo by capitalizing on her relationship with Duane and the gypsies; at the same time, the writers demonize Eve by alienating her from Duane and his gay friends. Unlike Lerner, the authors obviously concluded that it was preferable to have a predatory straight villain than a predatory bisexual one in 1970. Their choice was astute. Of the three musicals discussed in this chapter, *Applause* was by far the most popular and financially successful. The show managed to negotiate a careful balancing act. It capitalized on a built-in gay audience from the film (a gay cult classic) while simultaneously appealing to the values of a mainstream, straight audience—and titillating them at the same time.

Comden and Green break musical theatre tradition by creating Duane, an overtly gay character who is not an over-the-top screaming queen, a figure of ridicule, or a villain. In the film, lovable, tough Thelma Ritter played Margo's loyal, wisecracking maid with the heart of gold. Comden and Green turned the Thelma Ritter character into Duane. As originally played by Lee Roy Reams, Duane was nonthreatening and lovable. His career as a hairdresser is a stereotypical profession for a gay man, but he is primarily of interest because of his openness about his sexual identity and his loyalty to Margo. Duane's sexuality is established early in the script:

> *Margo*: Well, I deserve a good time tonight! Duane, how'd you like to escort two lonely ladies out on the town?
> *Duane*: I've got a date.
> *Margo*: Bring him along![85]

This is a laugh line, of course, but in 1970 it also brought a degree of shock mixed with recognition that gays *were* making themselves known and emerging from the closet. Margo's open acceptance of Duane's sexuality was fresh and topical for 1970 Broadway audiences.

Unlike Sebastian Baye, Duane is loving, trustworthy, and proud of his sexuality. When told that Margo's new show has received rave critical notices, he hugs her and jokingly remarks, "Good! Now I can buy that fun fur I've been laughing at! I'll put water on for your Sanka."[86] Although the character is explicitly gay, Comden and Green create no laughs at his expense, as Lerner does with Sebastian Baye. Instead, Duane functions as a tool to keep the plot moving. Like the Thelma Ritter character in the film, Duane is the first to warn Margo of Eve's usurpation and treachery:

> *Duane*: I saw her at Joe Allen's last night. She was table-for-twoing it with everybody's favorite producer.
> *Margo*: You don't like her, do you? (Duane rolls his eyes heavenward in disgust.) But Duane, she is marvelous! She only thinks of me.
> *Duane*: Let's say she thinks only about you. Studying you. The way you walk, the way you talk, the way you dress . . .[87]

This dialogue is taken verbatim from Thelma Ritter's dialogue in the film. How can one make the post-Stonewall homosexual more lovable and less threatening than cloning him as Thelma Ritter?

What Comden and Green have done is literalize identity in *Applause.* Unlike the texts of *Company* and *Coco,* which are enigmatic about their central characters, the text of *Applause* literalizes the sexuality of Eve and Duane. The wild card, however, is Margo, and this is where the text is incomplete. Margo is heterosexual; she ultimately retires from the Broadway stage to marry Bill Sampson and live happily in the country. Where the text is incomplete is the necessity for a larger-than-life diva to play Margo. If the text closes the sexuality of the characters, it reverts to the kind of performer as cocreator so popular in the pre–Rodgers and Hammerstein nonintegrated musical. *Applause* is a show that depends on a star performer. Writing of Broadway divas, John Clum accurately assesses Bacall's contribution to the original production:

> In this year after Stonewall, the creators of *Applause* acknowledged the relationship between diva and gay men. . . . It was a Grand Musical Debut for a camp figure, forties film siren Lauren Bacall. Bacall, another Broadway baritone, can't carry a tune, and her voice sounds

> lower than that of her leading man, Len Cariou. She can't really dance. She is a Presence, which means most of the musical work goes to the supporting cast. Bacall begins a number, but the ensemble quickly takes over. Her one ballad, "Hurry Back," is a dull, two-note affair for a singer with two notes. But Bacall is a celebrity, a star at a time in which there is a dire shortage of musical stars. And she represents those two essential aspects of the Broadway diva. She is a figure of nostalgia and she is a survivor in a show about survival.[88]

Bacall can get away with staying up all night and dancing with gypsies at a gay bar while managing to reassure straight audiences that ultimately marriage to a good man and a house with a white picket fence is better than being a celebrity. Like the vaudeville and burlesque stars of the 1920s, 1930s, and 1940s, and like the great female musical theatre stars of the 1950s and 1960s, she was able to control her audiences by negotiating their differences and appealing to a wide variety of spectators and readings.

Bacall herself is enigmatic and mysterious. That is the baggage she brings with her onstage. One remembers her famous film line about whistling to Bogart: just put your lips together and blow. One also remembers her campy portrayal of Amy in the film *Young Man with a Horn* (1950), in which she played a confused artist who amusingly could not decide whether she preferred men or women while she was married to Kirk Douglas. The intertextuality she brings from these film performances are part of her star persona. If the Comden-Green libretto defines Margo as heterosexual, Bacall transcends gendered categories and boundaries. As Clive Barnes described her in the *New York Post,* "Miss Bacall is probably going to be the Marlene Dietrich of the 1980s—she has that same enchantingly cool asexual sexuality."[89] Significantly, when the show was revived in the mid-1990s with Stephanie Powers, it folded quickly on the road. Although not open in the sense of the texts of *Company* or *Coco, Applause* is an incomplete text without a powerhouse, over-the-top star performance.

One can criticize *Company* and *Coco* for copping out in performance, for refusing to deal with the issues of sexual identity raised in their texts; however, the explicit is not always as interesting as the enigmatic, nor as lifelike. This allure of the unknown is true of nonmusicals as well. Brick, in *Cat on a Hot Tin Roof,* is fascinating because he remains ambiguous. The issue is not whether he has reciprocated his friend Skipper's homosexual desires; it is how a repressive society has made Brick perceive homosexuality. Williams and Kazan argued about the ending and finally settled on the hopeful version in which presumably Brick will resume sleeping with Maggie, which probably helped to sugarcoat the deeper issues the play raises. Wisely, William Dean Howells observed, "What the American public always wants is a tragedy with a happy ending."[90] *Cat* was a product of the mid-1950s, just as *Company, Coco,* and *Applause* were products of the aftermath of Stonewall. It will be exciting to see how new generations choose to deal with their ambiguities.

Thirty-five years after Stonewall, gay civil rights is more newsworthy than ever, as the issue of gay marriage has become a political hot potato. Although many contemporary musicals feature gay, bisexual, or gender-bender characters, one would never know it from the musicals chosen by the New York host committee for the 2004 Republican National Presidential Convention. According to veteran producer Emmanuel Azenberg, "Twenty percent of Republicans are evangelical, and they'd string up the guy who picked 'Movin' Out' or 'Avenue Q.' Whoever has to pick has to pick carefully."[91] Whereas such shows as *The Producers, Hairspray, Chicago,* and *Rent* were not approved by the committee, Republican delegates patronized *42nd Street, Wonderful Town, The Lion King, Beauty and the Beast,* and *Bombay Dreams.* The last was the only Republican-approved musical to feature men in drag. As Robert Hofler points out in an article for *Variety,* apparently cross-dressing is fine as long as one does it in India.[92]

Perhaps the greatest loss for Republican delegates, in terms of both entertainment and eye-opening ideology, was the lack of opportunity to see Hugh Jackman's performance as gay Australian cabaret singer Peter Allen in *The Boy from Oz* (2003). Allen, like the Margo Channing character in *Applause,* is written as a closed character. Whereas the text specifies that Margo is straight, the *Oz* script tells us that Allen is gay. Like Bacall, however, Jackman opens the role with an ambiguous sex appeal that registers with both straight and gay audiences. Jackman moves with a kinetic physicality that reads as hot; moreover, his charisma transforms a character who is written as selfish, egotistical, hedonistic, and flamboyant into a lovable protagonist. He is able to mainstream gayness in a way that was impossible for the real Peter Allen. Here is where performance subverts text. During the first act, Allen is caught in a sexual embrace with another man. During act 2, Allen brings home a trick with whom he falls in love and kisses him passionately. When I saw the show, not only were there no gasps, groans, or embarrassed giggles, the audience, clearly thrilled that Jackman had found someone to love, emitted a collective swoon at the steamy embrace. I deliberately make the distinction here between Jackman and Peter

Allen. In the following scene, Jackman, as Allen, tells his mother he has fallen in love with "someone." At first, the mother thinks it is a woman. When Jackman corrects her and tells that it is another man, she is taken aback for a moment, smiles, and indicates that this is just fine too. The audience was with her all the way. If the next scene had been a gay wedding, Jackman probably would have had them cheering.

It is one thing to laugh at cross-dressing comic caricatures, such as Roger de Bris in *The Producers* or even Harvey Fierstein's touching but campy impersonation of a slovenly but good-hearted mother in *Hairspray.* It is quite something else to play a gay character whose homosexuality is not an excuse for comedy and hold the audience in the palm of one's hand. It is difficult to imagine another major star succeeding with this role. The facile answer is that Jackman is an A-list movie star who is married. Perhaps the straight members of the audience assume that he is only playing a role; underneath the gay impersonation is a butch action hero. Perhaps the gay members of the audience are titillated by Jackman's possible sexual ambivalence—is he or isn't he? In either scenario, here is an old-fashioned, vaudeville star turn that is all the more remarkable because Jackman is a song-and-dance man, not a musical comedy diva or male comic. It is obvious he loves to perform in much the same way that Mary Martin made it obvious to her audiences that they could not possibly love her as much as she loved performing for them. In musicals women have traditionally evoked this kind of adulation: Martin, Merman, Carol Channing, Gwen Verdon, Barbara Harris, and Liza Minnelli come immediately to mind. Occasionally star comics such as Eddie Cantor, Jackie Gleason, Zero Mostel, and Nathan Lane have also produced this response. The only Broadway song-and-dance men I can think of who were capable of provoking this kind of audience worship were Jolson, George M. Cohan, and possibly Sammy Davis Jr.

Fortunately the vehicle in which Jackman is performing is a jerry-built musical comedy; otherwise this kind of vaudeville turn involving performer as cocreator would be impossible. I saw Jackman in the Trevor Nunn revival of *Oklahoma!* in London. He was fine but was hampered by being in a Rodgers and Hammerstein musical play with a fixed (and much better crafted) text. In *Oz,* he is able to ad-lib, carry on conversations with the audience, joke with latecomers, and bring audience members onstage to banter with him. Obviously he was not given this opportunity as Curly. The separation between performer and text is significant, for it permits Jackman to do what he does best: to entertain. In the process, he promotes an assimilationist strategy for gays that is comparable to the Jewish assimilationist strategies that Cantor and Jolson performed in the 1920s. I do not claim that this promotion is deliberate on Jackman's part by any means; nevertheless, it is the effect his performance seems to have produced on adoring audiences. Great entertainers, through talent and the sheer power of performance, do much to alter prejudice and change perceived notions of identity.

More than sixty years after *Oklahoma!*, vaudeville and musical comedy, despite formalistic histories that have long since dismissed them, are alive and well on Broadway. The struggle for autonomy between text and performer as cocreator is ongoing. On the one hand, an integrated musical such as Tony Kushner's sung-through *Caroline or Change* (2003) provides hope that whatever is wrong with society can be fixed. On the other hand, Jackman's powerhouse star turn in a jerry-built, vaudeville-like vehicle such as *Oz* does more to promote sexual tolerance at a time when gay marriage is a fiercely debated national topic than a room crammed with activists. Which is better? As far as I am concerned, they are both just fine.

Appendix

◆ ◆ ◆

Notes

◆ ◆ ◆

Works Cited and Consulted

◆ ◆ ◆

Index

◆ ◆ ◆ ◆ ◆ ◆ ◆

Appendix: Sources of Additional Information on Musicals

Libraries with Holdings of Material on Broadway Musicals

Since I discuss more than a hundred years' worth of musicals, if I were to cite each text separately, the bibliography would be a book in itself. The following libraries contain the libretti, scores, kinescopes, videotapes, films, or recordings of most of the musicals covered. In cases where I go into particular detail about a musical, I document the text, kinescope, videotape, film, or recording in a note.

Many kinescopes of musicals that were produced on television are available by title at the Museum of Television and Radio in New York and in Chicago. During the 1950s and 1960s, particularly, televised versions of Broadway musicals were frequently produced on series like *The Hallmark Hall of Fame, Producers' Showcase, Max Liebman Presents,* and *The Colgate Comedy Hour.* Frequently, shows are truncated, but they nevertheless offer the opportunity to see many stars at mid-century, some of whom perform their signature roles. Videotaped Broadway and off-Broadway shows can be seen by appointment at the New York Public Library for the Performing Arts at Lincoln Center. Vintage films of Broadway musicals from the 1920s and 1930s can be seen by appointment at the Museum of Modern Art in New York and at the Library of Congress in Washington.

Columbia University, New York: Butler Library
- Joseph Urban Collection

Library of Congress, Washington, DC
- Film Archives
- Leonard Bernstein Collection
- Bob Fosse–Gwen Verdon Collection

Victor Herbert Collection
Rodgers and Hammerstein Collection
Museum of Modern Art, New York
Film Division
Museum of the City of New York
Theatre Collection
Museum of Television and Radio, New York and Chicago
New York Public Library of the Performing Arts at Lincoln Center
Billy Rose Theatre Collection
New York Public Library: 42 Street Research Branch
Manuscript and Newspaper Division
Shubert Archive
Harold Washington Library: Chicago

Discographies of Original Cast Recordings

Original cast recordings are a significant source of information about musicals. It is beyond the parameters of this book to list all available cast recordings, and it is against the interests of scholarship to list a selection of my favorites. The following are discographies of musical comedies, operettas, revues, and integrated musicals that should prove helpful, although, to my knowledge, none is absolutely complete.

Hummell, David. *Collector's Guide to Musicals.* Metuchen, New Jersey: Scarecrow Press: 1984.

Lynch, Richard Chigley. *Broadway, Movie, T.V. and Studio Cast Music: 1985–1995.* Westport: Greenwood Press, 1996.

———. *Broadway on Record: Directory of Cast Recordings: 1931–1986.* Westport: Greenwood, 1987.

Portantiere, Michael. *The TheaterMania Guide to Musical Theater Recordings.* New York: Backstage, 2004.

Raymond, Jack. *Show Music on Record from the 1870s to the 1980s.* New York: Unger, 1982.

For recordings of early performances of musical comedy and operetta, see *Music of the York Stage* (Pearl CD GEMM CDS9050-2; 9053-8; 9056-8; 9059-61). This is a twelve CD collection and includes recordings of performers including Weber and Fields, Bert Williams, Lillian Russell, Nora Bayes, George S. Cohan, as well as performances by members of the original Broadway casts of early musicals by Cohan, Victor Herbert, Irving Berlin, and Jerome Kern.

◆ ◆ ◆ ◆ ◆ ◆ ◆

Notes

Preface

1. Throughout the book, I have used the English spelling of *theatre,* except where the American *theater* appears in quotations or citations. This is a preference based on the use of the English spelling in most journals and books that cover the field.

2. In an important piece about musical theatre scholarship, David Savran articulates several questions that bear examination in rehistoricizing musicals: the issue of authenticity, the evanescence of popularity, the importance of linking popular musical theatre with other forms of theatre and art that reflect cultural change, and the need to rehistoricize musical theatre from an author's medium to a more collaborative paradigm. See David Savran, "Toward a Historiography of the Popular."

3. See Greg Lawrence, *Dance with Demons: The Life of Jerome Robbins.*

1. Celebrating Incompleteness

1. Lawrence W. Levine, *Highbrow/Lowbrow: The Emergence of Cultural Hierarchy in America,* 3.

2. Roland Barthes, *Image, Music, Text,* 161.

3. Barthes, *Image, Music, Text,* 163.

4. Marvin Carlson, *Theories of the Theatre,* 445.

5. Peter Brook, *The Open Door: Thoughts on Acting and Theatre,* 63.

6. William E. Gruber, *Comic Theatres: Studies in Performance and Audience Response,* 2.

7. J. L. Styan, "Changeable Taffeta: Shakespeare's Characters in Performance," 136.

8. Gruber, *Comic Theatres,* 5.

9. Richard Taruskin, *Text and Act,* 12.

10. Quoted in Taruskin, *Text and Act,* 54.

11. Taruskin, *Text and Act,* 13.

12. See Michael A. Morrison, *John Barrymore: Shakespearean Actor,* 250–52.

13. Roland Jackson, "Editorial: Performance Practice and Its Critics—The Debate Goes On," 113.

14. Taruskin, *Text and Act,* 21.

15. Quoted in Paul de Man, *Blindness and Insight,* 49–50.

16. Quoted in Carlson, *Theories of the Theatre,* 459.

17. Brook, *Open Door,* 65–66.

18. Brook, *Open Door,* 66–67.

19. Joshua Logan, *Josh: My Up and Down, In and Out Life,* 263.

20. William G. Hyland, *Richard Rodgers,* 189. For Rodgers's comments on Logan's reenvisioning the show and tampering with the authenticity of the text, see Richard Rodgers, *Musical Stages.*

21. The term *poperetta* was coined by Denny Martin Flinn. See Flinn, *Musical! A Grand Tour,* 475.

22. Brook, *Open Door,* 60–61.

23. Michel Saint-Denis, *Theatre: The Rediscovery of Style,* 48, 50.

24. Quoted in Arthur Laurents, *Original Story by Arthur Laurents,* 378.

25. Laurents, *Original Story,* 378.

26. For a comprehensive study of the revue form, see Lee Davis, *Scandals and Follies: The Rise and Fall of the Great Broadway Revue;* see also Gerald Bordman, *American Musical Revue from* The Passing Show *to* Sugar Babies.

27. I thank Ralph Locke for this observation.

28. Even the name of the merry widow is subject to variation. In one version it is Hanna; in another, Sonia.

29. Gerald Bordman, *American Musical Theatre: A Chronicle,* 312.

30. For more on the genesis of the Princess Theatre shows, see Bordman, *American Musical Theatre,* 305.

31. Bill Gile, interview with author, January 26, 1998.

32. See Bordman, *American Musical Theatre,* 306.

33. Ethan Mordden, *Make Believe: The Broadway Musical in the 1920s,* 46.

34. Leslie Fiedler, *The Inadvertent Epic,* 13–42.

35. Susan McClary, *Georges Bizet: Carmen,* 146.

36. McClary, *Georges Bizet,* 116.

37. Paul Filmer, Val Rimmer, and Dave Walsh, "*Oklahoma!:* Ideology and Politics in the Vernacular Tradition of the American Musical," 381.

38. Andrea Most, "'You've Got to Be Carefully Taught': The Politics of Race in Rodgers and Hammerstein's *South Pacific,*" 310.

39. Greg Lawrence, *Dance with Demons: The Life of Jerome Robbins,* 82–83.

40. Quoted in Lawrence, *Dance with Demons,* 83.

41. See Richard Wagner, *Opera and Drama.* For a discussion of the guiding artistic hand necessary to reinforce the intentions of the composer, see Carl Dahlhaus, *Nineteenth-Century Music,* 196.

42. Quoted in Levine, *Highbrow/Lowbrow,* 145.

43. Quoted in Levine, *Highbrow/Lowbrow,* 1–2.

44. Levine, *Highbrow/Lowbrow,* 2.

45. See Taruskin, *Text and Act;* also, Jennifer Williams Brown, "On the Road with the 'Suitcase Aria': The Transmission of Borrowed Arias in Late Seventeenth-Century Italian Opera Revivals."

46. Quoted in Herbert G. Goldman, *Jolson: The Legend Comes to Life,* 113.

47. Donald Jay Grout, with Hermine Weigel Williams, *A Short History of Opera,* 213.

48. Patrick Barbier, *The World of the Castrati,* 215.

49. Curtis A. Price, Judith Milhous, and Robert D. Hume, *Italian Opera in Late Eighteenth-Century London,* vol. 1, *The King's Theatre, Haymarket, 1778–1791,* 29.

50. Grout, *Short History,* 219.

51. Price, Milhous, and Hume, *Italian Opera,* 30.

52. Brown, "On the Road."

53. Charles Burney, *Memoirs of the Life and Writings of the Abate Metastasio: In Which Are Incorporated Translations of His Principal Letters,* 2:325, 3:43.

54. Quoted in Grout, *Short History,* 269.

55. Charles Burney, *The Present State of Music in Germany, the Netherlands, and Provinces,* 2:262.

56. Quoted in Grout, *Short History,* 270. Handel also famously underestimated Gluck as knowing "no more of counterpoint than Waltz, my cook" (259).

57. See Dahlhaus, *Nineteenth-Century Music;* also Dahlhaus, *Between Romanticism and Modernism.*

58. Gerald Mast, *Can't Help Singing: The American Musical on Stage and Screen,* 203.

59. Alfred Drake and Celeste Holm of *Oklahoma!* and John Raitt of *Carousel* became stars, but not until they originated the roles of Curly, Ado Annie, and Billy Bigelow.

60. For more information on Gluck's reforms of opera seria, see Herbert Lindenberger, *Opera in History: from Monteverdi to Cage,* 49–64, 110, 127. Also see Dahlhaus, *Esthetics of Music;* Dahlhaus, "Ethos and Pathos in Gluck's 'Iphigenie auf Tauris'"; Patricia Howard, *Gluck and the Birth of Modern Opera;* and Grout, *Short History,* 258–81.

61. Quoted in Bordman, *American Musical Theatre,* 313.

62. Bordman, *American Musical Theatre,* 307–8.

63. Stanley Green, *Broadway Musicals Show by Show,* 45.

64. Logan, *Josh,* 102.

65. Logan, *Josh*, 104.

66. William McBrien, *Cole Porter*, 282. For Bennett's account, see George J. Ferencz, *"The Broadway Sound": The Autobiography and Selected Essays of Robert Russell Bennett.*

67. Bordman, *American Musical Theatre*, 366.

68. Ethel Merman and George Eells, *Merman*, 72.

69. McBrien, *Cole Porter*, 282–83.

70. See Merman and Eells, *Merman.*

71. Abe Burrows, *Honest, Abe: Is There Really No Business Like Show Business?*, 282.

72. Quoted in Meryle Secrest, *Somewhere for Me: A Biography of Richard Rodgers*, 318–19.

73. For more on star semiotics, see Michael Quinn, "Celebrity and the Semiotics of Acting"; also, Marvin Carlson, "The Haunted Stage: Recycling and Reception in the Theatre," 6.

74. Quoted in William Goldman, *The Season: A Candid Look at Broadway*, 170.

75. Brown, *Zero Mostel*, 230.

76. Quoted in Brown, *Zero Mostel*, 230.

77. Maria Karnilova, interview with author, May 12, 1983.

78. Brown, *Zero Mostel*, 231.

79. Quoted in Brown, *Zero Mostel*, 233.

80. Brown, *Zero Mostel*, 234.

81. Quoted in Brown, *Zero Mostel*, 235.

82. Bordman, *American Musical Theatre*, 667.

83. See Taruskin, *Text and Act*, 164–72.

84. See Brown, "On the Road," 3–25.

2. The Star as Cocreator: Performing Jewishness During the Melting Pot

1. For theoretical literature about the performance of identity, see Jill Dolan, *Geographies of Learning: Theory and Practice, Activism and Performance;* Judith Butler, "Performative Acts and Gender Constitution: An Essay in Phenomenology and Feminist Theory"; Butler, *Gender Trouble;* Butler, *Bodies That Matter;* and Eve Kosofsky Sedgwick, *Epistemology of the Closet.*

2. Andrea Most, *Making Americans: Jews and the Broadway Musical.*

3. Lawrence J. Epstein, *The Haunted Smile: The Story of Jewish Comedians in America*, 23–33.

4. Gerald Bordman, *American Musical Theatre*, 580.

5. Stanley Green, *The Great Clowns of Broadway*, 114.

6. Green, *Great Clowns of Broadway*, 125.

7. For further reading, see David Krasner, *Resistance, Parody, and Double Consciousness in African American Theatre, 1895–1910;* Thomas L. Riis, *Just Before Jazz: Black Musical Theatre in New York, 1890–1915;* Allen Woll, *Black Musical Theatre*

from Coontown *to* Dreamgirls; Michael Rogin, *Blackface, White Noise: Jewish Immigrants in the Hollywood Melting Pot;* Ann Douglas, *Terrible Honesty: Mongrel Manhattan in the 1920s;* Eric Lott, *Love and Theft: Blackface Minstrelsy and the American Working Class;* Nadine George-Graves, *The Royalty of Negro Vaudeville: The Whitman Sisters and the Negotiation of Race, Gender and Class in African American Theater, 1900–1940;* Annemarie Bean, James V. Hatch, and Brooks McNamara, eds., *Inside the Minstrel Mask: Readings in Nineteenth-Century Blackface Minstrelsy;* William J. Mahar, *Behind the Burnt Cork Mask: Early Blackface, Minstrelsy, and Antebellum American Popular Culture;* and Ethel Waters, *His Eye Is on the Sparrow.*

8. Quoted in Lawrence W. Levine, *The Opening of the American Mind: Canons, Culture, and History,* 106.

9. Alexis de Tocqueville to Ernest de Chabrol, June 9, 1831, in Tocqueville, *Selected Letters on Politics and Society,* 38.

10. Ralph Waldo Emerson, *The Journals and Miscellaneous Notebooks of Ralph Waldo Emerson,* 299–300.

11. Herman Melville, *Redburn: His First Voyage,* 189–90.

12. See Israel Zangwill, *The Melting Pot.*

13. Zangwill, *Melting Pot,* 198.

14. Harley Erdman, *Staging the Jew: The Performance of an American Ethnicity, 1860–1920,* 138.

15. For more information on Eastern European and Mediterranean immigration during this period, see Thomas J. Archdeacon, *Becoming American: An Ethnic History,* 112–71. For the influence of social Darwinism and racism on the nativist movement and on eugenics, see John Higham, *Strangers in the Land: Patterns of American Nativism, 1860–1925,* 131–57.

16. Quoted in Karen Brodkin, *How Jews Became White Folks and What That Says about Race in America,* 28.

17. See Madison Grant, *The Passing of the Great Race, or the Racial Basis of European History.*

18. Quoted in Brodkin, *How Jews Became White Folks,* 28.

19. Levine, *Opening of the American Mind,* 111.

20. Lewis S. Gannett, "Is America Anti-Semitic?," 330–31.

21. Erdman, *Staging the Jew,* 117.

22. See Horace M. Kallen, *Culture and Democracy in the United States.*

23. Levine, *Opening of the American Mind,* 113; also see Kallen, *Culture and Democracy.*

24. See Stephen J. Whitfield, *In Search of Jewish American Culture,* 148–49.

25. Brodkin, *How Jews Became White Folks,* 189.

26. Brodkin, *How Jews Became White Folks,* 60.

27. Brodkin, *How Jews Became White Folks,* 104–5.

28. Most, *Making Americans,* 14.

29. Most, *Making Americans,* 13.

30. "Whiteness," like other racial identities (and like gender), can be performed and is the function of white cultural production's imagery of itself. See Richard Dyer, *White.*

31. Bordman, *American Musical Theatre,* 386.

32. Epstein, *Haunted Smile,* 86.

33. Zeppo replaced Gummo when the latter was drafted during World War I.

34. Barbara W. Grossman, *Funny Woman: The Life and Times of Fanny Brice,* 101.

35. Quoted in Norman Katkov, *The Fabulous Fanny,* 205.

36. According to Grossman, Brice appeared only once in blackface, in *The Ziegfeld Follies of 1917.* Grossman acknowledges Helen Armstead-Johnson's claim that Brice introduced "Lovie Joe" in brown face, although according to Grossman, no apparent evidence supports this. See also Helen Armstead-Johnson, "Blacks in Vaudeville: Broadway and Beyond," 83.

37. Fanny Brice as told to Palma Wayne, "Fannie of the Follies, Part 1," 139.

38. Brice, "Fannie of the Follies," 139.

39. Douglas, *Terrible Honesty,* 57.

40. Quoted in Douglas, *Terrible Honesty,* 56.

41. See Douglas, *Terrible Honesty;* Lott, *Love and Theft.*

42. Douglas, *Terrible Honesty,* 76.

43. Herbert G. Goldman, *Jolson: The Legend Comes to Life,* 76.

44. On the limits of assimilation and Jewish and Irish blackface, see Michael Bronski, *The Pleasure Principle: Sex, Backlash, and the Struggle for Gay Freedom,* 37–53. For Jewish blackface, see Rogin.

45. For Irish blackface, see Noel Ignatiev, *How the Irish Became White;* Douglas C. Riach, "Blacks and Blackface on the Irish Stage, 1830–1860"; Lott, *Love and Theft,* 94–97, 148–49; Rogin, *Blackface, White Noise,* 56–8; and Bronski, *Pleasure Principle,* 38–42.

For Jewish blackface, see Rogin, *Blackface, White Noise;* Lott, *Love and Theft;* Bronski, *Pleasure Principle,* 38–52; Douglas, *Terrible Honesty,* 73–107, 346–86; Riis, *Just Before Jazz;* Robert C. Toll, *Blacking Up;* Mel Watkins, *On the Real Side: Laughing, Lying and Signifying—The Underground Tradition of African-American Humor;* and William Torbert Leonard, *Masquerade in Black.* For a female Jewish performer's recollections of her days in blackface, see Sophie Tucker, *Some of These Days,* 33–42.

46. Whitfield, *In Search of Jewish American Culture,* 150.

47. Roger D. Abrahams, *Singing the Master: The Emergence of African-American Culture in the Plantation South,* 155.

48. Krasner, *Resistance,* 12.

49. For audience demographics on Broadway between 1910 and 1930, see Richard Butsch, *The Making of American Audiences: From Stage to Television, 1750–1990,* 81–94; and Michael Marks Davis Jr., *The Exploitation of Pleasure: A Study of Commercial Recreations in New York City,* 30–39.

50. Butsch, *Making of American Audiences*, 81–94.

51. Butsch, *Making of American Audiences*, 115.

52. Elbert Hubbard, *In the Spotlight*, 20. For more on diverse spectatorships within vaudeville, see Edwin Milton Royle, "The Vaudeville Theatre," 487.

53. Alison M. Kibler, *Rank Ladies: Gender and Cultural Hierarchy in American Vaudeville*, 93–94.

54. Peter Bailey, "Conspiracies of Meaning: Music Hall and the Knowingness of Popular Culture," 138–70.

55. Tucker, *Some of These Days*, 95.

56. See Epstein, *Haunted Smile*, 82–83.

57. See Leo Rosten, *The Joys of Yiddish*, 84.

58. Epstein, *Haunted Smile*, 37.

59. Bordman, *American Musical Theatre*, 458.

60. Epstein, *Haunted Smile*, 38.

61. Rosten, *Joys of Yiddish*, 84.

62. Quoted in "Rose," 743.

63. Florenz Ziegfeld, "Picking Out Pretty Girls for the Stage," 121.

64. Linda Mizejewski, *Ziegfeld Girl: Image and Icon in Culture and Cinema*, 116; also see Martha Banta, *Imaging American Women: Idea and Ideals in Cultural History*, 112–13.

65. Samuel S. Janus, "The Great Jewish-American Comedians' Identity Crisis," 259–65.

66. Rachel M. Brownstein, *Tragic Muse: Rachel of the Comédie-Française*, 83.

67. Riis, *Just Before Jazz*, 32.

68. Andrea Dworkin, *Scapegoat: The Jews, Israel, and Women's Liberation*, 318. The quoted matter within the quotation from Dworkin is from Brownstein, *Tragic Muse*, 130.

69. Laura Doyle, *Bordering on the Body: The Racial Matrix of Modern Fiction and Culture*, 21.

70. James Shapiro, *Shakespeare and the Jews*, 89–111.

71. See Marjorie Garber, *Vested Interests: Cross-Dressing and Cultural Anxiety*, 226.

72. Cited in Garber, *Vested Interests*, 228.

73. Dworkin, *Scapegoat*, 319.

74. Garber, *Vested Interests*, 228. For Jewishness and its perceived pathology on the stage, also see Sander L. Gilman, *Difference and Pathology: Stereotypes of Sexuality, Race, and Madness;* Gilman, *Freud, Race, and Gender;* and Gilman, *The Jew's Body.*

75. Dworkin, *Scapegoat*, 102.

76. Dworkin, *Scapegoat*, 95.

77. Garber, *Vested Interests*, 306–8.

78. Dworkin, *Scapegoat*, 102.

79. Dworkin, *Scapegoat*, 102.

80. *Whoopee!* quoted in Bordman, *American Musical Theatre,* 446.

81. Depending on his whim, Cantor interpolated a wide variety of songs in this spot on stage: "Hungry Women," "My Blackbirds are Bluebirds Now," "Ever Since the Movies Learned to Talk," and the most famous, "My Baby Just Cares for Me," written for the film. See Ethan Mordden, *Broadway Babies: The People Who Made the American Musical,* 65.

82. Douglas Gilbert, *American Vaudeville: Its Life and Times,* 79–80.

83. Quoted in Gary Giddins, *Bing Crosby: A Pocketful of Dreams—The Early Years, 1903–1940,* 79.

84. Royle, "Vaudeville Theatre," 485–95.

85. Herbert G. Goldman, *Banjo Eyes: Eddie Cantor and the Birth of Modern Stardom,* 66.

86. Goldman, *Banjo Eyes,* 57–58.

87. Goldman, *Banjo Eyes,* 58.

88. See Hilary Harris, "Failing 'White Woman': Interrogating the Performance of Respectability," 187; and Kate Davy, "Outing Whiteness: A Femininst/Lesbian Project," 204.

89. Dyer, *White,* 29.

90. Mizejewski, *Ziegfeld Girl,* 153.

91. Goldman, *Jolson,* 81.

92. Goldman, *Jolson,* 66.

93. See *Wonder Bar,* Warner Brothers, 1934.

94. See Douglas, *Terrible Honesty,* 363.

95. Goldman, *Jolson,* 142–43.

96. *Big Boy,* Warner Brothers, 1930.

97. *Big Boy.*

98. *Big Boy.*

99. *Big Boy.*

100. Rogin, *Blackface, White Noise,* 105.

101. Douglas, *Terrible Honesty,* 361.

102. Garber, *Vested Interests,* 277.

103. William A. Henry III, "Beyond the Melting Pot," 28.

104. Holland Cotter, "Beyond Multiculturalism: A Way to a New Freedom in Art," 28.

105. Cotter, "Beyond Multiculturalism," 1, 28.

106. Henry, "Beyond the Melting Pot," 42.

3. Unfinished Business

1. Gerald Mast, *Can't Help Singing: The American Musical on Stage and Screen.*

2. Foster Hirsch, *Harold Prince and the American Musical Theatre,* 21.

3. Quoted in Hirsch, *Harold Prince,* 20.

4. Hirsch, *Harold Prince,* 20.

5. Ethan Mordden, *Make Believe: The Broadway Musical in the 1920s,* 46.

6. Although O'Neill's early reputation was established with the Pulitzer Prize–winning *Beyond the Forest,* it would be inaccurate to classify O'Neill as a realistic playwright, since he spent much of his career after the realistic *Forest* experimenting with a variety of dramatic styles and genres.

7. Brenda Murphy, *American Realism and American Drama, 1880–1940,* 8.

8. See William Dean Howells, "Editor's Study," July 1886, 318.

9. Quoted in *New York Times,* September 11, 1927, sec. 8, p. 1, col. 3.

10. Lorraine Arnal McLean, *Dorothy Donnelly: A Life in the Theatre,* 83. For more on Sheldon and both his personal and professional relationship with Donnelly, see Eric Wollencroft Barnes, *The Man Who Lived Twice,* 70–71.

11. Gerald Bordman, *American Operetta from* H.M.S. Pinafore *to* Sweeney Todd, 115.

12. Ann Douglas, *Terrible Honesty: Mongrel Manhattan in the 1920s,* 21.

13. Oscar Wilde, *The Importance of Being Earnest,* 58.

14. Before *Show Boat,* Urban was perhaps best known for his imaginative, pointillist designs, notably for the *Ziegfeld Follies.* He began designing the *Follies* in 1915, the same year that Robert Edmund Jones introduced his groundbreaking designs to Broadway with *The Man Who Married a Dumb Wife.* Both were among the first to apply elements of the New Stagecraft to the American commercial theatre.

15. Bordman, *American Musical Theatre: A Chronicle,* 434.

16. Douglas, *Terrible Honesty,* 533.

17. See Bordman, *American Musical Theatre,* 417.

18. Bordman, *American Musical Theatre,* 433.

19. Richard Barrios, *A Song in the Dark: The Birth of the Film Musical,* 302–3.

20. Hugh Fordin, *Getting to Know Him: A Biography of Oscar Hammerstein II,* 93–95.

21. Jon Bradshaw, *Dreams That Money Can Buy: A Biography of Libby Holman,* 66.

22. Bradshaw, *Dreams That Money Can Buy,* 65–67.

23. Bradshaw, *Dreams That Money Can Buy,* 66–67.

24. William Goldman, *The Season: A Candid Look at Broadway,* 171.

25. Mark Fearnow, *The American Stage and the Great Depression: A Cultural History of the Grotesque,* 130.

26. Albert Bermel, *Farce,* 21.

27. Fearnow, *American Stage,* 129.

28. Eric Bentley, *Life of the Drama,* 245.

29. Fearnow, *American Stage,* 145.

30. Joan Peyser, *The Memory of All That,* 140–42.

31. Richard Traubner, *Operetta: A Theatrical History,* 155.

32. Traubner, *Operetta,* 415.

33. Bordman, *American Musical Theatre,* 582.

34. Quoted in Peyser, *Memory of All That,* 192.

35. *Leave It to Me* is probably best remembered as the show in which Mary Martin made her Broadway debut, singing the striptease "My Heart Belongs to Daddy" in a Siberian railway station, flanked by chorus boys Gene Kelly and Van Johnson. See Bordman, *American Musical Theatre,* 513.

36. Hollis Alpert, *Life and Times of* Porgy and Bess: *The Story of an American Classic,* 278.

37. Quoted in Alpert, *Life and Times,* 137.

38. Alpert, *Life and Times,* 140.

39. Quoted in Alpert, *Life and Times,* 270.

40. Quoted in Alpert, *Life and Times,* 305.

41. Hirsch, *Harold Prince,* 14.

42. See Traubner, *Operetta,* 320–21.

43. Lockridge quoted in Bordman, *American Musical Theatre,* 483.

44. Joshua Logan, *Josh: My Up and Down, In and Out Life,* 110.

45. Wendy Smith, *Real Life Drama: The Group Theatre and America, 1931–1940,* 261.

46. Smith, *Real Life Drama,* 281.

47. Harold Clurman, *The Fervent Years,* 177.

48. Green quoted in Smith, *Real Life Drama,* 278.

49. Marc Blitzstein emulated the Brecht-Weill *Rise and Fall of the City of Mahagonny* (1931) with *The Cradle Will Rock* (1938), which takes place in a mythic American city, Steeltown, run by an autocratic Mr. Mister; however, Blitzstein's work also failed to achieve popular success.

50. Quoted in Bordman, *American Musical Theatre,* 523.

51. Fearnow, *American Stage,* 20–21.

52. The choir has since changed. Three major New York revivals (1969, 1979, and 2002) all failed to earn back their investment. For more on these revivals, see Bruce Kirle, "Reconciliation, Resolution, and the Political Role of *Oklahoma!* in American Consciousness," 271–74.

53. Thornton Wilder, "Some Thoughts on Playwriting."

54. William Dean Howells, "Editor's Study," August 1891, 478.

55. Elia Kazan, *A Life,* 295.

56. See Bruce McConachie, "The 'Oriental' Musicals of Rodgers and Hammerstein and the U.S. War in Southeast Asia."

57. See Andrea Most, "'You've Got to Be Carefully Taught': The Politics of Race in Rodgers and Hammerstein's *South Pacific.*"

58. Meryle Secrest, *Somewhere for Me: A Biography of Richard Rodgers,* 291–92.

59. Kazan, *Life,* 345.

60. Goldman, *Season,* 359.

61. Ethan Mordden, *Rodgers and Hammerstein,* 97.

62. Mordden, *Rodgers and Hammerstein,* 33.

63. Mordden, *Rodgers and Hammerstein,* 97–98.

64. Perhaps de Mille's staging experiments were more than Hammerstein had bargained for. Hammerstein stepped in during rehearsals and directed some of the scenes himself, whether because de Mille had too much on her plate or because her innovative, ballet theatre staging became of concern.

65. Quoted in Hirsch, *Harold Prince,* 21.

66. Richard Rodgers and Oscar Hammerstein, introduction to *Allegro,* 116.

67. Alan Jay Lerner, *The Musical Theatre: A Celebration,* 170–71.

68. Cheryl Crawford, *One Naked Individual,* 168.

69. See David Garfield, *A Player's Place: The Story of the Actors Studio,* 69–70.

70. Quoted in Hirsch, *Harold Prince,* 162.

71. Quoted in John Storey, *An Introduction to Cultural Theory and Popular Culture.*

72. Quoted in Hirsch, *Harold Prince,* 120.

73. Joe Masteroff, John Kander, and Fred Ebb, *Cabaret,* 93.

74. Frank Rich, "At Last, 9/11 Has Its Own Musical."

75. Rich, "At Last."

76. John Lahr, "Talkers and Talkers."

77. Quoted in Hirsch, *Harold Prince,* 15.

78. Quoted in Hirsch, *Harold Prince,* 15.

79. See Tom Eyen and Bruce Kirle, *Kama Sutra.*

80. See Marvin Carlson, "The Haunted Stage: Recycling and Reception in the Theatre"; see also Carlson, *The Haunted Stage: The Theatre as Memory Machine;* Carlson, *Theatre Semiotics;* and Carlson, *Places of Performance.*

81. Categories overlap. For instance, *Jesus Christ Superstar* is a rock-poperetta-concept musical.

82. See Hirsch, *Harold Prince,* 169.

83. Hirsch, *Harold Prince,* 169.

4. Popular Musicals as Utopia

1. Jane Baldwin, *Michel Saint-Denis and the Shaping of the Modern Actor,* 2–3.

2. Richard Dyer, "Entertainment and Utopia," 376.

3. For a discussion of history versus memory, see Michael Kammen, *Mystic Chords of Memory: The Transformation of Tradition in American Culture,* 655–88.

4. Steven Carr, *Hollywood and Anti-Semitism: A Cultural History up to World War II,* 3.

5. Carr, *Hollywood and Anti-Semitism,* 39.

6. Populists attacked the American Theatrical Syndicate, founded in 1896 by Abraham Erlanger, Marc Klaw, Al Hayman, Charles Frohman, Samuel Nix, and Fred Zimmerman, on the basis of race. The syndicate controlled legitimate theatre throughout the United States during the first decade of the twentieth century, after which control was usurped by the Shubert brothers, also Jews. *Life,* the humor

magazine popular during the late nineteenth and early twentieth centuries, printed cartoons and editorials that railed against the Jewish theatrical trust. The cartoons portrayed Jewish producers and theatrical managers as sexually rapacious, money-grubbing, and physically repulsive. See Carr, *Hollywood and Anti-Semitism,* 45–53.

7. Michael Kazin, *The Populist Persuasion: An American History,* 2.

8. Carr, *Hollywood and Anti-Semitism,* 38–39.

9. Carr, *Hollywood and Anti-Semitism,* 178.

10. Kazin, *Populist Persuasion,* 131–32.

11. Hugh Fordin, *Getting to Know Him: A Biography of Oscar Hammerstein II,* 142–43.

12. Quoted in Fordin, *Getting to Know Him,* 143.

13. Hammerstein's interventionist stance came back to haunt him during the McCarthy era, when the State Department cited his involvement with the Hollywood League Against Nazism as a questionable activity, since the antifascist organization was suspected of sheltering communists. He responded that if communists were also members of the League, they were united by a common goal against fascism rather than by an agenda promoting communism: "If there were a forest fire outside of Los Angeles and we all ran out with buckets to pour water on it, I would not ask the man at my shoulder what his philosophy was." See Fordin, *Getting to Know Him,* 143.

14. Quoted in Carr, *Hollywood and Anti-Semitism,* 159.

15. Carr, *Hollywood and Anti-Semitism,* 160.

16. Carr, *Hollywood and Anti-Semitism,* 172.

17. Carr, *Hollywood and Anti-Semitism,* 238.

18. Fordin, *Getting to Know Him,* 211.

19. Fordin, *Getting to Know Him,* 211.

20. Kazin, *Populist Persuasion,* 158.

21. Kazin, *Populist Persuasion,* 159.

22. See Joseph Gaer, *The First Round: The Story of the* CIO *Political Action Committee,* 17.

23. See Andrea Most, "'We Know We Belong to the Land': The Theatricality of Assimilation in Rodgers and Hammerstein's *Oklahoma!*"

24. Most, "'We Know We Belong to the Land,'" 77–78.

25. See Michael Rogin, *Blackface, White Noise: Jewish Immigrants in the Hollywood Melting Pot.*

26. Jacquelyn Kilpatrick, *Celluloid Indians: Native-Americans and Film,* xvi–xvii. For a list of books, articles, and reviews of films from 1911 through 1985 that investigate the misrepresentation of the Native American in movies, see Gretchen M. Bataille and Charles L. P. Silet, *Images of American Indians on Film: An Annotated Bibliography.* See also Gretchen M. Bataille and Charles L. P. Silet, "The Entertaining Anachronism: Indians in American Film"; Roy Harvey Pearce, *Savagism*

and Civilization: A Study of the Indian and the American Mind; and Raymond William Stedman, *Shadows of the Indian: Stereotypes in American Culture.*

27. Ella Shohat and Robert Stam, *Unthinking Eurocentrism: Multiculturalism and the Media,* 119.

28. Carr, *Hollywood and Anti-Semitism,* 3–4.

29. Kilpatrick, *Celluloid Indians,* xvii.

30. Curtis Dahl, *Robert Montgomery Bird,* 79.

31. Andrea Most, "'Big Chief Izzy Horowitz': Theatricality and Jewish Identity in the Wild West," 336–37.

32. Lynn Riggs, *Green Grow the Lilacs,* 107–8.

33. Riggs, *Green Grow the Lilacs,* 161.

34. See Israel Zangwill, *The Melting Pot.*

35. Paul Filmer, Val Rimmer, and Dave Walsh, "*Oklahoma!:* Ideology and Politics in the Vernacular Tradition of the American Musical," 386.

36. Meryle Secrest, *Somewhere for Me: A Biography of Richard Rodgers,* 245.

37. The Jud character is named Jeeter in Riggs's play.

38. Max Wilk, *The Story of Oklahoma!,* 155.

39. Buloff can be heard on *Oklahoma!,* vol. 2, with Joseph Buloff, Betty Garde, and Alfred Drake, original cast recording Decca A-383.23M Personality Series, 1945. The album features three songs not on the 1943 cast album. The two volumes are combined in the 1993 CD re-release.

40. William G. Hyland, *Richard Rodgers,* 144. For more on Buloff's career, see Luba Kadison and Joseph Buloff, with Irving Genn, *On Stage, Off Stage: Memories of a Lifetime in the Yiddish Theatre.*

41. Carr, *Hollywood and Anti-Semitism,* 281.

42. For more on the Nunn revival, see Bruce Kirle, "Reconciliation, Resolution, and the Political Role of *Oklahoma!* in American Consciousness," 271–74.

43. Charles Kaiser, *1968 in America,* 153.

44. Robert Doty, "Growth of Overt Homosexuality in City Provokes Wide Concern," *New York Times,* December 17, 1963, quoted in Michael Bronski, *The Pleasure Principle: Sex, Backlash, and the Struggle for Gay Freedom,* 217.

45. Bronski, *Pleasure Principle,* 217.

46. Martin Duberman, *Stonewall,* 98.

47. Sally Banes, *Greenwich Village 1963: Avant-Garde Performance and the Effervescent Body,* 10.

48. Robert Brustein, *Dumbocracy in America: Studies in the Theatre of Guilt, 1987–1994,* 51.

49. For a discussion of pop music in the early 1960s, including Motown, see Kaiser, *1968 in America,* 209.

50. Kaiser, *1968 in America,* xxi.

51. Quoted in Stuart W. Little, "Robbins Casts Middle-Aged Dancers."

52. Quoted in Little, "Robbins Casts Middle-Aged Dancers."

53. Jared Brown, *Zero Mostel: A Biography,* 217.

54. Greg Lawrence, *Dance with Demons: The Life of Jerome Robbins,* 349, 336.

55. Quoted in Lawrence, *Dance with Demons,* 336.

56. Walter Kerr, "'Fiddler on the Roof.'"

57. William Goldman, *The Season: A Candid Look at Broadway,* 149.

58. Goldman, *Season,* 149–50.

59. Quoted in Richard Piro, *Black Fiddler,* 112.

60. Quoted in Piro, *Black Fiddler,* 112.

61. Quoted in Ken Mandelbaum, *A Chorus Line and the Musicals of Michael Bennett,* 170–71.

62. John Fiske, *Understanding Popular Culture,* 8.

63. John M. Clum, *Acting Gay: Male Homosexuality in Modern Drama,* 301.

64. Bruce J. Schulman, *The Seventies: The Great Shift in American Culture, Society, and Politics,* 79.

65. Schulman, *Seventies,* 16.

66. Mandelbaum, *Chorus Line,* 74.

67. Mandelbaum, *Chorus Line,* 146–47.

68. George Wachtel, "A Study of the New York Audience for the Broadway Theatre, 1980," 10.

69. Bernard Rosenberg and Ernest Harburg, *The Broadway Musical: Collaboration in Commerce and Art,* 40.

70. Sheridan Morley and Ruth Leon, *Mr. Producer,* 74.

71. Lawrence Grossberg, *We Gotta Get Out of This Place: Popular Conservatism and Postmodern Culture,* 174.

72. Grossberg, *We Gotta Get Out,* 275–76.

73. Brustein, *Dumbocracy,* 118.

74. Brustein, *Dumbocracy,* 16.

75. Augustine, *Confessions,* 55–56.

76. D. A. Miller, *Place for Us [Essay on the Broadway Musical],* 57.

77. Miller, *Place for Us,* 57.

78. Margo Jefferson, "Moseying Along in a Grand Old Land."

79. Clive Barnes, "Everything's Goin' Its Way."

5. Enigmatic Characters and the Post-Stonewall Musical

1. Eric Bentley, *The Life of the Drama,* 68–69.

2. See Manfred Pfister, *The Theory and Analysis of Drama,* 181.

3. According to Judy Insell, who worked for Lerner during the filming of *Paint Your Wagon,* director Joshua Logan was responsible for insisting that Lerner fashion a marriage in which two men share the same wife, which only underscores the precarious autonomy of authorial intent in the process of creating a musical onstage or on film.

4. See John M. Clum, *Something for the Boys: Musical Theatre and Gay Culture.*

5. Quoted in Charles Kaiser, *The Gay Metropolis, 1940–1996,* 96.

6. Edmund White, *States of Desire: Travels in Gay America,* 259.

7. George Chauncey, *Gay New York: Gender, Urban Culture and the Making of the Gay Male World, 1890–1940,* 355.

8. Chauncey, *Gay New York,* 327.

9. Chauncey, *Gay New York,* 331.

10. Percy Hammond, "Review."

11. Chauncey, *Gay New York,* 313.

12. Quoted in Kaier Curtin, *We Can Always Call Them Bulgarians: The Emergence of Lesbians and Gay Men on the American Stage,* 154–89.

13. Quoted in Gerald Bordman, *American Theatre: A Chronicle of Comedy and Drama, 1930–1969,* 107–8.

14. Chauncey, *Gay New York,* 356.

15. For more on these allegedly gay sex crimes against young boys in the late 1930s and 1940s, see Estelle Freedman, "'Uncontrolled Desires': The Response to the Sexual Psychopath, 1920–1960"; John D'Emilio, "The Homosexual Menace: The Politics of Sexuality in Cold War America"; Allan Berube, *Coming Out under Fire: The History of Gay Men and Women in World War Two;* and George Chauncey, "The Postwar Sex Crime Panic."

16. Ralph H. Major Jr., "New Moral Menace to Our Youth," 104.

17. Chauncey, *Gay New York,* 226.

18. Chauncey, *Gay New York,* 286.

19. Chauncey, *Gay New York,* 286.

20. Cole Porter and Moss Hart, *Jubilee.*

21. Quoted in Kaiser, *Gay Metropolis, 1940–1996,* 16. Ironically, during the 1960s, Watts was sympathetic to homosexual playwrights and was one of the greatest supporters of Albee and Williams when both were suffering critical brickbats from others.

22. See Ethan Mordden, *Coming Up Roses: The Broadway Musical in the 1950s.*

23. Kaiser, *Gay Metropolis, 1940–1996,* 93.

24. See Sally Banes, *Greenwich Village 1963: Avant-Garde Performance and the Effervescent Body;* Martin Duberman, *Stonewall;* also David Carter, *Stonewall.*

25. Alan Sinfield, *Out on Stage: Lesbian and Gay Theatre in the Twentieth Century,* 297.

26. Duberman, *Stonewall,* 221.

27. Quoted in Kaiser, *Gay Metropolis, 1940–1996,* 168.

28. Michel Foucault, "Sexual Choice, Sexual Act: Foucault and Homosexuality," 301.

29. Quoted in Kaiser, *Gay Metropolis, 1940–1996,* 6.

30. Quoted in Duberman, *Stonewall,* 61.

31. Quoted in Sinfield, *Out on Stage,* 298.

32. Quoted in Kaiser, *Gay Metropolis, 1940–1996,* 189.

33. A critically acclaimed off-Broadway revival of the Pirandello play was produced at the Martinique Theatre in 1963 and ran for 528 performances.

34. Ironically Eyen wanted the kind of mainstream success he ridiculed and eventually collaborated with Michael Bennett on *Dream Girls* (1981) as librettist and lyricist. Also see Tom Eyen and Bruce Kirle, *Kama Sutra.*

35. Howard Taubman, "Modern Primer: Helpful Hints to Tell Appearances from Truth."

36. Taubman, "Modern Primer".

37. Richard Schechner, "Who's Afraid of Edward Albee?," 64.

38. Quoted in Mel Gussow, *Edward Albee: A Singular Journey,* 220.

39. Quoted in Gussow, *Edward Albee,* 249.

40. Quoted in John M. Clum, *Acting Gay: Male Homosexuality in Modern Drama,* 180.

41. Kaiser, *Gay Metropolis, 1940–1996,* 165.

42. William Goldman, *The Season: A Candid Look at Broadway,* 237.

43. Goldman, *Season,* 239.

44. Arthur Laurents, *Original Story by Arthur Laurents,* 270.

45. Greg Lawrence, *Dance with Demons: The Life of Jerome Robbins,* 155–71.

46. Duberman, *Stonewall,* 190–91.

47. Arguing that Judy Garland's funeral had no connection to the Stonewall riots, David Carter maintains that the demonstrators were a new breed of homosexual and had no interest in Garland, an icon for older homosexuals. He also argues that drag queens, though involved in the riots, were not the principal demonstrators. Carter's conclusions seem overstated and facile to me, since it was Stonewall that helped create a new breed of homosexual; changes in gay identity did not occur overnight. Moreover, the bravery of the drag queens who defied the New York City police force inspired the support of others. See Carter, *Stonewall.*

48. The fifteen musicals are *Jimmy* (October 23, 1969), *Buck White* (December 2, 1969), *La Strada* (December 14, 1969), *Coco* (December 18, 1969), *Gantry* (February 4, 1970), *Georgy* (February 26, 1970), *Purlie* (March 15, 1970), *Blood Red Roses* (March 22, 1970), *Minnie's Boys* (March 26, 1970), *Look to the Lillies* (March 29, 1970), *Applause* (March 30, 1970), *Cry for Us All* (April 8, 1970), *The Boy Friend* (April 18, 1970), *Park* (April 22, 1970), and *Company* (April 26, 1970). Only one of the fifteen, *The Boy Friend,* was a revival. Although *Oh, Calcutta!* was financially successful, it preceded the Stonewall riot, as did *Hair.* Both shows also opened off-Broadway before transferring to regular Broadway runs.

49. See Foster Hirsch, *Harold Prince and the American Musical Theatre,* 87.

50. Quoted in Craig Zadan, *Sondheim and Company,* 124.

51. See Hirsch, *Harold Prince,* 87.

52. John M. Clum, *Something for the Boys: Musical Theatre and Gay Culture,* 222.

53. George Furth and Stephen Sondheim, *Company,* 42.

54. Quoted in Meryle Secrest, *Stephen Sondheim: A Life,* 371.

55. D. A. Miller, *Place for Us [Essay on the Broadway Musical],* 125.

56. Joanne Gordon, *Art Isn't Easy: The Theatre of Stephen Sondheim,* 55.

57. Secrest, *Stephen Sondheim,* 180.

58. Quoted in Kevin Kelly, *One Singular Sensation,* 69.

59. Quoted in Clum, *Something for the Boys,* 224.

60. Sinfield, *Out on Stage,* 292.

61. Alan Jay Lerner, *Coco,* act 2, scene 3, page 27.

62. Lerner, *Coco,* 2.2.11.

63. Lerner, *Coco,* 2.3.28.

64. Rick Altman, "The American Film Musical: Paradigmatic Structure and Mediatory Function," 197.

65. Lerner, *Coco,* 1.5.42.

66. Quoted in Steven Suskin, *More Opening Nights on Broadway: A Critical Quotebook of the Musical Theatre, 1965–1981,* 179.

67. Lerner, *Coco,* 1.6.54.

68. Lerner, *Coco,* 1.5.43.

69. Mark Steyn, *Broadway Babies Say Goodnight: Musicals Then and Now,* 198.

70. Goldman, *Season,* 238.

71. Quoted in Steven Bach, *Dazzler: The Life and Times of Moss Hart,* 224.

72. Bach, *Dazzler,* 224–25.

73. Bach, *Dazzler,* 213–16.

74. Ethan Mordden, *Beautiful Mornin': The Broadway Musical in the 1940s,* 61.

75. Lerner, *Coco,* 1.6.54.

76. Benthall, Hepburn's choice to direct, was reportedly so ineffectual, not to mention unfamiliar with musicals, that Bennett basically assumed the role of director during rehearsals.

77. Allegedly Chanel was delighted to learn that Hepburn had been chosen to play her in the musical. She later was bitterly disappointed when she found out it was the wrong Hepburn—Katharine, rather than Audrey.

78. Darwin Porter, *Katherine the Great: A Lifetime of Secrets . . . Revealed.*

79. Vito Russo, *The Celluloid Closet: Homosexuality in the Movies,* 94.

80. Russo, *Celluloid Closet,* 101.

81. Joseph L. Mankiewicz, "All about the Women in 'All about Eve,'" 38.

82. *Applause,* liner notes, original Broadway cast recording, 1971, ABC records, ABD-OCS-11.

83. See Sinfield, *Out on Stage,* 297.

84. Svetlana McLee Grody and Dorothy Daniels Lister, *Conversations with Choreographers,* 82.

85. Betty Comden and Adolph Green, *Applause,* 473.

86. Comden and Green, *Applause,* 477.

87. Comden and Green, *Applause,* 490.

88. Clum, *Something for the Boys,* 180.

89. Quoted in Suskin, *More Opening Nights,* 61.

90. Quoted in Edith Wharton, *A Backward Glance,* 147.

91. Quoted in Robert Hofler, "Strangers in Paradise: Delegates, Pols, Protesters Heading for Culture Clash," 52.

92. Hofler, "Strangers in Paradise," 1.

◆ ◆ ◆ ◆ ◆ ◆ ◆

Works Cited and Consulted

Abrahams, Roger D. *Singing the Master: The Emergence of African-American Culture in the Plantation South.* New York: Pantheon, 1992.

Acocella, Joan. "Stagestruck: What the Broadway Revivals Have Wrought." *New Yorker,* May 15, 2000, 98–101.

Allen, Robert Clyde. *A Horrible Prettiness.* Chapel Hill: University of North Carolina Press, 1991.

Alpert, Hollis. *The Life and Times of* Porgy and Bess: *The Story of an American Classic.* New York: Knopf, 1990.

Altman, Rick. *The American Film Musical.* Bloomington: Indiana University Press, 1987.

———. "The American Film Musical: Paradigmatic Structure and Mediatory Function." In *Genre: The Musical,* edited by Rick Altman, 197–207. London: Routledge, 1981.

Archdeacon, Thomas J. *Becoming American: An Ethnic History.* New York: Free Press, 1983.

Armstead-Johnson, Helen. "Blacks in Vaudeville: Broadway and Beyond." In *American Popular Entertainment,* edited by Myron Mattlaw. Westport, CT: Greenwood, 1979.

Atkinson, Brooks. *Broadway.* New York: Limelight, 1970.

Augustine. *Confessions.* Translated by R. S. Pine-Coffin. Baltimore: Penguin, 1961.

Bach, Steven. *Dazzler: The Life and Times of Moss Hart.* New York: Knopf, 2001.

Bailey, Peter. "Conspiracies of Meaning: Music Hall and the Knowingness of Popular Culture." *Past and Present* 144 (August 1994): 138–70.

Baldwin, Jane. *Michel Saint-Denis and the Shaping of the Modern Actor.* Westport, CT: Praeger, 2003.

Banes, Sally. *Greenwich Village 1963: Avant-Garde Performance and the Effervescent Body.* Durham, NC: Duke University Press, 1993.

Banfield, Stephen. *Sondheim's Broadway Musicals.* Ann Arbor: University of Michigan Press, 1993.

Banta, Martha. *Imaging American Women: Idea and Ideals in Cultural History.* New York: Columbia University Press, 1987.

Barbier, Patrick. *The World of the Castrati.* Translated by Margaret Crosland. London: Souvenir, 1996.

Barnes, Clive. "Everything's Goin' Its Way." *New York Post,* March 22, 2002. http://www.nypost.com/theatre/40632.htm.

Barnes, Eric Wollencroft. *The Man Who Lived Twice.* New York: Scribner, 1956.

Barrios, Richard. *A Song in the Dark: The Birth of the Musical Film.* New York: Oxford University Press, 1995.

Barthes, Roland. *Image, Music, Text.* Translated by Stephen Heath. New York: Hill and Wang, 1977.

Bataille, Gretchen M., and Charles L. P. Silet. "The Entertaining Anachronism: Indians in American Film." In *The Kaleidoscopic Land: How Hollywood Views Ethnic Groups,* edited by Randall M. Miller. Englewood, NJ: Ozer, 1980.

———. *Images of American Indians on Film: An Annotated Bibliography.* New York: Garland, 1985.

Bean, Annemarie, James V. Hatch, and Brooks McNamara, editors. *Inside the Minstrel Mask: Readings in Nineteenth-Century Blackface Minstrelsy.* Hanover, NH: Wesleyan University Press, 1996.

Becker, George. *Realism in Modern Literature.* New York: Ungar, 1980.

Bentley, Eric. *The Life of the Drama.* New York: Atheneum, 1964.

Bergreen, Laurence. *As Thousands Cheer: The Life of Irving Berlin.* New York: Viking, 1990.

Bermel, Albert. *Farce.* New York: Simon, 1982.

Berube, Allan. *Coming Out under Fire: The History of Gay Men and Women in World War Two.* New York: Free Press, 1990.

Bianconi, Lorenzo, and Giorgio Pestelli, editors. *Opera Production and Its Resources.* Translated by Lydia G. Cochrane. Chicago: University of Chicago Press, 1998.

Big Boy. Warner Brothers film. Starring Al Jolson, 1930. Library of Congress, Washington, DC.

Block, Geoffrey. *Enchanted Evenings: The Broadway Musical from Show Boat to Sondheim.* New York: Oxford University Press, 1997.

Bordman, Gerald. *American Musical Comedy from* Adonis *to* Dreamgirls. New York: Oxford University Press, 1985.

———. *The American Musical Revue from* The Passing Show *to* Sugar Babies. New York: Oxford University Press, 1985.

———. *American Musical Theatre: A Chronicle.* New York: Oxford University Press, 1978.

———. *American Operetta from* H.M.S. Pinafore *to* Sweeney Todd. New York: Oxford University Press, 1981.

———. *American Theatre: A Chronicle of Comedy and Drama, 1914–1930.* New York: Oxford, University Press, 1985.

———. *American Theatre: A Chronicle of Comedy and Drama, 1930–1969.* New York: Oxford University Press, 1996.

———. *Days to Be Happy, Years to Be Sad: The Life and Music of Vincent Youmans.* New York: Oxford University Press, 1982.

Bradshaw, Jon. *Dreams That Money Can Buy: A Biography of Libby Holman.* New York: Morrow, 1985.

Brett, Philip, Elizabeth Wood, and Gary C. Thomas, editors. *Queering the Pitch: The New Gay and Lesbian Musicology.* London: Routledge, 1994.

Brice, Fanny, as told to Palma Wayne. "Fanny of the Follies, Part 1." *Cosmopolitan,* February 1936, 139.

Brodkin, Karen. *How Jews Became White Folks and What That Says About Race in America.* New Brunswick, NJ: Rutgers University Press, 2000.

Bronski, Michael. *The Pleasure Principle: Sex, Backlash, and the Struggle for Gay Freedom.* New York: St. Martin's, 1998.

Brook, Peter. *The Open Door: Thoughts on Acting and Theatre.* New York: Theatre Communications Group, 1995.

Brown, Jared. *Zero Mostel.* New York: Atheneum, 1989.

Brown, Jennifer Williams. "On the Road with the 'Suitcase Aria': The Transmission of Borrowed Arias in Late Seventeenth-Century Italian Opera Revivals." *Journal of Musicological Research* 15:1–2 (1995): 3–25.

Brownstein, Rachel M. *Tragic Muse: Rachel of the Comédie-Française.* New York: Knopf, 1993.

Brustein, Robert. *Dumbocracy in America: Studies in the Theatre of Guilt, 1987–1994.* Chicago: Dee, 1994.

Burney, Charles. *Memoirs of the Life and Writings of the Abate Matastasio: In Which Are Incorporated Translations of His Principal Letters.* 3 volumes. London: Robinson, 1796.

———. *The Present State of Music in Germany, the Netherlands, and Provinces.* 2 volumes. London: Becket, 1773.

Burrows, Abe. *Honest, Abe: Is There Really No Business Like Show Business?* Boston: Little, Brown, 1980.

Butler, Judith. *Bodies That Matter.* New York: Routledge, 1993.

———. *Gender Trouble.* New York: Routledge, 1990.

———. "Performative Acts and Gender Constitution: An Essay in Phenomenology and Feminist Theory." In *Performing Feminisms: Feminist Critical Theory and Theatre,* edited by Sue Ellen Case, 270–82. Baltimore: Johns Hopkins University Press, 1990.

Butsch, Richard. *The Making of American Audiences: From Stage to Television, 1750–1990.* Cambridge: Cambridge University Press, 2000.

Carlson, Marvin. "The Haunted Stage: Recycling and Reception in the Theatre." *Theatre Survey* 35 (May 1994): 5–18.

———. *The Haunted Stage: The Theatre as Memory Machine.* Ann Arbor: University of Michigan Press, 2001.

———. *Places of Performance.* Ithaca, NY: Cornell University Press, 1989.

———. *Theatre Semiotics.* Bloomington: University of Indiana Press, 1990.

———. *Theories of the Theatre.* Ithaca, NY: Cornell University Press, 1984.

Carr, Steven. *Hollywood and Anti-Semitism: A Cultural History up to World War II.* Cambridge: Cambridge University Press, 2001.

Carter, David. *Stonewall.* New York: St. Martin's, 2004.

Chapin, Ted. *Everything Was Possible.* New York: Knopf, 2003.

Chauncey, George. *Gay New York: Gender, Urban Culture and the Making of the Gay Male World, 1890–1940.* New York: Basic, 1994.

———. "The Postwar Sex Crime Panic." In *True Stories from the American Past,* edited by William Graebner. New York: McGraw, 1993.

Clum, John M. *Acting Gay: Male Homosexuality in Modern Drama.* New York: Columbia University Press, 1992.

———. *Something for the Boys: Musical Theatre and Gay Culture.* New York: St. Martin's, 1999.

Clurman, Harold. *The Collected Works of Harold Clurman,* edited by Marjorie Logia and Glenn Young. New York: Applause, 1994.

———. *The Fervent Years.* New York: Hill and Wang, 1945.

Comden, Betty, and Adolph Green. *Applause.* In *Great Musicals of the American Theatre,* vol. 2., edited by Stanley Richards (Radnor, PA: Chiton, 1977).

Corio, Ann. *This Was Burlesque.* New York: Madison Square Press, 1968.

Cotter, Holland. "Beyond Multiculturalism: A Way to a New Freedom in Art." *New York Times,* July 19, 2001, sec. 2, pp. 1, 28.

Crawford, Cheryl. *One Naked Individual.* New York: Bobbs-Merrill, 1977.

Creekmur, Corey K., and Alexander Doty, editors. *Out in Culture: Gay, Lesbian, and Queer Essays on Popular Culture.* Durham: Duke University Press, 1995.

Curtin, Kaier. *We Can Always Call Them Bulgarians: The Emergence of Lesbians and Gay Men on the American Stage.* Boston: Alyson, 1987.

Dahl, Curtis. *Robert Montgomery Bird.* New York: Twayne, 1963.

Dahlhaus, Carl. *Between Romanticism and Modernism.* Translated by Mary Whittal. Berkeley: University of California Press, 1980.

———. *Esthetics of Music.* Translated by William W. Austin. Cambridge: Cambridge University Press, 1982.

———. "Ethos and Pathos in Gluck's 'Iphigenie auf Tauris.'" *Die Musikforschung* 17 (1974): 289–300.

———. *Nineteenth-Century Music,* translated by J. Bradford Robinson. Berkeley: University of California Press, 1989.

Davis, Lee. *Scandals and Follies: The Rise and Fall of the Great Broadway Revue.* New York: Limelight, 2000.

Davis, Michael Marks, Jr. *The Exploitation of Pleasure: A Study of Commercial Recreations in New York City.* New York: Russell Sage Foundation, 1911.

Davy, Kate. "Outing Whiteness: A Feminist/Lesbian Project." *Theatre Journal* 47:3 (1995): 189–206.

de Man, Paul. *Blindness and Insight.* Minneapolis: University of Minnesota Press, 1983.

Demastes, William W. *Beyond Naturalism: A New Realism in American Theatre.* London: Greenwood, 1988.

D'Emilio, John. "The Homosexual Menace: The Politics of Sexuality in Cold War America." In *Passion and Power: Sexuality in History,* edited by Kathy Peiss and Christina Simmons, 226–40. Philadelphia: Temple University Press, 1989.

Dietz, Howard. *Dancing in the Dark.* New York: Quadrangle–New York Times Book Company, 1974.

Dinnerstein, Leonard, and David M. Reimers. *Ethnic Americans: A History of Immigration.* New York: Columbia University Press, 1999.

Dolan, Jill. "Geographies of Learning: Theatre Studies, Performance Studies, and the 'Performative.'" *Theatre Journal* 45:4 (1993): 417–41.

———. *Geographies of Learning: Theory and Practice, Activism and Performance.* Middletown, CT: Wesleyan University Press, 2001.

Doty, Alexander. *Making Things Perfectly Queer: Interpreting Mass Culture.* Minneapolis: University of Minnesota Press, 1993.

Douglas, Ann. *Terrible Honesty: Mongrel Manhattan in the 1920s.* New York: Farrar, 1995.

Doyle, Laura. *Bordering on the Body: The Racial Matrix of Modern Fiction and Culture.* New York: Oxford University Press, 1994.

Duberman, Martin. *Stonewall.* New York: Plume, 1993.

Dufresne, Claude. *La Belle histoire de l'opérette: d'Offenbach a nos jours.* Paris: Editions Solar, 1997.

———. *Histoire de l'Opérette.* Paris: Fernand Nathan, 1981.

Dworkin, Andrea. *Scapegoat: The Jews, Israel, and Women's Liberation.* New York: Free Press, 2000.

Dyer, Richard. "Entertainment and Utopia." In *The Cultural Studies Reader,* edited by Simon During. London: Routledge, 1993, 371–81.

———. *Heavenly Bodies: Film Stars and Society.* New York: St. Martin's, 1986.

———. *The Matter of Images: Essays on Representations.* New York: Routledge, 1993.

———. *Only Entertainment.* New York: Routledge, 1992.

———. "*A Star Is Born* and the Construction of Authenticity." In *Stardom: Industry of Desire,* edited by Christine Gledhill, 132–40. New York: Routledge, 1991.

———. *White.* London: Routledge, 1997.

Eells, George. *The Life That Late He Led: A Biography of Cole Porter.* New York: Putnam's, 1967.

Emerson, Ralph Waldo. *The Journals and Miscellaneous Notebooks of Ralph Waldo Emerson.* Cambridge: Harvard University Press, 1971.

Engel, Lehman. *The American Musical Theater.* New York: Collier, 1975.

Epstein, Lawrence J. *The Haunted Smile: The Story of Jewish Comedians in America.* New York: Public Affairs, 2001.

Erdman, Harley. *Staging the Jew: The Performance of an American Ethnicity, 1860–1920.* New Brunswick, NJ: Rutgers University Press, 1997.

Erenberg, Lewis A. *Steppin' Out.* Westport, CT: Greenwood, 1981.

Everett, William A., and Paul R. Laird. *The Cambridge Companion to the Musical.* Cambridge: Cambridge University Press, 2002.

Eyen, Tom, and Bruce Kirle. *Caution: A Love Story.* Clipping file. Lincoln Center Library for the Performing Arts in New York, Billy Rose Theatre Collection.

———. *Kama Sutra.* In *Ten Plays by Tom Eyen.* New York: French, 1971.

Farneth, David, with Elmar Juchem and Dave Stein. *Kurt Weill: A Life in Pictures and Documents.* Woodstock, NY: Overlook, 2000.

Fearnow, Mark. *The American Stage and the Great Depression: A Cultural History of the Grotesque.* Cambridge: Cambridge University Press, 1997.

Ferencz, George J., editor. *"The Broadway Sound": The Autobiography and Selected Essays of Robert Russell Bennett.* Rochester, NY: University of Rochester Press, 1999.

Feuer, Jane. *The Hollywood Musical.* Bloomington: Indiana University Press, 1993.

Fiedler, Leslie. *The Inadvertent Epic.* New York: Simon, 1979.

Fields, Armond, and L. Marc Fields. *From the Bowery to Broadway: Lew Fields and the Roots of American Popular Theatre.* New York: Oxford University Press, 1993.

Filmer, Paul, Val Rimmer, and Dave Walsh. "*Oklahoma!:* Ideology and Politics in the Vernacular Tradition of the American Musical." *Popular Music* 18:3 (1999): 381–95.

Fiske, John. *Understanding Popular Culture.* London: Unwin Hyman, 1989.

Flinn, Denny Martin. *Musical! A Grand Tour.* New York: Schirmer, 1997.

Fordin, Hugh. *Getting to Know Him: A Biography of Oscar Hammerstein II.* New York: Ungar, 1977.

Foucault, Michel. "Sexual Choice, Sexual Act: Foucault and Homosexuality." In *Michel Foucault: Interviews and Other Writings 1977–1984,* edited by Lawrence D. Kritzman and translated by Alan Sheridan, 286–306. New York: Routledge, 1988.

Freedland, Michael. *Jolson.* New York: Stein, 1972.

Freedman, Estelle. "'Uncontrolled Desires': The Response to the Sexual Psychopath, 1920–1960." In *Passion and Power: Sexuality in History,* edited by Kathy Peiss and Christina Simmons, 199–225. Philadelphia: Temple University Press, 1989.

Furth, George, and Stephen Sondheim. *Company.* New York: Theatre Communications Groups, 1996.

Gaer, Joseph. *The First Round: The Story of the CIO Political Action Committee.* New York: Duell, 1944.

Gannett, Lewis S. "Is America Anti-Semitic?" *Nation,* March 21, 1923, 330–31.

Gänzl, Kurt. *Song and Dance.* New York: Smithmark, 1995.

Garber, Marjorie. *Vested Interests: Cross-Dressing and Cultural Anxiety.* New York: Routledge, 1997.

Garfield, David. *A Player's Place: The Story of the Actors Studio.* New York: MacMillan, 1980.

Gassner, John. *Form and Idea in Modern Theatre.* New York: Dryden, 1956.

George-Graves, Nadine. *The Royalty of Negro Vaudeville: The Whitman Sisters and the Negotiation of Race, Gender and Class in African American Theater, 1900–1940.* New York: St. Martin's, 2000.

Giddons, Gary. *Bing Crosby: A Pocketful of Dreams—The Early Years, 1903–1940.* New York: Little, Brown, 2001.

Gilbert, Douglas. *American Vaudeville: Its Life and Times.* New York: Whittlesey, 1940.

Gilman, Sander L. *Difference and Pathology: Stereotypes of Sexuality, Race, and Madness.* Ithaca: Cornell University Press, 1985.

———. *Freud, Race, and Gender.* Princeton: Princeton University Press, 1993.

———. *The Jew's Body.* New York: Routledge, 1991.

Glazer, Nathan, and Daniel P. Moynihan. *Beyond the Melting Pot: The Negroes, Puerto Ricans, Jews, Italians, and Irish of New York City.* Cambridge: MIT Press, 1995.

Glenn, Susan A. *Female Spectacle: The Theatrical Roots of Modern Feminism.* Cambridge: Harvard University Press, 2000.

Golden, Eve. *Anna Held and the Birth of Ziegfeld's Broadway.* Lexington: University Press of Kentucky, 2000.

Goldman, Herbert G. *Banjo Eyes: Eddie Cantor and the Birth of Modern Stardom.* New York: Oxford University Press, 1997.

———. *Fanny Brice.* New York: Oxford University Press, 1992.

———. *Jolson: The Legend Comes to Life.* New York: Oxford University Press, 1988.

Goldman, William. *The Season: A Candid Look at Broadway.* New York: Harcourt, 1969.

Goodhart, Danro, editor. *Reading Stephen Sondheim.* New York: Garland, 2000.

Gordon, Joanne. *Art Isn't Easy: The Theatre of Stephen Sondheim.* New York: Knopf, 1998.

Gorelik, Mordecai. *New Theatres for Old.* New York: French, 1940.

Grant, Madison. *The Passing of the Great Race, or the Racial Basis of European History.* New York: Scribner, 1916.

Grant, Mark N. *The Rise and Fall of the Broadway Musical.* Boston: Northeastern University Press, 2004.

Green, Benny. *Let's Face the Music: The Golden Age of Popular Song.* New York: Pavilion, 1989.

Green, Stanley. *Broadway Musicals Show by Show.* Milwaukee: Hal Leonard, 1985.

———. *Encyclopedia of the Musical Theatre.* New York: Dodd, 1976.

———. *The Great Clowns of Broadway.* New York: Oxford University Press, 1994.

———. *Ring Bells! Sing Songs!: Broadway Musicals of the 1930s.* New Rochelle, NY: Arlington, 1971.

———. *The World of Musical Comedy.* South Brunswick, NJ: Barnes, 1974.

Grody, Svetlana McLee, and Dorothy Daniels Lister. *Conversations with Choreographers.* Portsmouth, NH: Heinemann, 1996.

Grossberg, Lawrence. *We Gotta Get Out of This Place: Popular Conservatism and Postmodern Culture.* New York: Routledge, 1992.

Grossman, Barbara W. *Funny Woman: The Life and Times of Fanny Brice.* Bloomington: Indiana University Press, 1991.

Grout, Donald Jay, with Hermine Weigel Williams. *A Short History of Opera.* 3rd ed. New York: Columbia University Press, 1988.

Gruber, William E. *Comic Theaters: Studies in Performance and Audience Response.* Athens: University of Georgia Press, 1996.

Gussow, Mel. *Edward Albee: A Singular Journey.* New York: Simon, 1999.

Hamm, Charles. *Irving Berlin: Songs from the Melting Pot: The Formative Years, 1907–1914.* New York: Oxford University Press, 1997.

Hammond, Percy. "Review." *New York Tribune,* September 18, 1924.

Harris, Andrew B. *Broadway Theatre.* London: Routledge, 1994.

Harris, Hilary. "Failing 'White Women': Interrogating the Performance of Respectability." *Theatre Journal* 52:2 (2000): 183–209.

Harris, Warren G. *The Other Marilyn: A Biography of Marilyn Miller.* New York: Arbor, 1985.

Hart, Dorothy. *Thou Swell, Thou Witty: The Life and Lyrics of Lorenz Hart.* New York: Harper, 1976.

Henderson, Amy, and Dwight Blocker Bowers. *Red, Hot, and Blue: A Smithsonian Salute to the American Musical.* Washington: Smithsonian Institution, 1996.

Henderson, Mary C. *The City and the Theatre.* Clifton, NJ: White, 1973.

Henry, William A., III. "Beyond the Melting Pot." *Time,* April 9, 1990, 28–44.

Higham, Charles. *Ziegfeld.* Chicago: Regnery, 1972.

Higham, John. *Strangers in the Land: Patterns of American Nativism, 1860–1925.* New Brunswick, NJ: Rutgers University Press, 1955.

Hirsch, Foster. *The Boys from Syracuse: The Shuberts' Theatrical Empire.* Carbondale: Southern Illinois University Press, 1998.

———. *Harold Prince and the American Musical Theatre.* Cambridge: Cambridge University Press, 1989.

———. *Kurt Weill on Stage: From Berlin to Broadway.* New York: Knopf, 2002.

Hoch, Danny. *Jails, Hospitals, and Hip-Hop and Some People.* New York: Villard, 1998.

Hofler, Robert. "Strangers in Paradise: Delegates, Pols, Protesters Heading for Culture Clash." *Variety,* June 28–July 11, 2004, 1, 52.

Howard, Patricia. *Gluck and the Birth of Modern Opera.* London: Barrie and Rockliff, 1963; reprint New York: St. Martin's, 1964.

Howells, William Dean. "Editor's Study." *Harper's Monthly* 73 (July 1886): 314–19.

———. "Editor's Study." *Harper's Monthly* 83 (August 1891): 476–81.

———. "Life and Letters." *Harper's Weekly* 39 (December 28, 1895): 1236–37.

———. "The Plays of Eugene Brieux." *North American Review* 201 (March 1915): 402–11.

Hubbard, Elbert. *In the Spotlight.* East Aurora, NY: Roycrofters, 1917.

Hyland, William G. *Richard Rodgers.* New Haven: Yale University Press, 1998.

Ignatiev, Noel. *How the Irish Became White.* New York: Routledge, 1995.

Jablonski, Edward, and Lawrence D. Stewart. *The Gershwin Years.* New York: Da Capo, 1958.

Jackson, Arthur. *The Best Musicals of the Century.* New York: Crown, 1977.

Jackson, Roland. "Editorial: Performance, Practice and Its Critics—The Debate Goes On." *Performance Practice Review* 4 (1991): 113.

Janus, Samuel S. "The Great Jewish-American Comedians' Identity Crisis." *American Journal of Psychoanalysis* (Fall 1980): 259–65.

Jefferson, Margo. "Moseying Along in a Grand Old Land." *New York Times,* April 14, 2002, sec. 2, p. 5.

Jones, John Bush. *Our Musicals, Ourselves.* Lebanon, NH: Brandeis University Press, 2003.

Kadison, Luba, and Joseph Buloff, with Irving Genn. *On Stage, Off Stage: Memories of a Lifetime in the Yiddish Theatre.* Cambridge: Harvard University Press, 1992.

Kair, Curtin. *We Can Always Call Them Bulgarians: The Emergence of Lesbians and Gay Men on the American Stage.* Boston: Alyson, 1987.

Kaiser, Charles. *The Gay Metropolis, 1940–1996.* Boston: Houghton, 1996.

———. *1968 in America.* New York: Grove, 1988.

Kallen, Horace M. *Culture and Democracy in the United States.* New Brunswick, NJ: Transaction, 1998.

Kammen, Michael. *American Culture American Tastes: Social Change and the 20th Century.* New York: Knopf, 1999.

———. *Mystic Chords of Memory: The Transformation of Tradition in American Culture.* New York: Vintage, 1993.

Katkov, Norman. *The Fabulous Fanny.* New York: Knopf, 1953.

Kazan, Elia. *A Life.* New York: Knopf, 1988.

Kazin, Michael. *The Populist Persuasion: An American History.* Ithaca, NY: Cornell University Press, 1995.

Kelly, Kevin. *One Singular Sensation.* New York: Doubleday, 1990.

Kennedy, Michael Patrick, and John Muir. *Musicals.* New York: Harper, 1997.

Kerman, Joseph. *Opera as Drama.* New York: Vintage, 1956.

Kerr, Walter. "'Fiddler on the Roof.'" *New York Herald Tribune,* September 22, 2004. In "New York Theatre Reviews, 1964," 216. New York Public Library for the Performing Arts at Lincoln Center.

Kibler, M. Allison. *Rank Ladies: Gender and Cultural Hierarchy in American Vaudeville.* Chapel Hill: University of North Carolina Press, 1999.

Kilpatrick, Jacquelyn. *Celluloid Indians: Native Americans and Film.* Lincoln: University of Nebraska Press, 1999.

Kimball, Robert, and Alfred Simon. *The Gershwins.* New York: Atheneum, 1973.

Kirle, Bruce. "Reconciliation, Resolution, and the Political Role of *Oklahoma!* in American Consciousness." *Theatre Journal* 55:2 (2003): 251–74.

Knapp, Raymond. *The American Musical and the Formation of National Identity.* Princeton: Princeton University Press, 2005.

Koestenbaum, Wayne. *The Queen's Throat: Opera, Homosexuality, and the Mystery of Desire.* New York: Vintage, 1993.

Koger, Alicia Kae. "Trends in Musical Theatre Scholarship: An Essay in Historiography." *New England Theatre Journal* 3 (1992): 69–83.

Krasner, David. *Resistance, Parody, and Double Consciousness in African American Theatre, 1895–1910.* New York: St. Martin's, 1997.

Kreuger, Miles. *Showboat: The Story of a Classic American Musical.* New York: Oxford University Press, 1977.

Lahr, John. "Talkers and Talkers." *New Yorker,* May 3, 2004, 101.

Lamb, Andrew. *150 Years of Popular Musical Theatre.* New Haven: Yale University Press, 2000.

Laurents, Arthur. *Original Story by Arthur Laurents.* New York: Knopf, 2000.

Lawrence, Greg. *Dance with Demons: The Life of Jerome Robbins.* New York: Putnam, 2001.

Lawson-Peebles, Robert, ed. *Approaches to the American Musical.* Exeter, Eng.: Exeter University Press, 1996.

Leonard, William Torbert. *Masquerade in Black.* Metuchen, NJ: Scarecrow, 1968.

Lerner, Alan Jay. *Coco.* Typescript, file RM6795. Billy Rose Theatre Collection, New York Public Library for the Performing Arts at Lincoln Center.

———. *The Musical Theatre: A Celebration.* New York: McGraw, 1987.

Levine, Lawrence W. *Highbrow Lowbrow: The Emergence of Cultural Hierarchy in America.* Cambridge: Harvard University Press, 1988.

———. *The Opening of the American Mind: Canons, Culture, and History.* Boston: Beacon, 1996.

Lewis, Robert. *Slings and Arrows: Theatre in My Life.* New York: Stein and Day, 1984.

Lindenberger, Herbert. *Opera in History: From Monteverdi to Cage.* Stanford: Stanford University Press, 1998.

Little, Stuart W. "Robbins Casts Middle-Aged Dancers." *New York Herald Tribune,* June 11, 1964, n.p. In *Fiddler on the Roof* clipping file. Billy Rose Theatre Collection, New York Public Library for the Performing Arts at Lincoln Center.

Litton, Glenn, and Cecil Smith. *Musical Comedy in America.* New York: Routledge, 1981.

Locke, Ralph. "What Are These Women Doing in Opera?" in *En Travesti: Women, Gender, Subversion, Opera,* edited by Corinne E. Blackmer and Patricia Juliana Smith. New York: Columbia University Press, 1995, 59–98.

Loesser, Susan. *A Most Remarkable Fella.* New York: Donald I. Fine, 1993.

Logan, Joshua. *Josh: My Up and Down, In and Out Life.* New York: Delacorte, 1976.

Loney, Glenn, editor. *Musical Theatre in America: Papers and Proceedings of the Conference on the Musical Theatre in America.* Westport, CT: Greenwood, 1984.

Lott, Eric. *Love and Theft: Blackface Minstrelsy and the American Working Class.* New York: Oxford University Press, 1993.

Lynes, Russell. *The Lively Audience.* New York: Harper, 1985.

Mahar, William J. *Behind the Burnt Cork Mask: Early Blackface, Minstrelsy, and Antebellum American Popular Culture.* Urbana: University of Illinois Press, 1999.

Major, Ralph H. Jr. "New Moral Menace to Our Youth." *Coronet,* September 28, 1950, 104.

Mandelbaum, Ken. *A Chorus Line and the Musicals of Michael Bennett.* New York: St. Martin's, 1989.

Mankiewicz, Joseph. "All about the Women in 'All about Eve.'" *New York Magazine,* October 16, 1972, 38–47.

Marshall, Bill, and Robynn Stilwell. *Musicals: Hollywood and Beyond.* Exeter, Eng.: Cromwell, 2000.

Martin, Mary. *My Heart Belongs.* New York: Quill, 1984.

Marx, Samuel. *Rodgers and Hart: Bewitched, Bothered and Bedeviled.* New York: Putnam, 1976.

Masson, Alain. *Comédie musicale.* Paris: Stock/Cinema, 1981.

Mast, Gerald. *Can't Help Singing: The American Musical on Stage and Screen.* Woodstock, NY: Overlook, 1987.

Masteroff, Joe, John Kander, and Fred Ebb. *Cabaret.* New York: Random, 1967.

McBrien, William. *Cole Porter.* New York: Knopf, 1998.

McClary, Susan. *Conventional Wisdom: The Content of Musical Form.* Berkeley: University of California Press, 2000.

———. *Feminine Endings: Music, Gender, and Sexuality.* Minneapolis: University of Minnesota Press, 1991.

———. *Georges Bizet, Carmen.* Cambridge Opera Handbooks. Cambridge: Cambridge University Press, 1992.

McConachie, Bruce A. "The 'Oriental' Musicals of Rodgers and Hammerstein and the U.S. War in Southeast Asia." *Theatre Journal* 46 (October 1995): 385–98.

McLean, Albert F., Jr. *American Vaudeville as Ritual.* Lexington: University of Kentucky Press, 1965.

McLean, Lorraine Arnal. *Dorothy Donnelly: A Life in the Theatre.* Jefferson, NC: McFarland, 1999.

Melville, Herman. *Redburn: His First Voyage.* New York: Boni, 1924.

Merman, Ethel, and George Eells. *Merman.* New York: Simon, 1978.

Meyer, Moe, editor. *Politics and Poetics of Camp.* London: Routledge, 1994.

Meyerson, Harold, and Ernie Harburg. *Who Put the Rainbow in the Wizard of Oz?: Yip Harburg, Lyricist.* Ann Arbor: University of Michigan Press, 1993.

Miller, D. A. *Place for Us [Essay on the Broadway Musical].* Cambridge: Harvard University Press, 1998.

Mizejewski, Linda. *Ziegfeld Girl: Image and Icon in Culture and Cinema.* Durham: Duke University Press, 1999.

Mordden, Ethan. *The American Theatre.* New York: Oxford University Press, 1981.

———. *Beautiful Mornin': The Broadway Musical in the 1940s.* New York: Oxford University Press, 1999.

———. *Broadway Babies: The People Who Made the American Musical.* New York: Oxford University Press, 1983.

———. *Coming Up Roses: The Broadway Musical in the 1950s.* New York: Oxford University Press, 1998.

———. *The Happiest Corpse I've Ever Seen: The Last 25 Years of the Broadway Musical.* New York: Palgrave, 2005

———. *Make Believe: The Broadway Musical in the 1920s.* New York: Oxford University Press, 1997.

———. *One More Kiss: The Broadway Musical in the 1970s.* New York: Palgrave, 2003.

———. *Open A New Window: The Broadway Musical in the 1960s.* New York: Palgrave, 2001.

———. *Rodgers and Hammerstein.* New York: Abrams, 1992.

———. *Sing for Your Supper: The Broadway Musical in the 1930s.* New York: Palgrave, 2005

Morley, Sheridan, and Ruth Leon. *Mr. Producer.* London: Weidenfield, 1998.

Morrison, Michael A. *John Barrymore: Shakespearean Actor. Cambridge: Cambridge University Press, 1997.*

Most, Andrea. "'Big Chief Izzy Horowitz': Theatricality and Jewish Identity in the Wild West." American Jewish History 87 (May 1999): 313–41.

———. *Making Americans: Jews and the Broadway Musical.* Cambridge: Harvard University Press, 2004.

———. "'We Know We Belong to the Land': The Theatricality of Assimilation in Rodgers and Hammerstein's *Oklahoma!*." *PMLA* 113:1 (1998): 77–89.

———. "'You've Got To Be Carefully Taught': The Politics of Race in Rodgers and Hammerstein's *South Pacific.*" *Theatre Journal* 52:3 (October 2000): 307–37.

Murphy, Brenda. *American Realism and American Drama, 1880–1940.* Cambridge: Cambridge University Press, 1987.

Nasaw, David. *Going Out: The Rise and Fall of Public Amusements.* New York: Basic, 1997.

Pearce, Roy Harvey. *Savagism and Civilization: A Study of the Indian and the American Mind.* Baltimore: Johns Hopkins University Press, 1965.

Peiss, Kathy. *Cheap Amusements: Working Women and Leisure in Turn-of-the-Century New York.* Philadelphia: Temple University Press, 1986.

Petty, Frederick C. *Italian Opera in London: 1760–1800.* Ann Arbor: UMI Research Press, 1972.

Peyser, Joan. *The Memory of All That.* New York: Simon, 1993.

Pfister, Manfred. *The Theory and Analysis of Drama.* Cambridge: Cambridge University Press, 1988.

Phillips, Julien. *Stars of the Ziegfeld Follies.* Minneapolis: Lerner, 1972.

Piro, Richard. *Black Fiddler.* New York: Morrow, 1971.

Porter, Cole, and Moss Hart. *Jubilee.* Unpublished manuscript, 1936. Billy Rose Theatre Collection, New York Public Library for the Performing Arts at Lincoln Center.

Porter, Darwin. *Katherine the Great: A Lifetime of Secrets . . . Revealed.* New York: Blood Moon, 2004.

Price, Curtis, Judith Milhous, and Robert D. Hume. *Italian Opera in Late Eighteenth-Century London.* Vol. 1, *The King's Theatre, Haymarket, 1778–1791.* Oxford, Eng.: Clarendon, 1995.

Prince, Harold. *Contradictions: Notes on Twenty-Six Years in the Theatre.* New York: Dodd, 1974.

Quinn, Michael. "Celebrity and the Semiotics of Acting." *New Theatre Quarterly* 6 (May 1990): 154–61.

Radway, Janice A. *A Feeling for Books: The Book-of-the-Month Club, Literary Taste, and Middle-Class Desire.* Chapel Hill: University of North Carolina Press, 1997.

Riach, Douglas C. "Blacks and Blackface on the Irish Stage, 1830–1860." *American Studies* 7 (Fall 1981): 231–42.

Rich, Frank. "At Last 9/11 Has Its Own Musical." *New York Times,* May 2, 2004, sec. 2, p. 14.

———. *Hot Seat: Theatre Criticism for The New York Times, 1980–1993.* New York: Random, 1998.

Riggs, Lynn. *Green Grow the Lilacs.* New York: French, 1931.

Riis, Thomas L. *Just Before Jazz: Black Musical Theatre in New York, 1890–1915.* Washington, DC: Smithsonian Institution Press, 1989.

Rodgers, Richard, and Oscar Hammerstein. Introduction to *Allegro.* In *Six Plays by Rodgers and Hammerstein.* New York: Random, 1953.

Rodgers, Richard. *Musical Stages.* New York: Random, 1975.

Rogin, Michael. *Blackface, White Noise: Jewish Immigrants in the Hollywood Melting Pot.* Berkeley: University of California Press, 1998.

"Rose." *Dramatic Mirror,* November 19, 1921, 743.

Rosenberg, Bernard, and Ernest Harburg. *The Broadway Musical: Collaboration in Commerce and Art.* New York: New York University Press, 1993.

Rosselli, John. *The Opera Industry in Italy from Cimarosa to Verdi.* Cambridge: Cambridge University Press, 1984.

Rosten, Leo. *The Joys of Yiddish.* New York: Pocket, 1970.

Royle, Edwin Milton. "The Vaudeville Theatre." *Scribner's Magazine* 26 (October 1899): 485–95.

Russo, Vito. *The Celluloid Closet: Homosexuality in the Movies.* New York: Harper, 1985.

Saint-Denis, Michel. *Theatre: The Rediscovery of Style.* New York: Theatre Arts, 1960.

Sanders, Ronald. *The Days Grow Short: The Life and Music of Kurt Weill.* New York: Holt, 1980.

Savran, David. "Toward a Historiography of the Popular." *Theatre Survey* 45 (October 2004): 211–17.

Schechner, Richard. "Who's Afraid of Edward Albee?" In *Edward Albee: A Collection of Critical Essays,* edited by C. W. E. Bigsby. Englewood Cliffs, NJ: Prentice-Hall, 1975.

Schulman, Bruce J. *The Seventies: The Great Shift in American Culture, Society, and Politics.* New York: Free Press, 2001.

Secrest, Meryle. *Somewhere for Me: A Biography of Richard Rodgers.* New York: Knopf, 2001.

———. *Stephen Sondheim: A Life.* New York: Knopf, 1998.

Sedgwick, Eve Kosofsky. *Epistemology of the Closet.* Berkeley: University of California Press, 1990.

Seldes, Gilbert. *The Seven Lively Arts.* Reprinted with an introduction by Michael Kammen. Mineola, NY: Dover, 2001.

Shapiro, Doris. *We Danced All Night.* New York: Morrow, 1990.

Shapiro, James. *Shakespeare and the Jews.* New York: Columbia University Press, 1996.

Sheward, David. *It's a Hit: The Back Stage Book of Longest-Running Shows, 1884 to the Present.* New York: Back Stage, 1994.

Shohat, Ella, and Robert Stam. *Unthinking Eurocentrism: Multiculturalism and the Media.* London: Routledge, 1994.

Sinfield, Alan. *Out on Stage: Lesbian and Gay Theatre in the Twentieth Century.* New Haven: Yale University Press, 1999.

Singer, Barry. *The Last Years of Musical Theater and Beyond.* New York: Applause, 2004.

Slide, Anthony, editor. *Selected Vaudeville Criticism.* Metuchen, NJ: Scarecrow, 1988.

Smith, Wendy. *Real Life Drama: The Group Theatre and America, 1931–1940.* New York: Grove, 1990.

Snyder, Robert W. *The Voice of the City: Vaudeville and Popular Culture in New York.* New York: Oxford University Press, 1989.

Stagg, Jerry. *The Brothers Shubert.* New York: Random, 1968.

Staples, Shirley. *Male-Female Comedy Teams in American Vaudeville.* Ann Arbor: UMI Research, 1984.

Stedman, Raymond William. *Shadows of the Indian: Stereotypes in American Culture.* Norman: University of Oklahoma Press, 1982.

Stein, Charles W., editor. *American Vaudeville as Seen by Its Contemporaries.* New York: Knopf, 1984.

Stein, Gertrude. *The Geographical History of America; or, The Relation of Human Nature to the Human Mind.* Baltimore: Johns Hopkins University Press, 1995. First published 1936 by Random House, New York.

Steyn, Mark. *Broadway Babies Say Goodnight: Musicals Then and Now.* London: Faber, 1998.

Storey, John. *An Introduction to Cultural Theory and Popular Culture.* Athens: University of Georgia Press, 1998.

Styan, J. L. "Changeable Taffeta: Shakespeare's Characters in Performance." In *Shakespeare: The Theatrical Dimension.* Edited by Philip C. McGuire and David A. Samuelson. New York: AMS, 1979.

Suskin, Steven. *More Opening Nights on Broadway: A Critical Quotebook of the Musical Theatre, 1965–1981.* New York: Schirmer, 1997.

———. *Opening Nights on Broadway: A Critical Quotebook of the Musical Theatre, 1943–1964.* New York: Schirmer, 1990.

Swain, Joseph P. *The Broadway Musical: A Critical and Musical Survey.* New York: Oxford University Press, 1990.

Taruskin, Richard. *Text and Act.* New York: Oxford University Press, 1995.

Taubman, Howard. "Modern Primer: Helpful Hints to Tell Appearances from Truth." *New York Times,* April 28, 1963, sec. 2, p. 1+.

Toll, Robert C. *Blacking Up.* New York: Oxford University Press, 1974.

———. *The Entertainment Machine: American Show Business in the Twentieth Century.* New York: Oxford University Press, 1982.

Toqueville, Alexis de. *Selected Letters on Politics and Society,* edited by Roger Boesche. Berkeley: University of California Press, 1985.

Traubner, Richard. *Operetta: A Theatrical History.* Oxford: Oxford University Press, 1983.

Tucker, Sophie. *Some of These Days.* New York: Garden City, 1946.

Van Leer, David. *The Queening of America: Gay Culture in Straight Society.* New York: Routledge, 1995.

Wachtel, George, sponsored by League of New York Theatres. *A Study of the New York Audience for the Broadway Theatre, 1980.* Data collected by Consumer

Behavior, Inc. Billy Rose Theatre Collection, New York Public Library for the Performing Arts at Lincoln Center.

Wagner, Richard. *Opera and Drama.* Translated by Edwin Evans. New York: Scribner, 1913.

Waters, Ethel. *His Eye Is on the Sparrow.* New York: Doubleday, 1951.

Watkins, Mel. *On the Real Side: Laughing, Lying and Signifying—The Underground Tradition of African-American Humor.* New York: Simon, 1994.

Weill, Kurt, and Lotte Lenya. *Speak Low (When You Speak Love): The Letters of Kurt Weill and Lotte Lenya.* Translated and edited by Lys Symonette and Kim H. Kowalke. Berkeley: University of California, 1996.

Wharton, Edith. *A Backward Glance.* New York: Appleton, 1934.

White, Edmund. *States of Desire: Travels in Gay America.* New York: Dutton, 1980.

Whitfield, Stephen J. *In Search of Jewish American Culture.* Hanover: Brandeis University Press, 1997.

———. Introduction to *Culture and Democracy in the United States,* by Horace Kallen. New Brunswick, NJ: Transaction, 1998.

Wilde, Oscar. *The Importance of Being Earnest.* New York: Avon, 1965.

Wilder, Alec. *American Popular Song: The Great Innovators, 1900–1950.* New York: Oxford University Press, 1972.

Wilder, Thornton. "Some Thoughts on Playwriting." In *Dramatic Theory and Criticism: Greeks to Grotowski,* edited by Bernard F. Dukore. New York: Holt, 1974.

Wilk, Max. *The Story of Oklahoma!* New York: Grove, 1993.

Wolf, Stacy. "Mary Martin: Washin' That Man Right Outta Her Hair." In *Passing Performances: Queer Readings of Leading Players in American Theatre History,* edited by Robert A. Schanke and Kim Marra, 283–302. Ann Arbor: University of Michigan Press, 1998.

———. "'Never Gonna Be a Man/Catch Me If You Can/I Won't Grow Up': A Lesbian Account of Mary Martin as Peter Pan." *Theatre Journal* 49 (December 97): 493–509.

———. *A Problem Like Maria: Gender and Sexuality in the American Musical Theatre.* Ann Arbor: University of Michigan Press, 2002.

———. "The Queer Pleasures of Mary Martin and Broadway: *The Sound of Music* as a Lesbian Musical." *Modern Drama* 39 (Spring 1996): 51–63.

Woll, Alan. *Black Musical Theatre from* Coontown *to* Dreamgirls. New York: DaCapo, 1989.

Wonder Bar. Warner Brothers film. Starring Al Jolson, 1934. Library of Congress, Washington, DC.

Woodfield, Ian. *Opera and Drama in Eighteenth-Century London: The King's Theatre, Garrick and the Business of Performance.* Cambridge: Cambridge University Press, 2001.

Woolf, Virginia. "Middlebrow." In *The Death of the Moth and Other Essays by Virginia Woolf.* New York: Harcourt, 1942, 176–86.

Zadan, Craig. *Sondheim and Company.* New York: Harper, 1974.

Zangwill, Israel. *The Melting Pot.* New York: Macmillan, 1920.

Ziegfeld, Florenz. "Picking Out Pretty Girls for the Stage." *American Magazine* (December 1919): 121.

Ziegfeld, Richard E., and Paulette Ziegfeld. *The Ziegfeld Touch: The Life and Times of Florenz Ziegfeld, Jr.* New York: Abrams, 1993.

◆ ◆ ◆ ◆ ◆ ◆ ◆

Index

Bruce Kirle is a lecturer in music theatre at the Central School of Speech and Drama in London and a former associate professor of theatre at Roosevelt University in Chicago. He has published on the reflexive relationship between Broadway musicals and the shifting perceptions of American identity in *Theatre Journal,* and he received the Monette-Horwitz Dissertation Prize for 2001–2002 from CLAG (Center for Lesbian and Gay Studies). Before earning his doctorate, Kirle was a professional musical director. He began his career composing musicals at La MaMa in New York.

Theater in the Americas

The goal of the series is to publish a wide range of scholarship on theater and performance, defining theater in its broadest terms and including subjects that encompass all of the Americas.

The series focuses on the performance and production of theater and theater artists and practitioners but welcomes studies of dramatic literature as well. Meant to be inclusive, the series invites studies of traditional, experimental, and ethnic forms of theater; celebrations, festivals, and rituals that perform culture; and acts of civil disobedience that are performative in nature. We publish studies of theater and performance activities of all cultural groups within the Americas, including biographies of individuals, histories of theater companies, studies of cultural traditions, and collections of plays.